BIBLE WITHOUT THEOLOGY

The Bible
Without
Theology

The Theological Tradition
and Alternatives to It

ROBERT A. ODEN JR.

UNIVERSITY OF ILLINOIS PRESS

Urbana and Chicago

For Teresa with gratitude and love

First Illinois paperback edition, 2000
© 1987 by Robert A. Oden Jr.
Reprinted by arrangement with the author
Manufactured in the United States of America
⊗ This book is printed on acid-free paper.
P 5 4 3 2 1

Library of Congress Cataloging-in-Publication Data
Oden, Robert A.
The Bible without theology : the theological tradition
and alternatives to it / Robert A. Oden, Jr.
p. cm.
Originally published: San Francisco, CA : Harper & Row, ©1987
Includes bibliographical references (p.   )
ISBN 0-252-06870-x (pbk. : alk. paper)
1. Bible. O.T.—Criticism, interpretation, etc. I. Title.
BS1171.2.O34 2000
221.6'01—dc21   99-33950
CIP

Contents

Preface

The separate chapters in the present volume represent at once quite independent studies and also five variations upon a common theme. Their independence results from the disparateness of subject matter. The first two chapters are critical and historical summaries of broad areas within biblical study: first, the category of historical understanding as applied chiefly to ancient Israel; and second, the degree to which inquiry into the meaning and function of myth has been engaged fully within biblical research. The final three chapters are directly interpretive or analytic. Each seeks to heed warnings voiced in the broader discussions that begin the volume and then to focus upon a specific biblical text (Chapters 3 and 4) or theme (Chapter 5). What unites all these inquiries is their common critical stance to a particular tradition of understanding that has long dominated biblical study. This, quite obviously, is the theological tradition. The contributions of this main tradition are beyond counting and surely represent an essential first stage in the opening up of biblical materials to wider scrutiny. But all five studies here also argue that the theological tradition carries with it clear limitations that have threatened and perhaps still threaten to restrict the range of questions considered appropriate to raise of texts and themes in the Bible.

Both nouns in the title *Bible Without Theology* require some initial discussion. When not otherwise modified, a reference simply to the "Bible" in the present volume is almost always a reference to the Hebrew Bible. That is, the term *Bible* is limited to the Hebrew Bible alone (rather than including the New Testament under that heading) and generally the title *Hebrew Bible* is used while *Old Testament* is avoided. These practices may have seemed unusual and in need of sustained defense a generation ago. However, the plain if largely unarticulated foundation of method that supports this book is the comparative study of religion in the context of the modern university. Precisely this context has prompted an increasing willingness to label that collection of texts that runs from Genesis to 2 Chronicles (or from Genesis to Malachi) with terms other than and in addition to the specifically Christian title "Old Testament." Of course, since some of the essays here are devoted to the history of biblical scholarship, any attempt systematically to purge these pages of every reference to the Old Testament would be both artificial and anachronistic. Though the central focus throughout this volume is upon the religion of Israel and the Hebrew Bible, much of the discussion bears equally upon the study of early Christianity and the New Testament.

The terms *theology* or *the theological tradition* are also used here in a variety of senses that require some explication. Perhaps the chief sense is contextual. That is, a reference to "the theological tradition" is most often a reference to the intellectual and institutional setting of biblical study within the context of preparing students for the professional task of serving in a particular confessional, most often ecclesiastical, role. Though this is an entirely legitimate and proper context, its unusual status has perhaps been too little considered. Most academic disciplines train people to be students of a phenomenon, not apologetic advocates of a particular system of rituals and beliefs. Therein lies one difference between the theological approach to the Bible on the one hand and an approach based more generally in the history of religions, comparative religion, the anthropology of religion, and the like on the other hand. Secondly, the terms *theology* and *the theological tradition* are also here employed as a shorthand reference to a distinctive mode of argumentation. Recognizing that any attempt briefly to summarize theological argumentation is bound to be overly simplistic and to risk trivializing, such argumentation can still fairly be summarized as that in which appeal to concepts like "the mysterious" or "the workings of the divine will" is quite common. Put somewhat differently, within the theological tradition—at least as this bears upon and shapes biblical study—explanation by reference to the inexplicable is hardly unusual. Outside this tradition, that which is apparently inexplicable is rather that which cries out for explanation. In the formulation of the French anthropologist Claude Lévi-Strauss, whose works figure especially in Chapter 2, "a datum is not primary because it is incomprehensible."[1] However formulated, some such statement is hardly exceptional and governs almost all academic inquiry; it would seem to be rejected, however implicitly, by a well-trodden path of theological thinking for which the incomprehensible figures largely and precisely as a primary datum. Here too, then, theology occupies a special and unusual place among academic disciplines. Part of the function of the chapters that follow is to trace and to further the process by which biblical study is moving into the center of the modern university. This process may require the jettisoning of much of the theological tradition.

Each of the five chapters here has been either composed entirely for the present volume or considerably recast from some earlier presentation.[2] In light of the audience presumed for the series in which this volume appears, translations from various languages into English appear with some frequency. Except where otherwise noted, these translations are my own, but I also cite whenever possible accessible translations of the works from which these citations appear.

Teachers, friends, academic allies and opponents alike will recognize their contributions to the arguments that I attempt to develop here, even as they may wish to disagree mildly or violently with my conclusions. My greatest debt of gratitude for the questions that prompted this book is beyond doubt owed to my colleagues in the Religion Department at Dartmouth College. But the opportunity to offer answers to these questions comes alone from the initial suggestion and then from the continual encouragement of the editor of this series, John J. Collins.

Robert A. Oden Jr.
Dartmouth College

1. Historical Understanding and Understanding the Religion of Israel

1. UNDERSTANDING "TRADITIONS" OF SCHOLARSHIP

When the intellectual history of the twentieth century comes to be written, the following will loom large among the noteworthy discoveries of the latter half of this century: the discovery of the surprisingly revealing and broadly applicable conclusions that can result from the study of individual traditions of learning. Like most discoveries, this is in fact a rediscovery. The enterprise of closely following the development of a single area of investigation is not really a new one. But this enterprise's most recent applications have reached conclusions that have generated both excitement and controversy in the past quarter of a century.

In important ways, the heightened interest in following the histories of particular areas of learning began with the publication of Thomas Kuhn's *The Structure of Scientific Revolutions*.[1] As is widely known, his central argument was that the standard and accepted view of how learning progresses in science was incorrect. Scientific progress was seen as gradual and linear. Such progress was "development-by-accumulation" in a steady "process of accretion."[2] Kuhn's investigations of a number of advances within the natural sciences persuaded him that these advances came about through nothing like such gradual, linear progress. Rather, science develops much more dramatically, through revolutions signalled by what Kuhn came to call paradigm shifts. Kuhn defined these paradigms as "universally recognized scientific achievements that for a time provide model problems and solutions to a community of practitioners."[3] When such paradigms no longer seem able to make sense of new data, or of old data seen in a new way, there is a shift of paradigm that is soon apparent throughout an entire community of scholars. So dramatic is this shift that Kuhn is not afraid to speak of the "conversion" of scientists to a new paradigm, a new model of comprehension.[4] Another name for a shift like this is a scientific revolution. A scientific revolution thus is "a transformation of the world within which scientific work was done," and the history of science properly understood is the history of these "noncumulative developmental episodes in which an older paradigm is replaced in whole or in part by an incompatible new one."[5]

To say that the central argument of Kuhn's volume has sparked a controversy and that not all historians, philosophers of science, and social theorists agree with the volume's central thesis in all its details is a significant understatement.[6] However, even Kuhn's sharpest critics agree that a great deal is to be learned in pursuing the issue of central traditions of learning and of how these traditions quite unconsciously shape the working methods and the conclusions of those utilizing any model of understanding. Moreover, there is no question but that this issue is one of importance in areas of investigation well beyond that of the natural sciences. When asked whether his central thesis seemed applicable to other areas—to history, literature, and a host of additional academic disciplines—Kuhn answered that of course it was. Indeed, he went on to say, it was precisely the work already done in other disciplines that prompted him to apply his revolutionary model to the natural sciences.[7]

Whatever be the ultimate fate of the several specific arguments advanced in Kuhn's *The Structure of Scientific Revolutions,* he is surely right in claiming both that great dividends can accrue to those who look carefully at a particular tradition of learning and that doing just this has already paid dividends in areas outside the natural sciences. Within the area of concern in the present volume, T. K. Cheyne began his classic and still valuable inquiry into the history of Old Testament scholarship with the modest claim that "it is not unimportant to notice how the intellectual phases and material surroundings of a writer have affected his criticism."[8] Within a field long allied to that of biblical studies, that of classics and ancient history, the task of the scholar has long been understood to include not just the investigation of the ancient past but also the examination of influential students of antiquity. And some of the most brilliant advances of the past quarter century have come from the two classicists, Arnaldo Momigliano and M. I. Finley, who resolutely include within their central vision sustained inquiry into various intellectual traditions that have held the field for a time.[9]

Still, if scholars from widely disparate disciplines have observed that a neglected and vital subject for further research is that of the traditions in which the most influential thinkers of any discipline have stood, it remains true that there are a number of ways of conducting this further research. Some of these ways seem of more lasting value than others. Perhaps the least well controlled of these is to speak of the "influence" of a specific figure, usually from the field of literature or philosophy, upon the thought of others. Studies governed by this sort of general model abound in literary history, so that it is very common to read of the influence of various Italian sonnet styles upon Shakespeare, or of the influence of several turn-of-the-century anthropologists and mythographers upon T. S. Eliot. Such studies have also appeared in the domain of biblical scholarship. Of these, perhaps the best known are those that argue that the scholarship of F. C. Baur, the Tübingen historian of early Christianity, and of Julius Wellhausen, of whom I will speak at length, is heavily influenced by Hegel, or that the demythologizing program of Rudolf Bultmann is purely the result of the influence of various existentialist philosophers.[10]

While inquiries into the influence of a particular philosophy or philosopher upon the work of others are hardly without value, they often descend to the level of quite narrow debates designed to prove or refute the precise extent of the reputed influence. Further and more seriously, many such inquiries appear to fall into the fallacy of assuming that the truth of a proposition is dependent upon the circumstances of its discovery. That this is a fallacy might be clear from a single instance: Assuming that the truth of a proposition is dependent upon the circumstances of its discovery might demand that one argue that the penicillin discovered by the Scottish biologist Sir Alexander Fleming in 1928 was not effective in treating various infections, since Fleming made the discovery only because a *penicillium* mold accidentally contaminated a culture on which he was working.

Better controlled and more broadly useful ways of approaching the issue of an intellectual tradition's strengths and weaknesses are available. One of these, which is best seen as an instance of the sociology of knowledge, is the investigation of the complete set of institutional, economic, political, and personal affiliations of a particular community of scholars.[11] Though the present study will take a rather different direction, the potential significance of this · kind of sociological study for the history of biblical scholarship is great. For example, the institutional setting for the majority of biblical scholarship has long been that of the Christian seminary or of universities committed to training Christian ministers. This setting is quite different from that which exists today for the study of the Bible, especially in the United States, and from what has long existed for other disciplines. So, too, the field of biblical study has witnessed a far higher degree of "self-recruitment" than is true for other fields. To take the example of the nineteenth-century German university (the setting for almost all the material investigated in the present chapter), even if it is true that scholars in many disciplines were disproportionately the offspring of other scholars, this kind of self-recruitment has been demonstrated to have reached its peak in the particular discipline of theology.[12] A brief and very incomplete list of those Old Testament scholars of this period whose fathers were ordained Christian ministers reads like a list of many of the most important biblical scholars of the past two centuries: J. G. Eichhorn (1752–1827), W. M. L. de Wette (1780–1849), F. C. Baur (1792–1860), Hermann Hupfeld (1796–1866), Wilhelm Vatke (1806–1882), Julius Wellhausen (1844–1918), Albert Eichhorn (1856–1926), and Hermann Gunkel (1862–1932).

As with the inquiry into the influence that a specific thinker may have had upon a single scholar or upon an entire discipline, this kind of sociological study both poses special problems in the area of the logic of explanation and carries with it some clear dangers. That a biblical scholar was both the descendant of a Christian minister and was himself (and the scholars in question here are all males, which is also not without potential significance) employed by a Christian seminary need not alone account for all or any of his views. Certainly, sociologists of knowledge know this and attempt to put careful controls on their conclusions to guard against any facile generalizations. There seems little doubt that controlled research of this kind will eventually produce important results for the area of biblical scholarship.

A third way of engaging the history of an intellectual discipline is to be distinguished both from the discussion of specific influences and from the practice of the sociology of knowledge. This is the construction of intellectual history in its broadest sense. It is this method that will occupy our attention for the remainder of the present chapter. Rather than risking the trivialization of the work of committed, often brilliant scholars by tracing their central assumptions to a single mentor, and rather than speaking of the political, institutional, and personal loyalties of these same scholars, I wish instead to speak of an entire tradition of understanding in which biblical scholarship has long taken its stand. It is against this broad tradition of understanding, I believe, that the conclusions of the great nineteenth-century biblical scholars can be both best understood and most fairly evaluated. Nor is this purely a historical exercise. In important ways the tradition of understanding here surveyed has continued to shape the questions and answers of much Hebrew Bible study in the present century.

The intellectual paradigm in question here is a particular and definable way of understanding human history. This tradition for the practice of understanding history arose in Germany and exercised a powerful appeal to German biblical scholars. Because of this, and in company with others, I will generally refer to this paradigm as "the German tradition of historiography," or the like.

It is not, however, limited to Germany. As this historical paradigm shaped biblical study generally, as the conclusions of German biblical study made their way to other locations on the Continent and to England and the United States, and as the German university became the model for graduate education in the United States especially, many of the essentials of this tradition became a part of biblical study everywhere, however unconsciously.

This particular tradition of comprehending human phenomena made great claims for the discipline of history. History, its adherents never ceased to repeat, is a unique, indeed an autonomous, discipline. Because there is nothing in the world truly comparable to human beings and to their achievements, there is in turn no academic discipline fairly comparable to history.

The German historiographic tradition that made these claims and many others began to take clear shape at the end of the eighteenth century and during the first decades of the nineteenth century. It reached an initial peak in the years just before 1850. Then, after a period of doubts and of competition from other models of understanding, it was revived with a new combativeness in the decades around 1900. Debate about its possible merits and weaknesses has continued for much of the present century— and continues still.

The study of this historiographic tradition and its relationship to biblical study that will occupy our attention for the remainder of the present chapter offers three related arguments. (1) The first is, simply but most significantly, that biblical scholarship throughout the nineteenth century and beyond always saw itself as a part, often as the key part, of the broader tradition against which it arose. This is not, then, a question of "influence." Rather, the broader historiographic tradition and biblical study shared the same methods, the same goals, the same prejudices, and the same world of understanding. (2) Secondly, placing the study of the religion of Israel in this, its proper intellectual context, suggests some new ways to view what appear otherwise as puzzling debates and developments within biblical scholarship. (3) Finally, and most critically significant for the wider thesis of the present volume, an inquiry into the German historiographic tradition and its particular manifestations among biblical scholars reveals that the internal tensions, perhaps even the self-contradictions, of this tradition were and remain the internal tensions of biblical study.

Given these aims, the shape of what follows is dictated by an alternating concentration first upon the broader historical paradigm and then upon its manifestations in research devoted to the religion of Israel. Thus, after an account of the origins and key emphases of the entire historiographic tradition, there follows an attempt to demonstrate the workings of this tradition among two key biblical scholars from the period shortly after the mid-nineteenth century: Julius Wellhausen in Germany and William Robertson Smith in Great Britain. Similarly, a description of the crisis in confidence through which the broader tradition went in the years around the turn to the twentieth century precedes a concluding section devoted to the reflexes of this crisis among a group of biblical scholars for whom Hermann Gunkel spoke most clearly and most often. The detail in what follows may occasionally seem excessive, but it is essential to provide the reader with an adequate understanding of the forging of the alliance between theological history and biblical study.

2. THE GERMAN TRADITION OF HISTORICAL UNDERSTANDING

"Because it is now deeply entrenched in our thought, it is easy to forget that the tendency to view all matters in terms of their histories may itself have had a history."[13]

Among the many studies of the German tradition of historical understanding,[14] none fails to note the power of this tradition, a power so apparent that it gave to the entire nineteenth century the title "The Historical Century." Nor is there any doubt that it is a single concept of understanding with which we are here dealing. Despite the number and variety of names linked to this tradition, in Germany there was, as perhaps nowhere else, "one main tradition" behind which stood an interlocking set of "theoretical convictions in regard to the nature of history."[15] This single tradition, bolstered as it was by these firmly defended convictions, yielded what Georg Iggers, perhaps the most astute chronicler of the tradition, fairly calls "a comprehensive philosophy of life," one which subsumed all value judgments and all categories of logic, to the greater power of history's incomparable and unrepeatable progression.[16]

Though there are risks in periodizing human history, since all such periodization gains clarity at the risk of some accuracy,[17] the German historiographic tradition can usefully be seen both as originating in the eighteenth-century Enlightenment *(Aufklärung)* and as a protest against some Enlightenment views. For a long time, the latter alone was emphasized, and this tradition's polemical stance against rationality and against natural law were pointed to as fundamentally in conflict with the Enlightenment. Recently, however, this exaggerated view has received corrections. Intellectual historians have discovered that the essential premise of the German historiographic tradition—the premise that all inquiry into things human must begin with historical inquiry—is itself a result of Enlightenment thought.[18] Though this correction has been useful, it ought not to obscure the differences that those who shaped the German understanding of history intended between their views and Enlightenment views. Especially in such areas as the concentration upon individuals, upon artistic and intuitive comprehension as a replacement for what was seen as an Enlightenment stress upon "the cold light of reason," the tradition that was soon to proclaim itself with self-conscious pride is a distinct departure from the eighteenth-century Englightenment.[19]

If some risks accompany the schematizing of history into separate periods, the risks are greater in pointing to a single figure as the one who inaugurates a new historical epoch. Still, the arguments are powerful for discovering the theoretical basis for the German nistoriographic tradition in the thought of Johann Gottfried Herder (1744–1803).[20] Indeed, Herder's 1774 volume *Also a Philosophy of History for the "Development" of Humanity* has been labeled the "first formal statement" of the German stream of historical understanding.[21] Among the key theses of this book and of Herder's thought generally is that all nations and cultures are properly viewed as individual organisms, each with its own distinctive characteristics and defining "spirit." Every people ("Volk") should be viewed not as are the inert phenomena of nature but rather as "a genetic individual."[22] Nations, and every person in them, thus live under a divine mandate fully to develop their "unique individuality."[23] As vital for the further development of the German tradition of historical understanding as is Herder's insistence that every people is an individual organism, equally so is his strident claim that the history of any people can only be comprehended through acts of intuition and imagination. The historian, Herder said, must loathe metaphysical abstractions and purely rational constructs. The proper historian must rather work as does an artist or a poet.[24] Terms like *immediate, natural,* and *naive* are terms of high praise from Herder, as he sought to combat rationalism with "a kind of aesthetic submissiveness to each ancient depiction."[25]

Those German historians who came to maturity as the Enlightenment gave way to the Romantic era, and then their successors in the decades that followed, found in Herder's proclamations the keys for their ambitious program to compose the first authentic histories of humanity. Selecting representative scholars from the burgeoning German tradition of historical understanding is made difficult by the number of these, undoubtedly of the first rank, who were active during the nineteenth century. Still, the names of three historians do stand out: Wilhelm von Humboldt, Leopold von Ranke, and Johann Gustav Droysen. Emphasizing these three, as we will here, does mean omitting all but the most fleeting reference to further representatives of this tradition. Among the most important of these are Barthold Georg Niebuhr, Freidrich Carl von Savigny, and Theodor Mommsen, along with many others. Of these last named, the one to whom his successors pay the most reverential homage is clearly B. G. Niebuhr (1776–1831). Many historians claimed to find in Niebuhr's *Roman History* the first elaborated example of what the nascent German historiographic tradition could yield.[26] Niebuhr's history of Rome comprehends much of what we will discover to be the repeated emphases of this tradition. Already here we find a stress upon development and upon a unique kind of understanding that is a result of the combination of the careful analysis of sources with an intuitive art.

Even Niebuhr, however, did not attain the status among the saints of the German historiographic tradition achieved by the first of these figures to be discussed at length here, Wilhelm von Humboldt (1767–1835).[27] Paul R. Sweet, a recent biographer of Humboldt, well captures the power of Humboldt's thought by calling him the Jefferson of Germany. Sweet justifies the title with a brief list of the number of significant issues in nineteenth-century thought that find initial expression in Humboldt. These include the "character of humanistic education," the "nature of historical truth," "the German idealist way of thinking," and "what the Germans mean by *Bildung.* "[28] Humboldt's comments on the last of these concepts, the idea of *Bildung,* which came to mean something like the full development of one's capacities through education, already betray both his debt to Herder and a key aspect of the German idea of historical understanding. The full development of one's capacities, Humboldt stressed, came about not through reason but rather through "aesthetic feeling" or the "power of imagination."[29] Evident here, then, is that revolt against pure rationality that characterizes this entire tradition of learning. Similarly characteristic of this tradition, and similarly in the manner of Herder, Humboldt also began early in his career to argue that each nation and culture possessed its own "special individuality" and that the chief task of the historian was to pursue the spiritual progress of each instance of this national individuality. The historian is, then, in a sense a nation's "biographer."[30]

Fortunately for the intellectual historian, Humboldt composed a single essay that clearly summarizes many of his own theoretical positions—positions that were to become those of the entire tradition here surveyed. This essay is his "On the Task of the Historian," first published in 1822.[31] Humboldt begins his essay with a statement very like one for which Leopold von Ranke is most popularly known, a statement that appears to ground the historian's task in empirical investigation. "The historian's task," Humboldt writes, "is the representation of that which happened."[32] This initial emphasis upon empirical research is then filled out with Humboldt's warning that historical learning must not slide down into the arena of ideas, must not import foreign concepts from philosophy.[33] However, and in a way absolutely typical of the entire tradition of German historiography, Humboldt soon alters his focus to insist that the historian works above all "as a poet." Both poet and historian work creatively to shape "a whole" out of the particular fragmented data with which they deal. This creative, artistic task requires chiefly the faculty of "intuition."[34] Why must the historian work as a poet? And why must the historian utilize intuition? Because, Humboldt concludes, nations are individual organisms, each with its own distinctive spirit, and this spirit can only be apprehended through poetic and imaginative reconstruction.[35] For Humboldt, as for this tradition generally, "every human epoch bears its own, uniquely individual character."[36]

Brief as it is, Humboldt's essay on the historian's task boldly states each of the key propositions upon which the nineteenth-century German concept of history is based. It remains to document the continued life of these propositions in the works of two of Humboldt's successors. The first of these is Leopold von Ranke (1795–1886), the mere uttering of whose name is sufficient to call forth the historical sensibility personified.[37] Ranke is doubtlessly most widely known for a sentence from a preface to his early history of Europe, a sentence that has attained the status of an aphorism. The historian's chief aim, Ranke wrote in that preface, is "to portray what actually happened."[38] Like several claims early in Humboldt's key essay, this aphorism might appear to portray the historian as a pure empiricist, that is one who "insists that knowledge can be gained only through sense data and through inductions resulting from these data."[39] Certainly the general view of Ranke in many circles is that the Rankean historical method is a strictly objective and empiricist method.

In fact, however, it is clear that Ranke thought of such empirical research only as a first stage in the historian's task. He pursued the study of vast amounts of data only because these data gave him access to what he saw as the totalities and spiritual realities that lay behind and within history. It was the "hand of God" behind history that Ranke insisted the true historian was after.[40] Anyone, Ranke insisted, could collect and sift through mounds of information. What distinguished the historian was the ability to put this material together in a way that revealed the grand connections in history and the grander design behind history. The true historian, Ranke wrote in the preface to his *Universal History,* was one who traced "the course of the great connections which bind together and rule over all peoples."[41]

Just as did Herder and Humboldt, Ranke also viewed nations according to an organic analogy. Indeed, it was the truest identity of nations as individuals that lay behind Ranke's search for the connections between distinct historical data. Since nations are individuals, they too must be influenced by all kinds of larger developments around them, just as is any individual human being.[42] And how does one have access to comprehending the individuality of nations and the "hand of God" behind their separate and combined histories? Ranke answered in a way by now familiar: One works as does the artist or the poet, not in the coldly rational fashion of a natural scientist.[43]

It seems clear, then, that the conventional portrait of Ranke, based perhaps primarily upon the single sentence fragment for which Ranke is widely known, is incomplete. The biblical scholar Lothar Perlitt, for example, defends this portrait when he praises Ranke for perfecting Niebuhr's philological-critical method and for guarding against any Hegelian search for the overall design of history.[44] In fact, however, Ranke's search for reflections of metaphysical forces, for the "hand of God," behind historical phenomena is not that far from Hegel's philosophy of history.

Indeed, insofar as the idealist tradition of Hegel and others is based in the premise "that the ultimate reality of the universe lay in 'spirit' or 'idea' rather than in the data of sense perception," and insofar as one has access to this reality through intuition or poetic contemplation rather than through rational analysis, Ranke is very much in the Hegelian tradition.[45] Ranke therefore is a representative of this entire tradition. His thought is the result of the combination of two distinct tendencies. The result is, as Friedrich Meinecke says, a "compound of transcendent awe in the face of history . . . with perceptive, empirico-critical investigation."[46]

The third and final figure in the nineteenth-century historiographic tradition to be treated here is Johann Gustav Droysen (1808–1884),[47] the founder of the "Prussian School" of historians, who has been accorded more significance in recent studies of historiography. The result of this recent emphasis is that Droysen is today often ranked with Dilthey and with Marx among theoreticians of history.[48]

Droysen's early work was largely devoted to the history of Alexander the Great and of the Hellenistic era more generally. His history argued that the Hellenistic period played a key role in the development of humanity. Droysen portrayed this period as "the modern age of antiquity"; it produced the idea of universal history and thus prepared the world for Christianity.[49] The Hellenistic era was not to be seen, as it had been previously, as "a shabby decline from classical perfection" but rather as a key instance of "the continuing progress of spirit toward freedom."[50] Already in this work, then, Droysen reflects the larger historiographic tradition in his emphases upon human development and upon the role that history plays in revealing to humanity the plans of God. For both Droysen and the general tradition, history then becomes "an obvious complement to a knowledge of direct, scriptural revelation."[51] The significance accorded to historical work by all these nineteenth-century figures as an autonomous, even sacred, enterprise becomes ever clearer.

Given the frequency with which Droysen spoke in his work of the development of spirit and idea, a natural conclusion would be that Droysen, above all, plainly belongs in the camp of Hegelian historians. Droysen himself vehemently rejected any such suggestion.[52] This rejection, however, is typical of the larger tradition we are here surveying. Somewhat oddly, *both* insistent hints of an idealism very much like Hegel's philosophy of history *and* equally insistent denials that one was in any sense a Hegelian appear in the writings of every historian of consequence in the nineteenth-century German tradition. Here, too, the obvious conclusion is that Droysen's work represents an uneasy alliance of "critical historical science" with "idealistic historical philosophy."[53]

Just this alliance is seen throughout Droysen's lengthiest statement of the theoretical foundations of the German historiographic tradition, his *Principles of History*, which initially appeared in 1868.[54] Although this work had a complicated publication history, and although its pronouncements are notoriously cryptic and difficult, it has been called with little exaggeration "the most influential work on historical method ever published in Germany."[55] Droysen's description of historical thought is shot through with appeals both to empirical investigation and to the intuitive feel for history's larger processes. For example, he begins by praising Humboldt as the Bacon of historical science, because of Humboldt's reliance on careful investigation of empirical data.[56] But directly after this praise, Droysen then denies that understanding can come from any kind of rational or logical process. Historical thought is rather an "art," and historical comprehension comes "as an immediate intuition" through a process akin to divination.[57] The discipline of history is thus very different from that of the natural sciences. The latter can utilize general laws and can deduce valid conclusions from these laws. History works quite differently.

Droysen's *Principles of History* is also revealing for its stress upon the progressive development of humanity. Throughout the work we find statements about the development of "the moral world." The larger view of history reveals a process of restless awakening, with humanity progressing ever closer to the goal of full moral development, when humans will achieve greater awareness of themselves, the world, and God.[58] The success of this process depends, Droysen affirms, on the growing realization of individual freedom. Only if each individual human being can develop to his own potential can the overall historical spirit achieve its goal.

COMMON THEMES IN THE GERMAN HISTORIOGRAPHIC TRADITION

In spite of some differences of focus and of the choice of disparate nations and eras to be treated, it is overwhelmingly clear that all three of these historians stand firmly within a single tradition of understanding. What is impressive is the number of themes shared by Humboldt, Ranke, and Droysen. First, there is the conviction that nations and epochs are best viewed as individuals. This means initially that the historian's subject matter is to be treated as a living organism, like an individual human being. The historian searches for an appreciation of the unique individuality of every nation, and hence must not import foreign concepts into his construction of the life of that nation. The emphasis on individualism also means that for these historians the best society is that which allows every human being to develop his own individual characteristics most fully. Clearly, these views carried with them political implications.

Secondly, the various representatives of the German tradition of historical thought here summarized all view the writing of history as the tracing of human development. Humboldt, Ranke, Droysen, and others all "affirmed that the nature of any particular phenomenon was entirely comprehended in its development."[59] Further, the assessment of human change and growth accorded to history by each of these historians was a positive one. Some idea—a world spirit or the hand of God or the ethical world—was progressing through history, to a higher end.

Thirdly, there is throughout this tradition a loathing of all abstracting, theorizing, or law making. Indeed, Iggers's superb account of this tradition centers upon its "anti-conceptual" character. The tradition repeatedly rejected all abstract and purely conceptual thought, which was thought to risk emptying history of its vital reality.[60] It is this particular element within the nineteenth-century German view of history that accounts for the firm division advocated between natural science *(Naturwissenschaft)* on the one hand and the human science of history *(Geisteswissenschaft)* on the other. The same element accounts for the constant insistence that the historian work as does a poet or an artist, utilizing imagination, intuition, and divination rather than purely rational analysis.

Fourthly, every figure within this overall tradition elevates history to a special rank as an autonomous discipline. History is alone at the top of all learning because solely from historical investigation comes a glimpse of the guiding hand behind all human development. From historical investigation alone comes revelation. History, said Ranke, is "a holy work," which is best approached as one might approach prayer or worship.[61] The logic of this position is well summarized by a recent philosopher: "If all of reality is One, and the Divine is present in all the manifestations of this One, then what occurs within the process of history is itself a Revelation."[62]

Finally, and perhaps most obviously, this whole tradition is a representation of German idealism. This stance "holds that within natural human experience one can find the clue to an understanding of the ultimate nature of reality, and this clue is revealed through those traits which distinguish man as a spiritual being."[63] Whether any or all of the historians whose views were just summarized were specifically "Hegelians" is a question of lesser importance than is their fundamental standing in the broader idealistic stream. Droysen, as we have noted, denied he was a Hegelian. And yet his use of "the supra-empirical level of spirit" and his conviction that history's "movement from natural determinism to the freedom of ethical choice consists of a necessary logic" are both very much in keeping with Hegel's philosophy of history.[64] And the same might be said with fairness of others within this same tradition.

EMPIRICAL RESEARCH VERSUS INTUITIVE CONTEMPLATION

Before turning to a look at biblical historians, an issue directly related to the idealist foundations of the German tradition of historical understanding needs some further comment. This is the issue of the tension between this tradition's emphasis upon empirical, objective investigation on the one hand, and the equally firm emphasis upon intuiting history's larger process on the other. Perhaps we can enter into this discussion again by asking what the content of history's grander process was for these historians. If there is development within history, and if the historian must apprehend this development for his results to be worthy of the name of history, just what is it that develops? What develops is some sort of idea or spirit, something quite abstract—and this despite this entire tradition's otherwise steadfast refusal to grant any explanatory power to abstract concepts. However this apparent inconsistency be explained, it is undeniable that the ultimate keys to historical thought turn out to be some quite "elusive abstractions," concepts like a "spiritual principle" or "the hand of God."[65] Though the terms various nineteenth-century historians use in description of the larger processes of history differ in detail, they are without exception disconcertingly abstract, beyond discovery by any ordinary means of investigation. And, as Mandelbaum cogently argues, "all such conceptions are faced by fundamental empirical difficulties which they cannot overcome and cannot avoid."[66]

There thus appears to be a basic inconsistency, if not an essential contradiction, at the heart of this particular concept of historical understanding. So important is the realization of this potential contradiction, especially when we turn to biblical scholarship, that it is worth the risk of some redundancy in citing several recent scholars' formulations of this problem. Iggers, whose portrait of the German understanding of history has proved basic for all subsequent research in this area, has observed that despite the steadfastness with which those within this tradition claimed themselves free of any philosophical or political bias, in fact "German historicism, as a theory of history, possessed many of the characteristics of an ideology."[67] Indeed, in a perhaps curious way, it is precisely *the denial of philosophical presuppositions,* in the face of much evidence of the force of these presuppositions, that suggests most strongly that this tradition might be characterized as an ideology. Hans Frei's formulation of the central difficulty here is similarly forceful: "On the one hand, historicism was an apprehension of the specificity and irreducibly historical particularity of cultural change. But on the other hand, as a movement in German thought it led to the very opposite of this apprehension, to a vast universalization in defining the content of historical change."[68] Finally, the conclusion to a recent study of Droysen's thought is also relevant: By his emphasis upon the progress of "ethical powers" working toward individual freedom, Droysen's "interpretive categories remain ideologically fixed" and his claims for the autonomy of historical understanding are, in the end, mired "in the *Tendenzgeschichte* [partisanship] he wished so much to avoid."[69]

The results of this internal tension, between (1) scrupulous, objective investigation and (2) the imaginative search for the spiritual forces connecting phenomena, are everywhere apparent. At the very moment when the nineteenth-century German historians who shaped this tradition were advocating a careful relativism so that the historian sought to understand each nation on its own terms, as an individual, they were bringing into their own historical thought the most obvious kinds of value judgments. These judgments include a Protestant loathing for the Middle Ages, and especially for the Roman Catholic church, a distaste for the French and the results of the French Revolution, or a pronounced prejudice toward things German—judgments, one critic correctly notes, "so patently narrow that it is difficult to see any tendency toward relativism at all."[70] In short, following the dictates of this tradition led, inevitably, to anything but an objective portrait of matters "as they really were."

3. THE HISTORY OF ISRAEL IN THE NINETEENTH-CENTURY CONTEXT

The present context plainly prohibits anything like a fair portrait of the chief biblical scholars of the past several centuries or of their many and monumental contributions.[71] Still, before we move on to the mid-nineteenth century, it is worthy of note that critical biblical scholarship began, as did the broader movement of historical understanding, with the eighteenth-century Enlightenment. With the work of Richard Simon (1638–1712) and Jean Astruc (1684–1766) came the initial recognition that each of the Hebrew Bible's writings, and some of the sources behind each writing, had had a long history. Astruc, who was Louis XIV's physician, isolated within Genesis two "mémoires" according to the divine name that predominated in each and thus began a century's intense search for answers to the compositional history of the Pentateuch.[72] Passing over the contributions of J. G. Eichhorn (1752–1827), Karl David Ilgen (1763–1834), and others, the next vital stage in this search came with the demonstration by W. M. L. de Wette (1780–1849) that "the Book of the Law" that figures in the reform under King Josiah was identical with the Book of Deuteronomy or with some part of this book. In the work of de Wette, whose significance for the future path of biblical scholarship is difficult to overestimate, we can begin plainly to see that the study of the religion of Israel and of the Hebrew Bible had become a part of the the broad historiographic tradition surveyed in this chapter. Thus, in 1806 de Wette could confidently proclaim that "the general laws of hermeneutics are identical with the laws of historical interpretation," and a few years later that "the subject matter of biblical introduction is the history of the Bible."[73]

The immediate predecessors of Julius Wellhausen, to whom most of this section of the present study is devoted, include Heinrich Ewald (1803–1875), Eduard Reuss (1804–1891), Wilhelm Vatke (1806–1882), and Karl Heinrich Graf (1815–1869). The work of Reuss and of his student Graf was of especial significance for what would eventually become the most widely accepted model for the composition of the Pentateuch. Both Reuss and Graf concluded that the prophets pre-dated the "law," and hence that a major strand in the Pentateuch was to be dated well after the eighth century BC.

Julius Wellhausen

Since Julius Wellhausen (1844–1918) is remembered above all for his massive and systematic presentation of the argument that the prophets predate the law, it is plain that the separate pieces of this argument had been constructed before him. To say as much is to take nothing away from the achievement of Wellhausen, who is beyond all doubt one of the handful of scholars of genius ever to have devoted themselves to the study of Israelite religion.[74] Wellhausen was born in Hamelin, from which city, according to legend, the Pied Piper had cleared all rats in 1284. Wellhausen's opponents from the camp of orthodoxy would later cite this fact with some glee, seeing in it some evidence that Wellhausen was himself a Pied Piper for ill.[75] After an early brilliant career at Göttingen, where he studied under Ewald and others, Wellhausen was for a decade a professor at Greifswald. It was at Greifswald that he wrote the work of chief concern here, a volume now generally known as the *Prolegomena to the History of Ancient Israel.*[76] Wellhausen resigned from Greifswald in 1882. His letter of resignation is a classic testimony both to Wellhausen's integrity and to the internal tensions experienced by a historian who was also a theologian: "I became a theologian because the scientific treatment of the Bible interested me; only gradually did I come to understand that a professor of theology also has the practical task of preparing the students for service in the Protestant Church, and that I am not adequate to this practical task, but that instead despite all caution on my own part I make my hearers unfit for their office. Since then my theological professorship has been weighing heavily on my conscience."[77] The career of Wellhausen then ended where it had begun, at Göttingen, where from 1892 until his death he was a professor of Semitic languages.

Wellhausen's *Prolegomena,* as we have just noted, is best remembered for the comprehensive treatment of the sources of the Pentateuch and of other blocks of material in the Hebrew Bible for which Wellhausen similarly attempted to fix a chronology. The central thesis, that the prophets preceded the law, Wellhausen attributes to Graf, Reuss, and Vatke and less directly to the pioneering historical work of de Wette.[78] Wellhausen presents and defends this thesis not just with wide-ranging evidence from throughout the Hebrew Bible but also with a superb literary style.

Indeed, Wellhausen's beautifully metaphoric prose is matched by no other biblical scholar (least of all by Gunkel, whose literary abilities have been somewhat overrated) and by few historians anywhere.[79] So powerfully is the whole presented that Robertson Smith could write a few years later that, thanks to the work of Wellhausen above all, "nothing of vital importance for the historical study of the Old Testament religion remains uncertain."[80]

Our chief concern here, however, is not so much the status of the central thesis of the *Prolegomena*. We are concerned rather with the extraordinary extent to which the foundations of Wellhausen's arguments can be shown to correspond to the theoretical bases of the German tradition of historical understanding. This appears perhaps most clearly in the undisguised evaluative statements that run through the work. As Patrick Miller has recently observed, "one of the things that is always startling in reading Wellhausen is that along with the wealth of data he marshalled to argue his case there is a significant amount of value judgment running throughout the *Prolegomena*."[81] The first, and probably least startling, of these that is fully within the broader nineteenth-century historiographic tradition is Wellhausen's praise for anything that expresses or allows for human individualism. For example, Wellhausen leaves no doubt but that authentic religion entails "the spontaneous sacrifice of the individual" rather than "the prescribed sacrifice of the community."[82] That Wellhausen prefers the spontaneous to the prescribed has long been observed, but of even greater significance for his overall conception of religious development is his emphasis on individual freedom. Nor is this judgment limited to comments on sacrifice. The tribal period Wellhausen praises as the era that witnessed "the divineness of heroical self-sacrifice of the individual for the good of the nation."[83] So too Wellhausen's high regard for Israelite prophets is most truly a result of his vision of history progressing toward individual self-expression. For Wellhausen, the prophets are responsible for "the great metamorphosis" of Israelite religion.[84] The reason for the prophets' ability to effect such a change is what is of greatest interest. The importance of the prophets, writes Wellhausen, "rests on the individuals. . . . [The prophets are] always single, resting on nothing outside themselves. . . . [The prophets represent] the inspiration of awakened individuals. . . . They do not preach on set texts; they speak out of the spirit."[85] Individual freedom climaxes, of course, only in the New Testament, where Wellhausen finds expressed "the freedom of the children of God."[86]

Both this high praise for individual expression and the underlying belief that the world has progressed under providential design to allow for more and more such individual expression are, as we have seen, themes Wellhausen shares with the broader tradition of historical understanding. Wellhausen's reliance upon the basic historicist premise, that history represents an unceasing course of development, is clear throughout, even if this course is not always progressive for him. Thus, that prophetic individualism previously noted and responsible in Wellhausen's eyes for "ethical monotheism" is itself a result of "a progressive step which had been called forth simply by the course of events. The providence of God brought it about."[87] Such citations could be multiplied but are perhaps unnecessary in view of a most important sentence Wellhausen writes in the introduction to the *Prolegomena,* which explicitly presents his central assumption of method: "It is necessary to trace the succession of the three elements [the Jehovist, the Deuteronomic, and the Priestly] in detail, and at once to test and to fix each by reference to an independent standard, namely, the inner development of the history of Israel."[88] That "the inner development" of an individual nation's life should offer one "an independent standard" was self-evident *only* to those who stood squarely within a particular tradition of historical understanding—the tradition of Humboldt, Ranke, and Droysen. Moreover, just as that which develops in a nation's progress for these historians was morality or ethics, Wellhausen too finds in the moral the most significant arena of religious worth. The prophets, for Wellhausen, are moved "by ethical motives, which manifest themselves in them for the first time in history."[89] Again, in the most authentic representatives of Israelite religion, "sin or offence to the Deity is a thing of purely moral character. . . . Morality is that for the sake of which all other things exist; it is the alone essential thing in the world."[90]

Another vital area of agreement between Wellhausen and the broad stream of nineteenth-century historiography is a pronounced bias against all abstraction, theory, and nomothetic thought—even though both Wellhuasen and this broad stream were themselves deeply indebted to their own abstract concepts. It is this above all that accounts for Wellhausen's extraordinarily harsh condemnations of the Priestly Codex and for the work of the Chronicler. While the Jehovist (Wellhausen uses this to refer to a combination of the Yahwist and the Elohist) expresses "genuine antiquity," "sacred mystery," and "living poetic detail," the Priestly Codex represents "theological abstraction," "mere fact," and the "pedantry" of theory.[91] Again, further documentation is perhaps unnecessary. Throughout the *Prolegomena* we find the Priestly Code and the work of the Chronicler everywhere stigmatized as "an abstraction," "mechanical," "a theory," "a pattern," "a system," something static and beyond the reality of growth and development. As with the German historiographic tradition generally, what is here remarkable is Wellhausen's condemnation of the theoretical and the abstract on the one hand, and yet his fundamental reliance upon highly theoretical—and theological—abstractions on the other hand.

It seems clear, then, that the basic precepts of the German tradition of historical understanding are also the basic precepts out of which Wellhausen composes the history of Israelite religion and literature. That Wellhausen stands squarely within this tradition is a far more significant conclusion than is the issue of the extent to which he was or was not a Hegelian, an issue that has loomed large in the assessment of Wellhausen for many decades.[92] It has so partly because Wellhausen admitted his great debt to Vatke, who was openly Hegelian. For example, Wellhausen wrote in a letter to Vatke's son, "I have learned from none more, from few as much, as I have learned from your father. . . . Hegelian or not, that is immaterial to me."[93] But more basic and more important here, as in the case of Droysen for example, is the essential idealistic philosophy of history shared by so many in the nineteenth century.

Smend has recently written that "Wellhausen stood at as great a remove from Hegelian speculation as a German historian of the nineteenth century could without falling right out of context."[94] Smend's statement is well and carefully put. But the context of which he speaks, the context of both Wellhausen and the historians summarized earlier in this chapter, is the key to following the course of nineteenth-century biblical criticism. That this is the case, that Wellhausen is hardly alone in his situation within a broader stream of learning, can be made clear by a briefer glance at Robertson Smith.

WILLIAM ROBERTSON SMITH

The course of the career of William Robertson Smith (1846–1894) is in many ways not unlike that of Wellhausen. In May 1881, almost precisely a year before Wellhausen resigned his chair at Greifswald, Robertson Smith was removed from his chair at the Free Church of Scotland College in Aberdeen. He too moved to an allied field and in 1883 became the professor of Arabic at Cambridge. And Robertson Smith's work was in many ways as creative and influential as was that of Wellhausen. This is most especially true in the area of religion's social background and social impact. It is not going too far to claim that Robertson Smith "discovered" the social function of religions generally. And from a single sentence in his *The Religion of the Semites* arose an entire tradition of twentieth-century studies in religion, the sentence that reads: "Religion did not exist for the saving of souls but for the preservation and welfare of society."[95] What is of chief concern here, however, are not those areas in which Robertson Smith anticipated and shaped future studies, by those like Emile Durkheim, but rather the extent to which his portrait of the religion of Israel grows out of the historiographical tradition in which Wellhausen so clearly stands.

In his comparative study of Israelite religion, Robertson Smith offers continued praise for religious developments that result in the heightening of individual expression. For example, he labels both Judaism and Christianity *"positive* religions," by which he understands them to be religions "which did not grow up like the systems of ancient heathenism, under the action of unconscious forces operating silently from age to age, but trace their origin to the teaching of great religious innovators."[96] For Israel, the chief such innovators are the prophets, who acted under providential guidance to produce the uniquely individual and ethical religion of the Old Testament. While the preprophetic religious world thought "much of the community and little of the individual life," the prophets, acting according to "a series of special providences," ensured that Israel's religion would concern itself with "the welfare of every individual."[97] That this is the case, Robertson Smith argues, ought to be plain to anyone "who has faith enough to see the hand of God as clearly in a long providential development as in a sudden miracle."[98] Further, for Robertson Smith as for Wellhausen and the tradition behind both, what develops providentially in Israel's religion is not just an increase in individual freedom but also a heightened sense of the ethical. While other religions remained tied to a reward and punishment system of a purely "mechanical character," in "the religion of the Old Testament" the historian witnesses a "development of the higher sense of sin and responsibility."[99]

It was observed earlier that Wellhausen utters a surprising number of evaluative judgments in the course of his reconstruction of Israelite literary development. The same is true of Robertson Smith. Here, such judgments are if anything even more curious, given the high regard Robertson Smith has for the exercise of comparative religion. He opens *The Religion of the Semites* with the proclamations that "comparative religion . . . is indispensable to the future progress of Biblical research" and that the materials in the Old Testament "cannot be thoroughly comprehended until they are put into comparison with the religions of the nations akin to the Israelites."[100] Yet the remainder of the volume proves that Robertson Smith does not have in mind anything like the modern enterprise of comparative religion. It is not *comparison,* as objectively and fairly as is possible, that he exercises but rather a series of *contrasts* between the ethical, individual, fully developed religion of Israel on the one hand, and the restricted and communal religions of Israel's neighbors on the other. Thus, these other religions remained satisfied with a "crassly materialistic conception of the divine nature," while Israel alone "had learned to draw nigh to their God without the aid of sacrifice and offering."[101]

4. THE END OF THE NINETEENTH CENTURY AND THE "CRISIS" IN HISTORICAL UNDERSTANDING

The internal tension between empirical investigation and a reliance upon highly abstract, theoretical and theological, presuppositions that existed in the German historiographic tradition was noted with increasing frequency in the period from 1850 onward. The observation of this tension, and the implication that its presence might mean this tradition could not achieve anything like the full historical portraits it was after, was one of the sources for what came to be seen as a "crisis" in historical understanding as the nineteenth century came to a close. This crisis was met by a wide attempt on many fronts to reassert, with a new combativeness, the fundamental postulates of the German tradition of historical understanding. The "enemy" against which these combative blows were directed was largely positivism. Positivism was, of course, associated in its origin above all with the name of August Comte (1798–1857), who had argued that the best model for the explanation of any phenemenon was the model provided by the natural sciences. Many in Europe professed to see in the years following 1850 "a wave of anti-Hegelian positivist reaction," a reaction that "swept German intellectual (including theological) circles."[102] The historiographic tradition begun by Herder, Humboldt, and others responded to this perceived threat from positivism by attempting "to restore the Romantic sense of the historical and the ideal world."[103] As the nineteenth century came to a close, the battle lines were thus firmly drawn. On one side stood positivism; on the other stood a neo-idealist, neo-Romantic, anti-rationalist front that sought to restore the authentic spirit of historical understanding.

The sense that a formerly clear tradition of understanding was under attack and was no longer adopted uncritically by a new generation of thinkers was akin to a wider sense, which stretched far beyond the boundaries of the university, that the world had changed—and changed for the worse. There was continual talk of the evils of commercialism and materialism, of the destruction of the old culture and its ideal of the full development of human potential *(Bildung)*. What had replaced the former sense of history and poetry was now the ills of "mechanization, specialization, fragmentation."[104] In the 1870s, toward the ends of their lives, both Ranke and Theodor Mommsen expressed their dismay at what they claimed to see as "the dehumanizing tendencies of the time."[105] In roughly the same period, the letters of Droysen are filled with fulminations against "Positivism," "Materialism," and "the polytechnical Method."[106] The wider context of this "crisis" means, of course, that the term *positivism* was really a kind of catchall negative, utilized in much the same way that the term *Fascism* has been used in the present century. That is, positivism was not so much a particular model of understanding based upon the natural sciences as it was a symbol for all things against which the neo-Romanticism of the end of the nineteenth century wished to do battle.

Probably this era's most vital spokesman on behalf of a historical understanding that could retrieve the best of the former tradition and yet still be a proper science was Wilhelm Dilthey (1833–1911).[107] Dilthey can with justice be called the founder of historical hermeneutics, at least in the modern period. Hughes, for example, finds in his work "the first thoroughgoing and sophisticated confrontation of history with positivism and natural science."[108] It was Dilthey who first "truly perceived the epistemological inconsistency of the claim of the German 'historical school' to 'objectivity' as an uncritical mixture of the idealist and realist perspectives."[109]

In a sense, then, the problem Dilthey confronted is the problem at the base of the present study—and perhaps too the issue at the center of much of nineteenth-century thought. Where does historical understanding fit in the relationship between positivism and idealism, or between the natural sciences *(Naturwissenschaften)* and the human sciences *(Geisteswissenschaft)*.[110] And can historical understanding make claims to objectivity? Dilthey saw his task as that of guiding "a recalcitrant and rebellious historiography into the frame of science, after its autonomy *vis a vis* the natural sciences had been established."[111] His answer was to develop a notion of "understanding" *("Verstehen")* that he saw as both objective and yet still distinct from what existed in the natural sciences.

For our purposes, the precise content of Dilthey's notion of "understanding"[112] and an answer to the question of whether or not he was successful in defining a distinct role for historical understanding are less important than is the fact that Dilthey was representative of a widespread sense at the end of the nineteenth century that the German tradition of historical understanding needed reshaping and defending. That Dilthey did not stand alone is obvious. For example, the philosopher Wilhelm Windelband (1848–1915) also engaged in a sustained attempt to defend historical understanding and to distinguish it from the methods of natural science.[113] In a fashion by now quite familiar, Windelband's defense is partly that the historian works more imaginatively and intuitively than does the scientist, that the historian's task "in relation to what really happened, is similar to the task of the artist."[114] Others too engaged in a similar defense. They did so in sufficient numbers that one can accurately speak of the end of the nineteenth century as a period both of crisis and of nostalgic longing for the historical certainties that seemed to exist earlier in the century.

5. BIBLICAL SCHOLARSHIP AT THE END OF THE NINETEENTH CENTURY

Just as Wellhausen, Robertson Smith, and many others demonstrate repeatedly that the theoretical foundation of their scholarship is identical with that of the tradition of Herder, Humboldt, Ranke, and Droysen, so too there is a group of biblical scholars who worked in the years immediately following, the years at the end of the nineteenth century, whose works show them as full participants in the attempt to revitalize this same tradition of historical understanding. This group includes Albert Eichhorn, Hermann Gunkel, W. Wrede, Wilhelm Bousset, Ernst Troeltsch, and W. Heitmüller, all of whom were born within the first two decades following 1850, and a second group born only shortly thereafter: Hugo Gressmann, Hans Schmidt, Walter Baumgartner, Emil Balla, and Otto Pfleiderer. At one time or another, all of these scholars were associated with something commonly called the "History of Religions School."[115] As one of its members, Hugo Gressmann, frequently said, the title is not quite accurate if it suggests all these scholars worked together at a single location. Gressmann preferred the title "circle" or "movement."[116] Whatever be the most appropriate title, what is important here is that all these scholars shared an interest in defending the basic, German historiographic tradition and in defining their own work as an authentic representation of this tradition.

The History of Religions School's birthplace was the Göttingen of the 1880s, and its father was Albert Eichhorn. Even though Eichhorn wrote far less than did Gunkel or Gressmann, for example, the members of this school were unanimous in looking to him as their "undisputed spokesman."[117] Much that would become central to this school and much that demonstrates the school's participation in the end-of-the-century defense of historical understanding is implicit already in a set of twenty-four theses that Eichhorn defended publicly in 1886. The set includes the theses that "every explanation of a myth is false which does not bear in mind the origin and development of the myth" and that "the composition of history is an art" [118]—both of which might have been uttered by Herder. Gressmann attributes the great influence of Eichhorn over the others in the school to Eichhorn's passionate search for "the progress of human spiritual life," to his great "love for history and for historical development," and to his equally pronounced distaste for philosophy and natural science.[119] As

Gunkel was to later write in a letter to Gressmann, Eichhorn showed all of those in this school that the truth was to be found in "realities, not theories," and thus "in history and not in philosophy." '120

If Eichhorn was of early significance in shaping the essential concerns of the History of Religions School, it is the work of Johannes Heinrich Hermann Gunkel (1862–1932) that has had the greatest impact on twentieth-century biblical scholarship.[121] Gunkel's many contributions, all of which (including the form-critical method) are best seen against the background of the end-of-the-century reaffirmation of the German tradition of historical understanding, have justly been called "epoch making." Gunkel himself has been labeled "doubtless the most important Old Testament scholar since Wellhausen," one whose methods and goals "have been appropriated, in one fashion or another, by all who move in the mainstream of contemporary biblical studies."[122] Gunkel was the first (in 1889) to use the adjective *"religionsgeschichtliche"* ("History of Religions") to describe what this movement wanted to achieve. He was also the first openly to proclaim that he and the others in this school "stand at the beginning of a new epoch in the interpretation of Old Testament religious and literary history." '123 And his 1895 volume *Creation and Chaos*, which followed the life of a single mythic structure from Genesis in the Hebrew Bible through the Book of Revelation in the New Testament, marked the formal inauguration of the History of Religions School.

So voluminously did Gunkel write, and so plainly do his theoretical assumptions match those of the wider attempt to defend and reassert the basic postulates of the German tradition of historical understanding, that one can find evidence in his work for every one of these postulates. Just as Eichhorn had done in one of his public theses, Gunkel tirelessly repeated that to understand is to follow a phenomenon's providential growth. "We had come to see," Gunkel wrote in description of the origins of the History of Religions School, that the religion of Israel "can be understood only when it is understood in its history, in its growth and becoming."[124] What is it that progresses and develops in this religion? The same concept that progresses and develops for Wellhausen and the tradition in which he stood: the idea of human individualism. For Gunkel, the Old Testament yielded "the highest that was achieved anywhere throughout the East—human personality living its own life."[125] To the religion of Israel Gunkel attributes the very "origin of individualism."[126] If the Israelite prophets initiated this process, as they did in Gunkel's vision, the process is only complete in the New Testament. There, we see, Gunkel argues, that "in the teachings of Jesus everything centers about an ethical imperative born of supreme religious individualism."[127] The Old Testament, then, "is on a lower level, for in its pages religion deals in the first instance with national life, although it was out of this national religion that the higher religion of the individual gradually arose."[128]

How does one apprehend the central developmental message of the Old Testament? Here Gunkel speaks in a way that reveals most clearly his participation in the neo-Romantic, antipositivist revolt that characterized the final decade of the nineteenth century. One understands, Gunkel says again and again, not rationally, but poetically, not as a scientist but as an artist. Arguing that too much dry rationality has characterized biblical scholarship (in fact, there is very little that is anything like dry rationality), Gunkel pleads for "a certain flair or artistic sense."[129] Since exegesis is after the secret inner life, the spiritual fullness, of biblical literature, "exegesis in the highest sense is more an art than a science."[130] Gunkel says he began his scholarship to combat "the modernizings of exegetes who, without historical reflection and influenced by rationalism, know nothing of the 'effects' of the *pneuma* [spirit] and render 'Spirit' a pure abstraction."[131]

Further, such statements about biblical scholarship's task are buttressed by more general laments over the mechanical and impersonal course of recent events—laments we have seen to have been echoed everywhere in this era. Gunkel often railed against "materialism" and looked for a new religious awakening to return Germans to their spiritual roots.[132] In a sentence of extraordinary significance, a sentence that might serve as a kind of epigram for the real goals of Gunkel and the History of Religions School, Gunkel pauses in the midst of an essay on the Old Testament and offers the following reflection: "The conditions of modern life, especially in large cities, have become so unnatural, so complicated and chaotic, that the modern child . . . finds it extremely difficult to gain clear and simple conceptions."[133] This sentence is of vital significance partly because this nostalgic vision included also a specific nostalgia for the methods and aims of the German tradition of historical understanding—methods and aims that Gunkel, in company with others, knew to be under attack and in need of dramatic rearticulation.

The History of Religions School is often praised and perhaps chiefly remembered for its work in the area of comparative religion. According to the standard view, discoveries like that of the Amarna Tablets in 1887–88 led Gunkel and others to a new appreciation of the contribution that might come from such comparative work. Certainly, there is some truth to this conventional view. Gunkel did say, for example, that "the religion of the New Testament, in important, and even in some vital, points can be interpreted only in the light of the influence of extraneous religions."[134] However, whenever Gunkel, Gressmann, or others within this school were questioned about their comparative work, they replied with vigor that this was most emphatically *not* the central emphasis of this school. Gunkel, for example, repeatedly said that it was the history of *a religion* (i.e., biblical religion), not the history of *various religions,* that was his concern. The History of Religions School's title, Gunkel wrote, never meant "a dragging down of what is Biblical to the level of the non-Biblical." Rather, "the thoughts that then [in the period when this school was founded] filled our minds had arisen within theology itself. . . . Before our eyes, uplifting us and bearing us onward, stood a wondrous picture—the Religion of the Bible in all its glory and dignity."[135] Gressmann too wrote that the real "kernel of the movement" was never comparative work; it was rather the attempt to reconstruct "the history of a single religion."[136] Hence, this school did engage in a sort of comparative work. But it was comparative work very much like that of Robertson Smith or of Humboldt and Ranke. It was an enterprise that made claims to objectivity and yet whose central aim was plainly apologetic. The more comparative material was assembled, the more brightly shone the superiority of Israel's religion.

That the entire History of Religions movement was deeply immersed in the turn-of-the-century afterlife of the German idealist historiographic tradition is not solely a conclusion from data such as that just presented. The members of this school themselves readily granted this. Gressmann, for example, wrote that this school flourished despite some initial opposition precisely because its goals corresponded to "the general current of the era," a current defined as "an awakening sharpness of historical sensibility." Hence for Gressmann, "the appearance of the History of Religions School upon the theological scene is nothing but one manifestation of a larger, total movement which is now noticeable within scholarship everywhere."[137] The "larger, total movement" to which Gressmann refers is plainly an attempt to recapture the idealist and Romantic spirit of the historical tradition begun in Herder, to whom several of these scholars, and Gunkel especially, pay continued tribute. For Gunkel, the History of Religions School properly viewed is "nothing but a new wave of the mighty historical current set in motion by our great idealist thinkers and poets, which has affected our entire mental life, and has now long influenced our theological outlook also."[138] It comes as no surprise, then, that Gunkel finds in the Israelite prophets the expression of "the imperishable power of the Moral Idea," or that he believed always in "the revelatory power of history."[139]

When Gunkel and the others are thus placed within the particular context of turn-of-the-century polemics, the History of Religion School's so-called battle with Wellhausen becomes far more intelligible. Certainly, the members of this school were careful to voice their debts to Wellhausen. Gunkel, typically, claimed that he " 'was a true Wellhausian' " and that he and the others belonged in a sense to the larger school of Wellhausen.[140] But this movement's representatives also convicted Wellhausen for not being historical enough. For Gunkel, "Wellhausen falls into conflict with fundamental principles which are everywhere recognized in historical science" because "the cardinal principle of historical study is this: That we are unable to comprehend a person, a period, or a thought dissociated from its antecedents. . . . [Only such inquiry yields a] true and living understanding of the subject."[141]

This is the central accusation by this school against Wellhausen: not that he insufficiently utilized comparative materials, as is often claimed, but that his failure to go backward far enough behind the historical sources meant that Wellhausen was, in the end, *not* a true historian. But such a claim in isolation makes no sense at all. Surely Julius Wellhausen deserves the title of "historian" as much as anyone in the entire nineteenth century. But in the context of the decades of the 1890s and beyond, this claim makes a good deal of sense. Wellhausen is condemned, when he is, largely as a representative of the period between 1850 and 1890, a period that for Gunkel and for many others stood under the suspicion of making concessions to "positivism" and thus of not upholding the idealist historical tradition with sufficient vigor. In fact, there is very little even faintly positivist about Wellhausen's work. And he can compete admirably with Gunkel in his nostalgia for a rural, simpler world of greater poetry and less rationality or in his passion for pursuing the larger processes of history. So, too, can Wellhausen's nearest contemporaries. To the great Dutch scholar Abraham Kuenen, for example, a historian's task is completed only when he can offer a portrait "above all of spiritual life and activity," while for Bernhard Duhm the prophets are vital for their revolutionary break with demonism into "the spiritual sphere of ethics."[142] But Wellhausen and the others stood under indictment because the decades in which they worked stood under indictment. The battle with Wellhausen, then, is more a result of the History of Religions School's participation in the larger war against those positivistic powers seen to have emerged shortly after mid-century than it is a result of anything Wellausen did or failed to do.

It would be radically unfair to portray the History of Religions

School as a movement that produced no new results. Despite their denial that comparative work was anything like their central concern, that comparative work they inaugurated led eventually to attempts in the present century to do similar investigations with far more thoroughness. Too, their discovery of the cultic, liturgical life of many biblical genres and their more basic form-critical method of obtaining access to this life are both contributions of undoubted brilliance and fruitfulness. But the central motivating passion of this school is a passion to return to the idealist tradition of historical understanding. Indeed, to reread Herder or Humboldt, for example, after reading Gunkel is to come to the conclusion that few historians ever were in more fundamental agreement on theoretical principles—all the time, of course, inveighing against the presence of theory or abstraction in historical study— than were these three. This is true even in detail: Humboldt already in the 1790s accused the Enlightenment of possessing a faith in "mechanistic intellect", and Humboldt's statements on behalf of the simple naturalness of rural life and against urban life that destroyed individuality are strikingly like those of Gunkel.[143] This agreement in principle and detail between Herder, Humboldt, and others on the one hand and the History of Religions School on the other means that the internal inconsistency that threatens to invalidate the conclusions of the former poses the same threat to the conclusions of the latter.

6. CONCLUSION: OBJECTIVITY AND THE NINETEENTH-CENTURY HERITAGE

That the present century's biblical scholarship is massively indebted to the conclusions and the methods of Wellhausen, Gunkel, and the contemporaries of each need not be demonstrated here. The author of a recent account of the historical-critical method says with unquestionable correctness that "it is difficult to overestimate the significance the nineteenth century has for biblical interpretation. It made historical criticism *the* approved method of interpretation."[144] Where that debt is most notable, beyond the basic commitment to historical study, is precisely in that area of the internal tension implicit within nineteenth-century historical understanding to which we have repeatedly pointed. The nineteenth-century historical tradition made high claims for objectivity, for a portrait of matters as they really were, and for avoiding any philosophical commitments in favor of the data themselves. And yet both this tradition and its inheritors among biblical scholars everywhere are revealed to be founded upon obviously extra-empirical, theoretical, and theological commitments.

To choose but a single example in demonstration of this point, both nineteenth-century scholars and their successors in the present century repeat in almost liturgical fashion their methodological rooting in "the text itself." Gressman argues at length that the student of the Bible guard above all against importing any alien ideas into and upon the text itself.[145] So too, that same recent introduction to the historical-critical method just cited proclaims that the biblical historian's "first task" is "simply to hear the texts with which he is working. . . . to hear the text apart from the mass of biblical interpretation that has been laid over it in the history of its use."[146] Such advice is well meant. But just about the *only* tradition within learning ever to argue that such a naked confrontation with the text itself might be possible is the very historiographic tradition that is everywhere clothed in commitments to highly philosophical and theological principles—principles that come from somewhere beyond the text itself.

Let it be clear that the argument here presented is *not* that this tradition of learning is rooted in theory while other traditions are blissfully free from theory. The argument is rather that the claim of this particular historiographic tradition to be theory-free and hence to offer supremely objective conclusions is simply not sustainable. That this is the claim of this tradition is everywhere apparent. It appears in Perlitt's argument, as a part of his attempt to acquit Wellhausen of the charge of Hegelianism, that for Wellhausen "any general, comprehensive philosophical or theological systematic held no appeal."[147] And it appears in that polemic against the nomothetic model of the natural sciences to which every historian surveyed in this chapter gives voice. Nor are such claims limited to the nineteenth century. As M. I. Finley well formulates this issue, "Historians, one hears all the time, should get on with their proper business, the investigation of the concrete experiences of the past, and leave the 'philosophy of history' (which is a barren, abstract, and pretty useless activity anyway) to the philosophers. Unfortunately the historian is no mere chronicler, and he cannot do his work at all without assumptions and judgments."[148]

The particular assumptions and judgments of both the broad historical tradition of understanding and the reflexes of this in biblical scholarship are not just those of the idealist tradition. They are also those of specific commitments to equally specific traditions of faith. As early as the eighteenth century, J. G. Eichhorn defended historical criticism on the ground that such criticism will in the end " 'establish the credibility and truth of the gospel story on unshakable foundations.' "[149] Eichhorn is hardly alone in articulating such a view. F. C. Baur, too, said both that the " 'sole purpose' " of his research was " 'to comprehend the historically given in its pure objectivity' " and also that the results achieved would then " 'contend for the positivity of Christianity on scientific grounds.' "[150] Similarly, Gunkel can allege both that "Old Testament Science justly claims to be a fully qualified member of the circle of historical Sciences," and yet also that "the historical movement, by shedding new light on ancient Scriptures, is truly serving genuine religion."[151] Or, after offering a nearly identical defense of biblical history as objective in its methods and results, Gressmann too concludes that "the last goal of all our endeavors is to illuminate the essence and truth of the Christian religion."[152] If a historian begins any investigation with such a clear view in advance of what the results of that investigation will be, then it is obviously folly to lay claim to anything like objectivity.

Whether any research in the human sciences can aspire to, much less attain, something like purely objective results is, needless to say, no simple matter.[153] Once again, however, that is not the point at issue in the preceding argument. This point is rather that the recent origins of biblical scholarship are beyond doubt a monument to sustained industry, creativity, and piety. But the biblical scholarship of the past several centuries and for the most part still today, which is thoroughly and unapologetically theological scholarship, is no monument to disengaged objectivity. If it is true, as Iggers argues at length and with elaborate documentation, that the theoretical foundations of the German tradition of historical understanding have continued to live a life of their own in other disciplines "long after these theories had been abandoned or at least seriously questioned by philosophers and cultural scientists,"[154] of no discipline is this more true than it is of biblical scholarship.

There is, then, an important and unfortunate division between biblical study and a variety of other academic fields of inquiry. The latter joined in formulating a sustained critique of a model of historical understanding, a model that could not deliver on its promises to achieve objective historical reconstruction because its theoretical foundations prohibited precisely this. Biblical study, even into the present century, long seemed either unaware of the consequences of this critique or unwilling to allow these consequences to alter its portrait of Israelite religion. Though the motives responsible for such apparent ignorance or unwillingness are probably complex and beyond full recovery, among them surely was the congenialness of the idealist historiographic tradition for theology. This tradition allowed biblical scholars to absolutize and particularize the religion of Israel beyond any meaningful comparison, on the ground that every culture was an organic individual, incomparable with any other individual. The tradition also granted legitimacy to vague and unverifiable claims about the subtlety and yet the certainty of divine guidance to Israel's history, on the ground that authentic historical reconstruction would always discover the workings of God's hand. Finally, the same historiographic tradition supported the regular affirmations by theologians engaged in biblical research that their work was at once empirical and objective and yet capable of proving the unique superiority of biblical religion.

As we shall see in Chapter 2, this same split between the theological tradition of biblical study and the discoveries of those working within other academic fields occurred in the study of myth. Indeed, in mythological study the split quickly became a chasm that more and more distanced biblical scholars from significant developments occurring outside the enclosed arena of biblical study.

2. Interpreting Biblical Myths

1. THE STUDY OF MYTHS BY BIBLICAL SCHOLARS AND OTHERS

Inquiry into the meaning and function of myths, including the important and preliminary issue of the correct definition of myth, has long played an important role within biblical scholarship. However, since many scholars have proposed that any society's myths are an integral part of the ways in which that society presents to its members and to the wider world a full articulation of its deepest values and beliefs, the study of myths has also found a place in other disciplines. Anthropologists and classicists especially, but also historians, folklorists, sociologists, psychologists, and others have made a place within their own fields for the investigation of mythology. Such investigation has been pursued with especial intensity since approximately the mid-nineteenth century, when comprehensive and competing theories for the central functions of myth first became available.

The results of this wider inquiry into myths' meanings and functions suggest that the student of myth has today a number of methodological models to which he or she might turn when attempting to analyze a particular myth. Moreover, there is a long tradition, especially within anthropological circles, of subjecting each of these models to intense theoretical and empirical scrutiny, and of comparing at length the presumptive benefits and arguable pitfalls of each. It is thus all the more surprising that for many decades the clear majority of biblical scholars displayed a noteworthy hesitancy either to admit the presence of complete myths within the Hebrew Bible and the New Testament or to investigate fully the resources of other disciplines that might aid them in their attempts to interpret biblical myths. As we will see in the course of this chapter, there were some quite specific reasons for this hesitancy. But the presence of a pervasive tendency within biblical study stood behind, lent support to, and is of far greater significance than any of these specific reasons to avoid a full engagement with the study of myth. This has been the tendency to distinguish sharply between stories in the Bible on the one hand and the myths of all other cultures on the other hand. This distinction is of obvious theological usefulness. If biblical stories are unique, this offers supportive evidence to the confessional claim that these stories and the entire religion of Israel stem ultimately from divine instruction. Further, the distinction is itself a result of the understandable restriction of biblical study to theological concerns alone that has existed until quite recently.

This separation between theological interpretation of biblical stories on the one hand and the wider analysis of myths on the other meant that for the better part of a century the advances suggested in mythological analysis by anthropologists and others were only slowly utilized within biblical scholarship. Indeed, even when these suggested advances were applied to biblical materials, the application was most often accomplished in quite piecemeal fashion. The most common procedure was to select and apply what were considered the most obviously relevant portions of several different theories for the meaning and function of myth. Though such an eclectic approach is conventionally viewed as a virtue within biblical study, eclecticism here as elsewhere carries with it a clear danger—the danger that the several theoretical models from each of which small portions are selected may prove to be mutually contradictory. A more comprehensive analysis of the models used within mythological study demonstrates precisely this. Many of these models are so constructed as to simply prohibit the combination of portions of them with portions of other models without logical contradiction.

Against this background, the present chapter has two central goals. The first of these is to paint a brief portrait of the history of the discussion of myths within biblical study. This portrait is largely restricted to the mainstream, hence the theological stream, of biblical study. The second goal is to describe a half dozen of the past century's most influential, extra-theological models for the meaning and analysis of mythology. That students of the Bible have rarely appropriated the full fruits, or seen the wider implications, of any or all of these models is one of our conclusions. This conclusion is alone hardly a severe indictment. Very few scholars in any discipline have ever been able to enter into another discipline's conversations as equals. The only exceptions are the truly exceptional scholars like Max Weber. Still, that which for too long prohibited the total appropriation of advances in mythological study by biblical scholarship was the institutional and intellectual setting of such scholarship within a set of apologetic and theological concerns.

2. THE MYTHICAL VERSUS THE BIBLICAL

THE BEGINNINGS OF THE SCIENTIFIC STUDY OF MYTH

The more remote origins of mythological study lay within the biblical period itself. Already during the last four or five centuries before the Christian era there was lively interest in the genesis and reference of myths, especially the myths of other peoples. One of the most widely utilized explanations of myths in this era was a type of historical explanation that goes by the name of "Euhemerism." Euhemerism, to which we will return at greater length, locates the supernatural beings and occurrences in myths in the originally quite natural, if extraordinary, accomplishments of royalty and other cultural heroes. The feats of these heroes were magnified in the telling and retelling, until a story of a human hero became a myth of a supernatural being. Explanations of a generally Euhemeristic sort became especially popular among early apologists for Christianity, who distinguished between the truly miraculous acts of Jesus Christ on the one hand and the originally quite mundane accomplishments of those cultural heroes who are falsely seen as gods in all other religions.

Even given the existence for millennia of such modes of mythological analysis as Euhemerism, the scientific study of myths is usually and with fairness said to have begun at the end of the eighteenth and the beginning of the nineteenth centuries. Interest in and even a passionate concern for myths blossomed in this era. Perhaps the mere mention of the work of such scholars as Herder, whom we discussed in Chapter 1, or of the brothers Jacob (1785–1863) and Wilhelm (1786–1859) Grimm will serve to demonstrate this.

Several reasons account for the sudden increase in attention paid to myths during these years. Initially, the years of the rise in interest in myths coincide with the period of the birth of the Romantic movement. Among the emphases of this movement was that upon the human imagination and its earliest expressions in poetic myth. Romantic writers of all sorts argued that the human heart first spoke in poetry and in myth. Hence, there arose a desire to recover and to appreciate anew these ancient expressions of most authentic humanity.

Secondly, and as Chapter 1 has documented fully, the turn from the eighteenth to the nineteenth century witnessed both the birth of an intense historical consciousness and repeated calls for a truer understanding of all of human culture through historical inquiry. These calls were answered with alacrity. By the end of the first quarter of the nineteenth century new conclusions were available about the origins and development of many European nations, of ancient Greece and Rome, and of the lands that gave birth to the Hebrew Bible and the New Testament. Among these conclusions were those that suggested that many, perhaps most, biblical stories were nothing like the eyewitness testimony they had long been assumed to be. These stories were instead the products of long processes of community tradition. This conclusion suggested another: If biblical materials are the results of many centuries of orally and communally transmitted tales, then the process that led to the development of the Bible is the same process that lies behind the genesis of myth. Perhaps, then, biblical stories and myths might be open to the same sorts of analysis.

A third contribution of the nineteenth century to the scientific study of myth was the contribution of archaeology and allied philological work. This resulted, before the century's end, in the unearthing and translating of dozens of myths from Mesopotamia and elsewhere that were startlingly, in many quarters disturbingly, like several biblical narratives. By the final quarter of the nineteenth century, all who could read any one of several European languages would hear of a flood hero more ancient than Noah in a Mesopotamian version of Genesis 6–9 or of a first human called Adapa who was prevented by a Mesopotamian deity from attaining immortality.[1] Like the historical conclusions just noted, these discoveries and others to come would soon force scholars to face the issue of the possible presence of ancient myths in the Bible.

STRAUSS'S LIFE OF JESUS

One of those who early in the nineteenth century, to the great peril of his own career, did apply mythological study to the New Testament was the German scholar David Friedrich Strauss (1801–1874). The results of Strauss's application appeared in the first edition of his *Life of Jesus* published in 1835.[2] Strauss equated the "mythical" with the "miraculous," and on the basis of this equation subjected to analysis all of the mythical material in the Gospel accounts of Jesus. His argument was in many ways founded in the age-old theory of Euhemerism. Stories about Jesus, Strauss suggested, developed in much the way that stories about any remarkable person did. Whenever such a person dies, his memory is preserved in such a way that the historical quickly becomes the legendary and the mythical. That which is particularly notable about Strauss's *Life of Jesus* is the breadth to which he was willing to extend his basic thesis. Strauss made bold to argue that the mythical was present in the story of Jesus not just in the accounts of Jesus' conception and birth but also in the many details in the Gospel narratives—in the stories of Jesus' baptism, for example, or of the various healing and feeding miracles.

Given the early date of publication of Strauss's *Life of Jesus,* and given also the wide notoriety that the volume soon occasioned, Strauss was made to bear a burden that more properly belonged to the entire historical-critical approach to the Bible. For many people, a first acquaintance with the shocking conclusions of this approach coincided with their acquaintance, often at second- or thirdhand, with Stauss's volume. For such people, what was shocking was the most basic conclusion of both Strauss and his predecessors: that the accounts of Jesus in the New Testament or of other figures in the Hebrew Bible were not historically true. Scholars, including Strauss, could and did say that these accounts still remained true in another sense. Such statements did not alter the plain fact that the historical-critical method had reached conclusions that conflicted with many peoples' deeply held views about the reliability of the Bible.

The crisis prompted by Strauss's *Life of Jesus* had immediate and detrimental effects upon his career. More significantly for our purposes here, this crisis also yielded an effect upon biblical scholarship in general that lasted for about a century. However unconsciously perceived, this effect was the creation and then the steady strengthening of a hesitancy on the behalf of most biblical scholars to speak of the Bible and of myth in the same breath. The sole exception to this unwritten prohibition, the one way in which biblical scholars did permit the joint utterance of Bible and myth, was to deny the presence of myths in the Bible.

THE EXILE OF MYTH FROM THE BIBLE

The category "myth" was effectively exiled from the arena of biblical study for nearly a hundred years following the publication of Strauss's *Life of Jesus.* What had seemed to many scholars in the years leading up to the publication of this volume in 1835 as perhaps *the* chief problem in the historical study of the religions of Israel and of early Christianity—the problem of the Bible and mythology—simply ceased to exist. And this despite the undeniable fact that the number of extrabiblical myths with clear affinities to biblical narratives was far greater in the years following Strauss than in the preceding years.

The memory of the fate of Strauss and of his thesis was surely among the reasons for myth's exile from the field of biblical inquiry. The reason most offered for this exile, however, was something different, something far more direct and simple, far less personal. The problem of the Bible and mythology had ceased to be a problem, it was said on all fronts, because there are no myths, at least no complete myths, in either the Hebrew Bible or the New Testament.

Given the increase in the number and awareness of myths from Mesopotamia, Syria, Egypt and elsewhere so like biblical tales in many regards, what possible basis was there for this insistent denial that any complete myth is present in the Bible? And how can anyone exile an entire genre of literature from a collection of texts? The basis for the denial and the means of exile was a frontal assault, an assault apparently beyond counterattack: Myth was exiled from the Bible *by definition.*

The question of an adequate and fair definition for myth is so important that an entire section of the present chapter will be devoted to it. For now, what is noteworthy is that almost without exception biblical scholars in the century following Strauss relied upon a single such definition. This was that widely popularized by the Grimm brothers. A myth, according to this definition, was *a story about the gods.* The key to this definition for the tradition we are tracing here, is that the final noun, "gods," is in the plural. Both the Hebrew Bible and the New Testament, it was agreed, were of the highest significance in the development of human religions for their witness to the truth of monotheism. If, then, the heart of biblical religion was monotheism, there could be no talk of gods in the Bible. And if there was no talk of gods in the Bible, then there are in the Bible no myths.

So neatly and permanently did this definition sever mythology from the Bible that virtually every discussion that touched upon myth within the world of late nineteenth- and early twentieth-century biblical study rehearsed this definition and then the certain conclusion that ensued. Both Wellhausen and Robertson Smith, to whom a major part of Chapter 1 was devoted, use the conventional Grimm definition of myth. So too, and at greater length, does Hermann Gunkel, whose work has shaped the central questions asked by biblical scholars of the present century as has no one else's. Gunkel is an especially striking instance of the tension between mounting evidence for mythical material in the Bible on the one hand and the repeated denial of the presence of myths in the Bible on the other. Gunkel's *Creation and Chaos* (1895), which, it will be recalled, inaugurated the History of Religions School in the eyes of the members of this group, relies fundamentally upon extrabiblical materials. The volume's central thesis is that a single myth, the broadly defined myth of the defeat of a chaos dragon, is at the base of significant statements in the Bible about the beginning and end of the world. But despite the skill with which Gunkel defends this thesis, he, too, continued throughout his life to stand within the main camp of those who denied myths to the Bible. Though Gunkel's statements on myth in his voluminous publications are not entirely consistent, he remained consistent in defining myths as stories about the gods and in demanding that "for a story of the gods at least two gods are essential."[3] Since the Bible, Gunkel went on to say, was essentially monotheistic and "from its beginning tended toward monotheism," the Bible contains no complete myths. What the Bible does contain, Gunkel's own research forced him to admit, is "original myths" from other lands, myths that now appear in the Bible only "in comparatively faded colors." The story of the mating of divine beings with women in Genesis 6: 1–4, for example, was originally an elaborate myth but is now "nothing but a torso" of a complete myth.[4]

The simple and convenient view that all myths are stories about the gods continued to play the lead role in discussions by biblical scholars about myth and the Bible for a surprisingly long period in the twentieth century—surprisingly long since, as we will see, this definition was dismissed as unfair and inadequate by a wide range of scholars outside the area of biblical study. A look at almost any of the most widely used introductions to the Hebrew Bible or the New Testament, or at similarly influential biblical theologies, will show that this remained the case until very recently. The introductions of Eissfeldt, Weiser, and Fohrer, for example, introduced generations of students, and not just German students, to the Old Testament in the years between the 1930s and about 1970. Each one of these introductions presents, in remarkably similar language, the argument that a true myth demands a polytheistic background, that those stories that look mythical in the Old Testament are merely the decaying fragments of myths that originated elsewhere, and that there are thus no complete myths in the Old Testament.[5] The identical chain of reasoning appears, again, in the Old Testament theologies of Gerhard von Rad and G. E. Wright, different as these scholars' positions are in other areas. Both von Rad and Wright rehearse a version of this argument, then go on to contrast systematically the cyclical, naturalistic, and mythical thinking that they see as characteristic of Mesopotamia, Egypt, and Canaan, with the linear, historical, and antimythical thought process they find central to Israelite religion.[6] This last series of contrast will show how important the issue of mythical study is not only for the Bible but for comparative religion generally. For such scholars as Wright and von Rad, who hardly stand alone, the formula of "mythical versus biblical" becomes a key to the elaboration of what are in their view entirely different modes of thought. Needless to say, this formula leads necessarily to the affirmation that biblical thought is unique, an affirmation of great service to theology.

Long as the definition of myths as stories about the gods lived on in biblical study, it could not survive much beyond mid-century. Its end was inevitable, even if it outlived what anyone from without the circle of biblical scholars might have predicted, simply because developments in the study of myth more broadly demonstrated repeatedly the poverty of such a definition. One signal that the end of myth's exile from the Bible was imminent was the demythologization program begun about the time of the Second World War by the New Testament scholar Rudolf Bultmann (1884–1976). Though Bultmann rarely offers a succinct definition of myth, his discussion of the uses of myth plainly indicates that he is utilizing a definition that is both different from and broader than the conventional Grimm brothers' definition. Equally significant, Bultmann's understanding of myth is much more in keeping with what anthropologists, historians of religion, and others had been saying on the subject since the end of the nineteenth century. For Bultmann, as for many of these scholars in other fields, a myth is one of the ways in which any culture objectifies and symbolizes its entire world view. Thus understood, it is impossible to deny that much of the New Testament is mythical through and through. Not just the New Testament writers' notion of the physical cosmos as a three-storied edifice (heaven, earth, and hell), and not just the assumption that the earth is the arena of the activity of demons and other supernatural beings are mythical. More than these, for Bultmann "the whole conception of the world which is presupposed in the preaching of Jesus as in the New Testament generally is mythological."[7]

Anyone in the present century who wishes to appropriate the message of Jesus must then, according to Bultmann, demythologize the New Testament. Demythologizing does not mean ridding the Bible of mythology. It means rather translating this mythology. New Testament mythology requires translation because of the definition with which Bultmann begins. If a myth is the objectification and symbolization of any culture's world view, then the myth cannot function for a culture with a radically different world view.

The demythologizing program of Bultmann prompted, as any student of the fate of Strauss might ruefully have predicted, a controversy within and beyond theological circles similar in shape and intensity to that which Strauss's *Life of Jesus* generated. Bultmann was accused of substituting his own brand of existentialist philosophy for biblical thought and of raising this philosophy to the status of an independent mythology. Clearly, theological scholarship continued to hope that myths and biblical narratives might forever remain distinguishable. There must be, such thought seemed to urge, a fundamental difference between biblical thought on the one hand and all other categories of thought on the other.

Much as many may have regretted that Bultmann again so

pointedly raised this issue, much as they may have hoped that the problem of myth and the Bible had been solved once for all, other events soon demonstrated that Bultmann was not alone. The problem of myth and the Bible had been too long and too easily sidestepped by the maneuver of a simple definition. Thus, by the 1950s, studies began to appear that openly questioned the usefulness of the long regnant definition. Most directly to this point, G. H. Davies concluded a 1956 study on mythology with the affirmation that "mythology is a way of thinking and imagining about the divine rather than thinking and imagining about a number of gods" so that "the content of myth, whether polytheistic or otherwise is accidental to the nature of myth."[8] Within a few years of this study, John McKenzie surveyed some of the many theories of myth from scholars in disciplines beyond the biblical field. His survey convinced him that the Grimm brothers' definition, despite its long utilization within biblical study, was radically inadequate. Thus, the accompanying claim that the Bible was free of myth was no longer defensible.[9]

We can conclude this section with a brief glance at each of two important volumes, one from the 1960s and another from the 1970s. Neither volume rests upon the conventional denial of the category myth to the Bible. To the first of these volumes, B. S. Childs's *Myth and Reality in the Old Testament,* belongs the great credit of unmasking the inadequacy of defining myths as stories about the gods. Further, Childs goes well beyond this to note acutely the damage done by this definition. The damage is that the utilization of the Grimm brothers' definition created a "tendency among those using this definition to fail to see the essential problem of myth in the Old Testament."[10] For Childs, this problem is one that is perceived within biblical tradition itself. The Old Testament does contain material that is mythical, though it also contains material that is in tension with the mythical. Childs's identification of a biblical viewpoint that is antimythical does demonstrate that he still adheres to a theological commitment that wishes fundamentally to divide biblical thought from all other thought. This demonstration can hardly occasion surprise, so laudably forthright is Childs in all his work on his intended service to theology.

A second volume, F. M. Cross's *Canaanite Myth and Hebrew Epic*, goes further. Here, the argument is not chiefly theoretical, not intended as a contribution to the broader conversation about the study of myth generally. Cross's argument is rather driven by the force of newly available evidence. This evidence, which is largely that of the Syrian myths first uncovered in 1929 at the ancient city of Ugarit, persuades Cross of the bankruptcy of all attempts to prove that Israelite religion is discontinuous with the religions of Israel's neighbors. Rather, a pattern can be discerned within much biblical literature that is based upon the shape of a central cosmogonic myth of the Canaanites. The pattern is threefold: (1) A divine warrior battles against a god of chaos; (2) the divine warrior is victorious; and (3) the divine warrior becomes king and receives a royal palace. This pattern appears in some biblical texts in its pure, mythical form (Psalms 29, 89, or 93), in others in the form of a mixture of mythical with historical traditions (Psalm 77 or Isaiah 51:9–11). Such a mixture Cross finds to be characteristic of Israelite religion: "In Israel, myth and history always stood in strong tension, myth serving primarily to give a cosmic dimension and transcendent meaning to the historical, rarely functioning to dissolve history."[11]

Cross's notion of a "tension" between mythical thought and historical thought cannot but recall Childs's thesis that mythical material in the Bible often remains "in tension" with an alternate viewpoint. The similarity of these two scholars on this point is of potential significance. While both Childs and Cross have left far behind the former insistence that myths play no role in the Hebrew Bible, neither appears quite willing to entertain the possibility that mythical thought and mythical literature are at the very heart of Israel's religion. The possibility is a real one, and one which future studies of biblical religion must explore.

Nothing would be gained, and much lost, through any attempt to gainsay the recent progress by biblical scholars in returning openly to the issue of the presence of myths in the Bible. The speed of this progress in the past twenty years is stunning. But equally stunning is the century-long hiatus on behalf of biblical scholarship in making any real attempt to redefine myth on the basis of new discoveries and new theoretical advances. The hiatus can seem quite inexplicable—until and unless we recall biblical scholarship's long service to a particular model of theological historiography, which we have attempted to describe in Chapter 1. This model demanded that all things biblical be firmly and forever distinguished from the nonbiblical. The forcefulness of this foundational and long unquestioned distinction accounts for the otherwise inexplicable desire to divide the biblical from the mythical.

3. PROGRESS IN DEFINING MYTH

The historical survey just completed has repeatedly claimed that early definitions of myth have been jettisoned as scholars in a variety of related disciplines have struggled toward arriving at a definition that is at once serviceable and fair. Before we move on to a systematic summary of the available models we might utilize in analyzing a given myth, it is time that we return to this struggle. And a struggle it has been. Almost every attempt to define myth begins or ends with some admission that the task has been all but impossible. Some attempts go further still in the direction of despair. J. Rogerson, for example, laments that "finding an adequate and all-purpose definition of myth" is and remains an "impossible task."[12] In fact, there is little reason for such pessimism. A survey of some older and some more recent definitions of myth demonstrates well that there is now available a definition that satisfies most of the criteria so long sought.

Although the Greek word from which our term *myth* comes at one time meant only "a story," or "something said," without any suggestion of the truth or falseness of the story, by the time of the birth of the New Testament this word had come to be used as a label for something false—for a story and then later for any information that is not true. We still use the word *myth* in this sense, as when we speak of "the myth of nineteenth-century liberalism," or, some would say, of "the myth of meaningful tax reform." Within scholarly circles, however, myth has long been used in a more restricted sense to refer to a particular sort of story rather than to fabrications or to ideological smoke screens.

As we have noted, the definition of myth that came to dominate the early study of folklore throughout the nineteenth century was that made generally known by the publications of the Grimm brothers: A myth is a story about the gods. This definition, scholars in a variety of disciplines outside the theological camp have long argued, is inadequate because it implies both too much and too little. Its suggestion that myths must be limited to a polytheistic setting implies too much, thus unnecessarily removing from consideration a great many stories felt to be myths by both those who tell them and those who study them. Some myths do speak of the activities of a number of deities. Others tell of the deeds of a single deity. Others still, the classicist G. S. Kirk reminds us, "are not primarily about gods at all, and have no ancillary implications of sanctity or tabu."[13] If the limitation of the Grimm brothers' definition to a setting within polytheism implies too much, this definition's brevity suggests too little. To call a myth a story about the gods is too general. Surely, many scholars asserted, additional criteria are needed in the definition of myth beyond just "story" and "the gods."

Already by the close of the nineteenth century, there was wide agreement among anthropologists and the earliest students of comparative religion that to say myths are stories about the gods was to define myths most inadequately. A fair amount of the present century was then devoted to attempts to refine this definition. These attempts yielded such a variety of competing definitions that a complete listing of them would exhaust most of the pages in the present volume. Still, citing a few of these definitions, chiefly from the past several generations' most influential students of this phenomenon, will serve the useful purpose of demonstrating that there is some unity amidst all this apparent diversity—and hence that the problem of formulating an adequate definition of myth is in fact nothing like a problem beyond solution.

Any list, however brief, of the most important and influential scholars to have inquired after the meanings and functions of myth would have to include the name of Sir James George Frazer (1854–1941). Frazer is probably best known as the author of *The Golden Bough,* [14] an elaborate study of the origins of myths and religions that was updated and expanded through several editions rather in the manner of Calvin's *Institutes.* Though Frazer's various definitions of myth are nearly as numerous as the volumes of the latest editions of *The Golden Bough,* he did settle toward the end of his career upon a single definition. Myths, Frazer concluded, are "mistaken explanations of phenomena, whether of human life or of external nature."[15] Among Frazer's successors, Bronislaw Malinowski (1884–1942), a professor of anthropology at the London School of Economics for a period between the wars, wrote at length and often polemically on the subject of myths' functions. His polemical comments were often directed against "armchair" anthropologists, those whose theoretical conclusions were not supported by the years of extensive fieldwork that Malinowski demanded of any who wished to be heard in this area. Malinowski's emphasis on practical training in the field is reflected in a similar emphasis upon the practical in his comments on myth. Thus, for him a myth is "a pragmatic charter of primitive faith and moral wisdom."[16] Malinowski's influential stress upon the everyday functions of myths is something to which we will return when surveying methods of analyzing myths.

We can move more quickly through a collection of additional definitions that will bring us fully up to date. A post–World War II reference work on mythology, which may be found in almost any library, defined myth as "a story, presented as having actually occurred in a previous age, explaining the cosmological and supernatural traditions of a people, their gods, heroes, cultural traits, religious beliefs, etc."[17] Our generation's leading historian of religion, Mircea Eliade, proposes that we define myth as that which "narrates a sacred history; it relates an event that took place in primordial Time, the fabled time of 'beginnings.' . . . The actors in myths are Supernatural Beings."[18] T. H. Gaster, an American scholar associated with the view that links myths closely to rituals, defines a myth as "any presentation of the actual in terms of the ideal."[19] Moving closer to the present, the philosopher Paul Ricoeur finds myths to be "traditional narratives which tell of events which happened at the origin of time and which furnish the support of language to ritual actions."[20] And finally in this much abbreviated list, Walter Burkert, a scholar whose analyses of myth combine many of the latest methods, defines a myth as "a traditional tale with secondary, partial reference to something of collective importance."[21]

A first reading of the definitions selected here is likely to lead to the conclusion that scholars can as little agree on the correct definition of myth as they can on an issue like the date of the beginning, or the central cause, of the Renaissance. Further study, however, reveals that there are after all three important elements that most of these proposed definitions share. There is mounting agreement that a myth has to: (1) be in the form of a story; (2) be traditional, that is, to have been transmitted, almost always orally, within a communal setting and for a long period; and (3) treat characters who are in some sense or senses more than simply human. An additional and fourth criterion is also suggested by several of the definitions in the previous paragraph: A myth must also: (4) recount events from remote antiquity.

The definitions most widely utilized by contemporary folklorists (and folklore study is the area of the most sustained concentration upon myth) suggest that the three or four criteria just listed are indeed the tests that a given text or oral presentation must pass in order to qualify as a myth. Citing but a pair of these definitions well demonstrates this. The folklorist W. Bascom's article on the various genres of folk literature, an article cited frequently and approvingly by many others in the past two decades, concludes that "myths are prose narratives which, in the society in which they are told, are considered to be truthful accounts of what happened in the remote past. . . . their main characters are not usually human beings."[22] At nearly the same time, another scholar of the same phenomenon, Joseph Fontenrose, proposed a similar if somewhat simpler definition: Myths are "the traditional tales of the deeds of *daimones:* gods, spirits, and all sorts of supernatural or superhuman beings."[23]

Both these definitions include the criteria of story, traditional, and superhuman characters. That of Bascom adds the criterion of remote antiquity. Because the formulation of Fontenrose is more succinct, and because it omits the fourth criterion, that of remote antiquity, about which there is less agreement, his definition seems most likely to command general assent. It is the definition upon which all of the studies in the present volume continue to rely. Because of this reliance and in the interest of clarity (if at the cost of repetitiveness), this definition is worth restating: myths are *"the traditional tales of the deeds of daimones: gods, spirits, and all sorts of supernatural or superhuman beings."*

Before moving on to a discussion of some of the methods that have been proposed for analyzing any myth or group of myths, our treatment of the definitional problem must deal with one final issue. Given that great progress has been made in the attempt to formulate an adequate and acceptable definition of myth, what about the categories of legend and folktale? Are these to be distinguished one from another, and are both to be distinguished from myth? This is an important issue in the present context primarily because biblical scholarship has insisted for many years that many tales in the Bible must be seen not as myths but rather as legends or sagas or the like. Here there is much less agreement than has occurred recently in the case of the correct definition of myth, though it can at least be said that the certainty with which most biblical scholars wish to adhere to a distinction between myth on the one hand and legend or saga on the other hand is something with which many folklorists would find fault. Some of the latter, to be sure, do propose that myths are different and are to be analyzed differently from folktales (identified by contemporary folklorists with German *Märchen,* French *contes populaires*) and from legends (German *Sagen,* French *traditions populaires*).[24] Those who do adhere to these distinctions often go on to assert that folktales differ from myths in that the former are regarded less seriously or piously than are the latter. Legends, these same scholars argue, differ from myths both in setting (legends are set in eras less remote than are myths) and in characters (the characters of legends can be purely human). The point of central significance here, however, is that others disagree and express great doubts about the potential legitimacy or usefulness of any distinctions between myth on the one hand and folktales or legends on the other.[25] Directly to the point of the present volume, for example, Burkert convincingly argues that the distinction between myths and legends or sagas so beloved by biblical scholarship cannot survive the force of the available evidence. This distinction, Burkert concludes, is rather a part of a tradition of theological apology.[26] It is this same tradition that attempted, vainly in the end, to deny the presence of anything fully or properly mythical in the Bible.

4. THEORIES FOR ANALYZING MYTHS

BIBLICAL STORIES AS MYTHS

As we have seen, the course of twentieth-century research has yielded the increasingly more certain conclusion that there is mythical material in both the Hebrew Bible and the New Testament. Interestingly, however, for many years this conclusion was seen to apply primarily ur solely only to certain small sections within the Bible. These sections were essentially those for which an obvious parallel could be found among the mythological collections of ancient Israel's neighbors—the myths of Mesopotamia, Canaan, and Egypt. Of course, such parallels have appeared with unanticipated frequency because of the archaeological discoveries of the past few generations, so that even limiting the application of the label *myth* to those biblical narratives with ancient Near Eastern analogies has produced a fairly large pool of material. Today, it is not just the flood story in Genesis 6–9 or allusions to a battle between Yahweh and a cosmic monster (in Job, for example) that are seen as mythical. Included, too, are the portraits of Yahweh in the setting of a divine council's meeting (as in Psalm

82 or 2 Kings 22), any number of references to a cosmic mountain (in Ezekiel and several Psalms especially), and much more.

In light of the arguments presented here, however, even this greatly expanded list is far too limited. If a myth is a traditional narrative, at least one of whose characters is himself or herself superhuman or can perform superhuman feats, then a great deal of the Bible, and not just a scattering of "borrowings," is mythological. The patriarchal narratives in the Book of Genesis, in which many events are the result of the intervention of divine beings or of a deity, are myths. So, too, is the story of Moses and the Exodus from Egypt, a story filled with miraculous occurrences attributed to the action of a deity. And so, too, are many stories in the Deuteronomistic History (the Books of Deuteronomy through 2 Kings), the Chronicler's narrative, other stories in the Hebrew Bible, and the gospel narratives in the New Testament. If such a list sounds surprisingly comprehensive, it ought not. Any initial surprise is primarily the result of biblical scholars' long utilization of a narrow definition for myth, retained in the face of wide disagreement from other scholarly disciplines solely because the definition had the singular virtue of exiling myths from the Bible.

The realization that biblical narratives are mythical narratives carries with it an important implication. This implication is that the two-hundred-year history within the modern period of discussion and controversy about the origins, meanings, and functions of myths is a history to which biblical study might (perhaps must) profitably pay closer attention. As we noted in opening the present chapter, it would be unfair and inaccurate to allege that biblical scholars have paid no heed to this history. They have, but in a piecemeal and rarely systematic fashion. It thus becomes the aim of the following section to describe a number of the most significant stages in the history of the study of myth and to append to each description some account of the advantages and disadvantages of each model for the understanding of myth.[27] This latter task is of some significance, since it appears that several of the models to be described and assessed are still utilized by biblical scholars in apparent ignorance of the sharp criticism they have received in other quarters.

THE ANCESTORS OF MODERN THEORIES OF MYTH

Even if the scientific study of myth is conventionally said to have begun only sometime around the start of the nineteenth century, this hardly means that no theories for the origin and meaning of myth were available before this time. Mythographers in antiquity, and then again writers during the Renaissance, produced several such theories. Among the most popular was the view, to which we have already granted brief attention, that stories about human heroes, kings, and those who advanced civilization in other ways gradually attracted to themselves increasingly miraculous elements until a myth resulted. This theory might simply be called the historical explanation of myth, since it assumes that the key to the genesis of a myth is the history of its transmission. It is more often labeled *Euhemerism,* after a fourth-century B.C. novelist and geographer, Euhemerus of Messene. Euhemerus's travel tale, *Sacred Scripture,* recounted an imaginary trip to an island in the Indian Ocean. There the traveler discovered his key to mythology: that the deities worshipped on this island, and by extension elsewhere, were originally not deities at all but rather humans. So, too, the feats attributed to these deities were originally great acts of human prowess or courage. But they were hardly supernatural acts. If many well-educated people today are unaware of the name Euhemerus or of antiquity's attribution to him of this particular theory for the origin of myths, the theory itself continues to possess wide popularity. And much of biblical scholarship, in so far as it attempts to peel away the miraculous accretions to what are thought to be the original stories about, say, Moses or Jesus, is also Euhemeristic in impulse.

A more proximate ancestor to the theories of myth recounted later in this chapter was that developed largely by a single scholar, Friedrich Max Müller (1823–1900).[28] Müller was a philologist who became a professor of modern languages at Oxford University at about mid-century. His theory of myth was an ancillary product to a more general theory of the origin and development of many European languages. The discovery upon which both views were built was that which claimed to have found the ancestor of these languages in that spoken by the Aryan invaders of India in remotest antiquity. This language possessed several notable characteristics, among them a somewhat profligate tendency to both homonymy and polyonomy. When the Aryan language ceased to be spoken, and when those who spoke this language's descendant languages were no longer aware either of their own separate language's ancestry or of the special features of the Aryan language, some memorable confusions were set in motion. For the origin of myth, the most significant such confusion was the following: What once had been common nouns were incorrectly interpreted to be the names of gods and goddesses, and what once were fairly mundane accounts of natural phenomena were incorrectly interpreted as accounts of the wars, loves, and other activities of these deities. Myths thus begin as a result of ignorance and confusion, and the wrongly interpreted accounts once set in motion produce ever more elaborate mythologies. Since most of the original accounts were believed by Müller to be explanations of natural phenomena, especially those having to do with the course of the sun, this theory was to become known as "solar mythology."

Despite the great span of time that separates Euhemerus from Max Müller, the two models for the genesis of myth associated with each man are remarkably alike. Both Euhemerus and Müller begin with the assumption that myths are to be read literally—that they *are* about what they *appear* to be about. Both also assume that myths are fundamentally mistaken accounts of actual events or ordinary descriptions. For both, then, myths are the result of confusion and ignorance. Such assumptions fit without difficulty into any scheme that views human culture and human thought processes as evolving and improving within historical times. Since this scheme corresponds so well with the broader contours of nineteenth-century thought almost everywhere, Euhemerism and

Müller's solar mythology would only receive their sharpest criticisms after the close of that century. In the twentieth century, the conclusion of biologists, ethnographers, and others that human intelligence has not evolved within historical times has seemed so firmly based that no theory of myth based upon the assumption of such an evolution is any longer regarded with seriousness.

MYTHS ARE PRIMITIVE SCIENCE: THEY SEEK TO EXPLAIN

Another model for the interpretation of myth that arose in the nineteenth century is that which sets myth and science on the same linear line, and finds modern science to be the truest successor to primitive myth. Both myth and science are the result of an identical human need, the need for humans to have available explanations for all phenomena, especially those phenomena that seem initially baffling. Though the need that results in myth and science is the same, the two are not identical. Myths, because they arose early in human development when people simply knew less than do we, are incorrect explanations. Science, on the other hand, represents increasingly correct explanations. The world, then, has matured, and myths are a relic of humanity's immaturity.

Since the need, according to this view, to which both myths and science respond is an intellectual craving—the desire for adequate explanations for all phenomena—the view is often called the "intellectualist" theory. Its founder, E. B. Tylor (1832–1917), is also among the founders of the discipline of anthropology.[29] Among his other accomplishments, Tylor is remembered too for the idea of cultural "survivals," and for the argument that religion begins as "animism." The former idea holds that though human culture has evolved, various signs of its earlier state are evident in various "survivals," ideas and practices no longer strictly functional but still present in the human memory. Tylor's writings on animism were to be of even greater significance for the ensuing generations' study of the development of religion. Religions originate, according to Tylor, in the ascription of living souls *(anima)* to a wide variety of inanimate phenomena. Thus endowed with souls, these phenomena are eventually deified and worshipped.

Equipped with these fundamentals, Tylor felt able to construct an entire history of human religious development. Though the course of humanity's religious and cultural development has yielded many changes, something that has not changed, in his view, is the basic need to explain. This desire to know the causes of all phenomena is, then, reflected among early and primitive humans in mythology, and among moderns in science.

Myths are thus both historically conditioned and beyond history: the former because they represent a particular stage in human evolution, the latter because the need behind myths exists always and everywhere. One vitally important aspect of Tylor's theory of myth, an aspect that separates this theory sharply from many of the theories described later in this chapter, follows directly upon his view that both myth and science stem from the same impulse and are two stages of the same thing. This aspect is the following: Though myths may be wrong, they are neither irrational nor illogical. The craving for explanation that produced first myths, then science, is a desire satisfied only by reasoning and logic.

Even though Tylor's intellectualist theory of myth was born within a few years of the solar mythology of Max Müller, the two views have been accorded markedly different fates. Müller's view is largely a historical curiosity today, dependent as it is both upon a particular model of human mental progress and upon some highly speculative historical reconstructions. Tylor's theory, on the other hand, has found defenders both in the years immediately following its first articulation and much more recently. Among the former belongs James Frazer. Though Frazer also spoke on the behalf of the myth-ritual theory, as we will see, a theme rarely absent from his voluminous writings is that of myths as incorrect attempts to account for the causes of the world's puzzles. Indeed, this is perhaps clearest in Frazer's definition of myth cited earlier in this chapter: Myths, Frazer wrote, are "mistaken explanations of phenomena, whether of human life or of external nature." The definition is one that Tylor himself might have composed. The intellectualist theory, following Frazer and his near contemporaries, found few defenders for much of the twentieth century. However, the theory has been revived with enthusiasm of late by several anthropologists. Among these is Robin Horton, who lived and worked in Nigeria for many years. According to Horton, African traditional thought of many varieties utilizes quite different terminology from that of modern science, but the theoretical models upon which both rely are the same.[30]

What are the chief merits and demerits of the Tylorean intellectualist model for the origin and meaning of myths? Among the former, pride of place probably belongs to the proper credit this model gives to early and "primitive" humans for possessing the ability to think. Saying as much may seem odd and hardly distinctive. But given what other views on myth will say, and given especially the era in which Tylor first articulated this view, to say that Tylor's "primitives" can think is most distinctive. Many theorists contemporary with and later than Tylor denied to "savages" and others either the ability or the desire to think rationally. It is thus to the lasting credit of Tylor that he viewed early peoples as driven by the same intellectual needs and as possessing the same mental equipment as moderns. A second advantage of the Tylorean theory is that it accounts well for the literal level, even if it ignores any symbolic import, of many myths. Perhaps the majority of myths claim on the most obvious level to offer explanations —of meteorological phenomena, of personal or national fate, and so forth. This is clearly true of biblical myths, whose etiological (i. e., offering a causal explanation) level has long been of keen interest to scholars. Tylor proposed that we take these explanatory claims seriously; he acknowledged early humans' desire to know and yet in the end condemned as immature the results they achieved.

Aside from the refusal of the intellectualist theory to ponder at length the possible levels of myth beyond the literal, narrative level, this theory is also heir to other and potentially serious problems. First, the theory is very much in keeping with the era of its birth in assuming that humans have evolved in historical times. Tylor's primitives can think, but they remain quite ignorant. And they remain ignorant of any number of things about which the present century's anthropological work has found them anything but ignorant. Malinowski's field work, for example, demonstrated for him that his predecessors' lack of such firsthand exposure served them especially poorly in precisely this regard. The "savages" studied by Malinowski were, he concluded, as knowledgeable and competent in their own spheres as any twentieth-century scientist. "If," Malinowski argued, "by science be understood a body of rules and conceptions, embodied in material achievements and in a fixed form of tradition and carried on by some sort of social organization," then primitives display no inability to perform science.[31] And since these same peoples possess elaborate mythologies, it must be that these myths are performing some function different from that performed admirably by their science.

A second potential problem with the theory that views myths as immature science is that it offers no explanation for the social nature of myths.[32] Myths are born in a communal setting, and they continue to live only as long as they are the possession of an entire community. That something fundamental about myths is social is granted by almost every student of myth. It is not at all clear that the intellectualist model proposed by Tylor offers any reason for this social setting. If myths are the result of an innate human desire to explain the world, why should these explanations assume a communal level? Why should they not remain the possessions of separate individuals?

THE MYTH-RITUAL THEORY

A basic mistake committed by Tylor, and by the authors of every other theory summarized here, is, according to the advocates of the myth-ritual theory, that he and they neglect to study myths together with the rituals that accompany them. These scholars propose that myths and rituals are, inevitably, two parts of a larger, single phenomenon. To use an analogy borrowed from opera, an analogy much favored by myth-ritualists, the myth is simply the "libretto" to the entire performance. The myth-ritual complex is this entire performance. Several of those most heavily influenced by the myth-ritual view argued not only that all myths are simply a part of a larger complex that always includes a ritual component but also that many, perhaps most, myth-ritual complexes from the Near East and from the wider Mediterranean realm are structured according to a similar pattern. This pattern is one of (1) conflict, (2) disaster or death, (3) lamentation, and (4) rebirth. Because this particular structure was so favored by many myth-ritualists, their position is also sometimes called "pattern-ism."

William Robertson Smith, the nineteenth-century Scottish thinker whose vital contributions inaugurated the social study of religion and to whom a portion of Chapter 1 was devoted, was among the first to suggest that myths cannot be comprehended apart from their inevitably accompanying rituals. Robertson Smith further claimed that rituals arose *first* in the course of human history and only *later* were myths added to the complete myth-ritual performance. His creative inquiry into the origins of Semitic religions is based throughout upon the fundamental assumption that "in almost every case the myth was derived from the ritual, and not the ritual from the myth."[33] This extension of the basic myth-ritual view—myths are not only to be studied together with the rituals that always accompanied them, all myths themselves *originated* as rituals—is sometimes called the "strong" or the "bold" presentation of this position. A more moderate position, held by probably the majority of those within the myth-ritual camp, takes no firm stand on the issue of whether the myth or the ritual is the original component and simply states that these two are always to be studied together since they always appear together in any culture's religious life.

Toward the end of the nineteenth century Robertson Smith moved to Cambridge University after he was prohibited from continuing to lecture at the Free Church College in Aberdeen because of the alleged lack of orthodoxy in his views on biblical religion. Cambridge then became an early center for the broadcasting of the myth-ritual theory. Because of this, several British scholars who advocated this position are sometimes grouped together and labeled the "Cambridge School" of myth-ritualists. This "school" included the anthropologist Frazer and the classicists Jane Harrison (1850–1920), F. M. Cornford (1874–1943), A. B. Cook (1868–1952), and also Gilbert Murray (1866–1957), even though Murray became a professor at the other ancient English university, Oxford.[34] Whatever one's ultimate assessment of the myth-ritual position, many of the works of these scholars, and especially those of Harrison, remain well worth reading.[35] Most of this group might also be called "patternists" because they were persuaded not just that rituals accompanied all myths but also that the particular pattern noted previously is one that careful study shows to be behind many ancient religious performances, including Greek drama. Along with others, these same scholars insisted that the myth-ritual theory receives its best demonstration from Near Eastern evidence. For example, *Enuma Elish,* the Babylonian creation myth, was read as the "libretto" to the entire performance of the New Year "Akitu Festival" and hence was viewed in many circles as providing all the empirical proof that was needed to support the broader myth-ritual theory.

Both explicitly and implicitly, a great many (perhaps even a clear majority of) biblical scholars' works rely upon the myth-ritual theory in one or several of its various forms. This is true already of the studies of Gunkel, though his reliance upon this theory is largely implicit, and of the enormous number of works dependent upon Gunkel. It is more obviously true of the work of Gunkel's student Sigmund Mowinckel and of many others such as Ivan Engnell, A. R. Johnson, S. H. Hooke, and T. H. Gaster. The last two named are probably responsible for the widest applications of the myth-ritual theory. Hooke edited several volumes, the title of the first of which was simply *Myth and Ritual,* which applied the basic theory to biblical and other Near Eastern texts.[36] Gaster's central affirmation, which appears throughout his writings, is that Near Eastern myths are the reflections of "a pattern and a sequence of ritual acts which, from time immemorial, have characterized major seasonal festivals in most parts of the world."[37] The various mythic texts discovered at ancient Ugarit in Syria are read by

Gaster in such a way that they provide particular support for both the basic myth-ritual theory and for its "patternist" aspect. Gaster then goes on to discern this pattern, which is essentially identical with that posited by the earliest myth-ritualists, behind the structure of many biblical texts, including especially several Psalms (Ps. 29, 89, 93, 97, 99). Because Gaster is aware of the potential pitfalls of the "strong" myth-ritual position (that all myths originated as rituals), he repeatedly insists that he is defending and applying only the more moderate position (that myths and rituals are inseparable parts of a larger complex). However, Gaster's account of a chronological scheme according to which myths begin as the accompaniments to rituals but later are often separated from this context may hint that he, too, finds in ritual the originating element.[38]

Unlike the intellectualist position of Tylor and others, which went through a long decline before its recent revival, the myth-ritual theory has never suffered from a dearth of supporters even if few have been willing to go to the extremes of some of the Cambridge School. The theory's continued popularity is due in part to the force of evidence that suggests that some myths are beyond doubt linked with rituals. Several of the Ugaritic myths from ancient Syria recounting the actions of Baal, El, Anat, and others belong to this group, especially those that appear to include rubrics assigning different roles in the myth to different actors or groups. Since Israelite religion emerged from the Canaanite setting in which these Ugaritic myths lived, a likely conclusion becomes that some biblical myths are also part of a larger myth-ritual complex.

The myth-ritual theory is heir to a second advantage, in addition to its ability to account for those myths whose ritual context is undeniable. This is its frank awareness that myths rarely, if ever, exist in isolation. Myths rather appear to be a part of the fuller life of any society, and especially a part of the liturgy and cult of a society's religion. Indeed, it can be and has been argued that when severed from this life, myths die. It was the perception of just this that prompted Robertson Smith first to propose what would become the myth-ritual theory. He argued that scholars had before exhibited too clearly a tendency to abstract myth from its social and cultic context and then to concentrate upon doctrine alone. Robertson Smith wished to remedy this by looking rather at the larger religious life of any society, and his remedy began with the insistence that ritual action came first and hence that any adequate study of myth must look to this ritual action.

Unfortunately for the myth-ritual theory, the advantages that the theory initially appears to possess are at least balanced, and perhaps outweighed, by some grave disadvantages.[39] These disadvantages show up less in any theoretical assessments of the myth-ritual model than they do in the attempts practically to apply the model. The first deficit in this model is, then, the failure of empirical evidence widely to support the most fundamental presupposition of myth-ritualism: that myths are the inevitable accompaniments of rituals. If some myths do accompany rituals, a great many myths do not. Strikingly, it appears that in some cultures, among several in North America for example, myths are never connected with rituals. It will be remembered that Frazer, who figures so largely throughout the present discussion, was for a time a member of a lively circle of myth-ritualists. Yet this same scholar's lifelong and immense cataloguing of myths from almost everywhere convinced him in the end that the number of myths tied directly to rituals is "almost infinitesimally small, by comparison with myths which deal with other subjects and have had another origin."[40] Even more damagingly, the examples most favored by the early myth-ritualists, including Frazer for a number of years —the myths of Adonis, Attis, and Osiris, and of the alleged tie between the Babylonian creation myth and the Akitu Festival— all have more recently been shown to be supportive of a firm link of myth to ritual only if one utilizes very late evidence.[41] Earlier evidence shows no such link. Hence, one might even conclude, though it would not be prudent to do so, that the myth always comes first and any attachment to ritual is only a sign of the myth's degenerative status.

A further problem inherent in many applications of the myth-ritual theory is of even greater weight. This problem is one on the theoretical level, that of the logic of explanation. If a myth is to be explained by *reference* to the ritual that is asserted always to have accompanied it, then any such "explanation" is only worthy of the name if it concludes with the necessary further step of offering a comprehensive *explanation* of that ritual. And yet the majority of myth-ritualist "explanations" appear to fail just here: They offer a putative account of a myth's origin, but they then go no further. To say that *Enuma Elish* originated in and is an integral part of the Akitu Festival is to present a partial birth narrative of the myth; it is not to explain or interpret the myth. The same failure occurs in the argument that parts of the Book of Exodus stem from an early Israelite ritual. What must be forthcoming is an adequate explanation of the specific ritual alleged to accompany the myth.

Of course, if this problem is a severe one, it is also one that is in no sense beyond repair. We simply need an adequate theory of ritual, a model to explain the meanings and functions of ritual.[42] If this is forthcoming, and if it is then combined with those cases where myths and rituals do appear to be inextricably linked, then the myth-ritual position might prove to be most useful. There is a particular reason why biblical scholars might pay especial heed to the attempts to repair and refine the myth-ritual theory. This reason is the implicit dependence of so much biblical scholarship, well beyond the work of Mowinckel, Engnell, Gaster, and others, upon a version of myth-ritualism. For example, form criticism, that contextual method of literary criticism first suggested for biblical tradition by Gunkel and since then applied very widely, falls into this category. A foundation of form criticism is that an adequate interpretation of a biblical text is dependent upon the reconstruction of that text's setting in the religious life of ancient Israel. This setting is most usually a cultic, hence a ritual, setting. Form criticism thus assumes that an early form of many biblical texts, almost all of which are mythic, originally accompanied ritu-als. And this assumption is but a particular form of the central tenet of myth-ritualism. A comprehensive attempt to address and remedy the criticisms that can be leveled against myth-ritualism thus seems a clear need in the area of biblical research.

MYTHS AND THE MYTHOPOEIC MIND

This theory can usefully be thought of as the precise opposite of the intellectualist tradition inaugurated by the work of Tylor. That latter tradition viewed myths as explanatory and proposed to take seriously myths' literal meaning. The theory to which we now turn finds myths to be primarily expressive, rather than explanatory. This theory also finds little value in heeding the obvious, literal level in a myth. Rather, myths are here seen to be the results of something called "mythopoeic thought." Those who find this concept accurate and useful are persuaded that mythopoeic thought is not necessarily an earlier stage in the evolution toward modern thought. Here, too, this theory is distinguished from the intellectualist model of Tylor. Mythopoeic thought, according to some scholars, is not earlier thought but a different kind of thinking altogether. This sort of thinking is not so much logical and rational as it is expressive, poetic, and mystical. Logical and rational thought may seek to explain phenomena. Mythopoeic thought does not. The latter seeks rather an active participation with phenomena.

As much as with anyone else, the origins and fullest description of so-called mythopoeic thought are linked with the French anthropologist Lucien Lévy-Bruhl (1857–1939), even though Lévy-Bruhl abandoned this position near the end of his life.[43] Myths' chief function, according to Lévy-Bruhl, was expressive and participatory. Through relating a myth, a person or a group expresses the need to participate with the world. Here, participation is seen as an alternative to explanation. Myths, according to Lévy-Bruhl's earlier work, do not seek to explain. Indeed, the task of explanation is impossible for mythical thinking, since such thinking is mystical and refuses to make the distinctions between phenomena —between material things and mental representations, for example—upon which causal explanations are based. Lévy-Bruhl's alleged discovery of this last characteristic of mythical thought is responsible for his using the adjective *prelogical* in description of it. Whatever others who used this adjective may have thought, in fairness to Lévy-Bruhl, it is important to remember that he argued only that "primitives" did not (or did not usually) think logically. Lévy-Bruhl did not propose that such peoples were incapable of logic.[44]

Only an implicit reliance upon the myth-ritual theory and upon some version of Euhemerism compete with the notions of myth-opoeic and prelogical thought for frequency of utilization by biblical scholarship. Strikingly, even the most recent such scholarship continues to make reference to mythopoeic thought. This is surprising chiefly because the theory has been abandoned with some finality by anthropologists, philosophers, and others. Of course, that a theory has been abandoned in some circles is hardly itself a sufficient reason for all to turn their backs on it. In this case, however, the neglect accorded to mythopoeic thought seems well justified on other grounds. The most important of these is that twentieth-century fieldwork among the kinds of groups to whom Lévy-Bruhl attributed this thought has repeatedly failed to find any evidence that so-called primitive thought is mystical and participatory rather than rational and explanatory.[45] Plainly, biblical scholars cannot have discovered in any such recent field research statements defending the notion of mythopoeic thought. The chief source of this notion for biblical scholars appears rather to be the work of the philosopher Ernst Cassirer and of those dependent upon him.[46] Cassirer claimed to have found a distinctive type of thinking behind the production of myths. This sort of thinking he described in ways quite similar to Lévy-Bruhl: It was anti-empirical thought, and it was most emphatically not like any form of scientific reasoning.

The source to which many biblical scholars during the past forty years appealed most directly and most frequently for a defense of the existence of mythopoeic thought is the work of neither Lévy-Bruhl nor Cassirer. This source is rather an essay by H. and H. A. Frankfort entitled "Myth and Reality."[47] But this essay, written as the introduction to an extremely successful and often reprinted textbook on ancient Near Eastern thought, is itself a popularizing summary of the central views of the early Lévy-Bruhl and of Cassirer. The Frankforts propose here that the myths from the ancient Near East display a steadfast refusal to distinguish between subject and object—a refusal, that is, to make the distinction that is fundamental for all scientific thought. In language by now familiar, they argue that mythical thought is participatory rather than analytic and that such thought thus addresses the world as a personal "Thou" rather than seeking to explain the world as an impersonal object. "Primitive thought," the Frankforts maintain throughout this extraordinarily influential essay, "cannot recognize our view of an impersonal, mechanical, and lawlike functioning of causality."[48]

It might be argued that those scholars who propose that mythopoeic thought is the genesis of myths are to be granted some credit for their recognition that myths are a special and distinctive form of human expression that thus requires some equally distinctive modes of explanation. If so, this is just about the only positive comment that can today be made about the mythopoeic theory. Those who have actually lived for significant periods of time in the midst of communities of "primitives" have, of course, found abundant evidence for the distinctive and richly diverse kinds of cultural accomplishment each community has produced. But again and again, what these same fieldworkers have failed to discover is anything like a mode of thought that is different in kind from modern or scientific thought and that might be called mythopoeic thought. Individual people and separate groups of people will naturally emphasize different aspects of what it means to be a human being. But no consistent body of evidence comes close to suggesting that there is a fundamental cleavage between "primitive" thought and modern thought, much less that the former is distinctively mystical and irrational and the latter scientific and logical.

Students of myths outside the Bible have paid heed to the results of this century's painstaking fieldwork and to this work's rebuttal of any such construct as mythopoeic thought. Burkert's inquiry into the functions of Greek myths disposes at the outset of "the nostalgic idea of a golden age when a race of poetically minded primitives uttered myths instead of plain speech."[49] And Kirk's assessment of the theory of mythopoeic thought is similarly informed by the empirical results of field work and is thus similarly harsh: "The polarization between fully rational thought (which is usually held to begin, in the Western tradition, at some time after Thales) and non-rational or 'mythopoeic' thought is logically indefensible and historically absurd."[50] Biblical scholarship is arguably the only academic discipline in which such notions continue to go largely unrebutted. Moreover, here as in the discussion of myth-ritualism, it is important to remember that many voices within biblical study rely implicitly upon this particular theory even in the absence of direct reference to the term *mythopoeic.* Though there are some gratifying signs of a gradual shying away from that term, many biblical scholars continue to make reference to such constructs as "the Semitic mind" or "biblical thought," as if either or both of these were utterly distinctive. These constructs are most useful, again, as a part of the grander project that wishes to claim unique status for the Bible and for biblical patterns of thought—and hence for the ultimately super human origins of both. This grander project needs to be recognized for the apologetic edifice it is.

MYTHS' SOCIAL SETTING AND FUNCTIONS

A fourth theory for the origin and meaning of myth examines myth's extra-individual context. This theory's supporting evidence and explanatory power have meant that it continues to garner far more support than does the mythopoeic model. The social theory of myth takes its initial point of departure from the single aspect of myth to which all definitions of myth point. However much scholars have debated the merits of particular definitions, few if any of the proposed definitions omit the element of the "traditional." Myths are traditional stories, virtually everyone agrees. To say that myths are traditional stories is to observe that myths are generated in and persist in communal contexts. The theory under consideration here proposes to grant utmost serious-ness to this point of near universal consent. The function of myths, for this theory, thus becomes that of creating and cement-ing social bonds. Myths help to bring disparate people together into a single group, and then to establish and defend this group's larger identity.

This theory too, like others just chronicled, owes its clearest point of origin to perhaps the most creative student of myth and religion in the past century and a half, William Robertson Smith. It may be remembered that Robertson Smith found most wanting in contemporary studies of these phenomena any sustained awareness of the day-to-day, practical uses of religion and myth. Heeding these uses demonstrated for him that religion and myth functioned chiefly in group contexts. On the issue of sacrifice, for example, another area where Robertson Smith's thought marked a fundamental advance, he found sacrifice's primary function to be that not of appeasing a deity or granting to a deity a gift but rather of a meal shared between a deity on the one hand and a social unit on the other. Sacrifice thus performed the task of formally cement-ing social bonds. And what was true of sacrifice was also true of religion's other aspects.

Such thoughts led Robertson Smith ultimately to the conclusion that "religions did not exist for the saving of souls but for the preservation and welfare of society."[51] Only if we turn to the basic proclamations of thinkers like Marx or Freud can we find state-ments as powerfully constitutive of twentieth-century social thought as this brief conclusion of Robertson Smith. For example, Emile Durkheim (1858–1917) created an entire tradition of French sociology based upon this conclusion, and his *Elementary Forms of Religious Belief* pays generous tribute to Robertson Smith. Durk-heim's account of myths' function in this volume shows how well placed such tribute is: Myths, Durkheim wrote, are the means by which "the group periodically renews the sentiment which it has of itself and of its unity; at the same time, individuals are strength-ened in their social natures."[52]

So centrally have the arguments of Robertson Smith, Durkheim, and others been appropriated by a host of disciplines within the present century that elaboration upon these arguments runs the risk of documenting what have become truisms. Still, describing one application of this basic position to the study of a particular body of myths will prove useful. The example we choose comes from the work of the anthropologist Bronislaw Malinowski, who extended this line of thinking perhaps more consistently than did any other single scholar. Malinowski, we recall, lived for a period in the Southwest Pacific. It was this experience that persuaded him of the benefits of fieldwork and of the pitfalls of reaching any generalizations about human culture in its absence. The same experience persuaded Malinowski that myths are anything but speculative or intellectual exercises. The functions of myths are rather preeminently practical. His years' witnessing the performance of myths convinced him that no myth is "an intellectual explanation or an artistic imagery." Malinowski here disposes in a single phrase of both the Tylorean and the mythopoeic models. A myth's task in "primitive culture" is rather much more overtly functional. A myth "expresses, enhances, and codifies belief; it safeguards and enforces morality." A myth is "a pragmatic charter of primitive faith and moral wisdom."[53]

The frequency and urgency with which Malinowski utilized such terms as *function* or *charter* in the discussing of myth has led to this theory's receipt of the labels "functionalism" or "the char ter theory." As with other theories discussed in this chapter, here too biblical scholarship has long participated implicitly in functional models of myth, even if one has to look long and hard for many direct references to Durkheim or Malinowski. For example, many tales in the Bible are read as straightforward models for morally praiseworthy and religiously pious behavior. Other stories, those of the Exodus and the Conquest periods especially, are conventionally interpreted as stories that gave to ancient Israel a sense of national identity and pride. Such interpretations are founded squarely upon the functional model of myth. This is also true, if less overtly, of the periodic calls for biblical scholars to pay increased heed to Israel's social formation, calls issued both near the beginning of the present century and then again and very widely at the present. These demands to study Israelite literature as a reflection of Israelite social structures assume both that many biblical myths functioned to articulate and support group identity and that the modern scholar can reconstruct ancient Israelite social formations on the basis of evidence drawn primarily or wholly from myth. Both these assumptions are not without problematic aspects, and a continued reliance upon either depends unquestionably upon an adequate defense of the functional theory of myth.

The social context theory of myth, like others for which Robertson Smith was an early advocate, possesses the obvious attraction of calling for a comprehensive vision of the entire world of any culture's myths. Those standing within this tradition can thus argue well that they do not commit the potentially serious error of isolating a myth from its wider context. Ethnologists especially have rarely tired of labeling the views of Tylor, Frazer, and others as the views of library-bound, unrealistically detached scholars. Only such scholars, they go on to argue, could fail to recognize myths' practical, social functions.

Nor is this the only virtue to which the social context theory of myth is heir. Another is that which this theory shared with the intellectualist theory of Tylor, different as these two models are in other regards. This second, apparent advantage is again the seriousness with which the literal, narrative level of a myth is regarded. Some myths are most simply and most economically read as props for socially beneficial behavior. Virtue, heroism, patriotism, fidelity, integrity, and the like do win out in the end according to the story line of many myths. The social context or functional theory proposes that it is a vain exercise to look beyond this literal level. What myths say is what myths do.

So thoroughly has twentieth-century scholarship of many sorts adhered to and extended the central vision of Robertson Smith and Durkheim with regard to religions' and myths' social functions that it has been easy to overlook the weaknesses in this position. But weaknesses there are. These deserve a full hearing in the present context precisely because the social context theory has achieved, at least in some quarters, the status of a truism. First and most obviously, a social functional theory of myth seems incapable of dealing with the presence of the unusual, the bizarre, or the more wildly fanciful elements of myth. Any comprehensive list of mythical motifs, such as those that can be found in the standard Stith Thompson *Motif-Index of Folk-Literature,* [54] will reveal that which is clear in any case, that such elements play a large, perhaps even a dominant, role in myths. Animals become humans, and humans animals; people are transported vast distances in space and time; bodily functions are often exaggerated or reversed; mating or eating is done in variously unusual fashions; and so forth. Further, and perhaps more tellingly still, mythic motifs are not just strange or bizarre. These motifs are often socially disruptive or destructive, and yet they are participated in by the myths' heroes, by those who are successful in the end. The heroes of a great many myths cheat, lie, steal, commit incest, and the like. Consider, for example, the characters in the biblical patriarchal narratives (Gen. 12–50). According to one of the traditional sources of the Book of Genesis, Abraham marries his half sister, thus commiting incest. And Jacob, with his mother's aid, cheats both his father and his brother (see Chapter 4 on these stories). What is the possible function of such acts in the interest of social unity and stability? How can a mythic hero's performance of any number of illicit or disruptive acts play a role as a part of a charter for socially beneficial behavior? Were such heroes uniformly condemned for such acts, were they always to "grow up" out of such activity into more obviously praiseworthy behavior, then the myths that tell of them could with justice be seen as charters. But often this is not the case: the hero succeeds precisely on the basis of committing acts that would normally be condemned and receive harsh punishment.

Another major problem with the social functional theory of myth is a problem at the level of an often unarticulated and unexamined assumption upon which the theory rests. This assumption is the following: Social functionalist views of myth appear consistently to assume the existence of a one-for-one correspondence between empirical social conditions on the one hand and those social conditions that are described in myths on the other hand. That is, these views assume that a myth that speaks of, say, an egalitarian social formation, or of a particular set of inheritance rules, directly reflects the existence in the society from which the myth stems of an egalitarian social formation or of that particular set of inheritance rules. If this assumption appears in danger when ethnographic data clash with mythical data, then the normal strategy employed to rescue the assumption is to argue that the myth reflects empirical conditions from some long past, and now lost, social setting. Ethnographic research upon living societies does indeed demonstrate that this assumption can be justified in some cases. There are instances where a myth's social setting corresponds to the actual social formation of the society that produced the myth. However, this same research demonstrates that this assumption is hardly justified in all cases. Often, many or all of the aspects of the society that produced the myth are nothing like those portrayed in the myth, and appear never to have been so.[55]

This objection to the social functionalist mode of mythical interpretation ought, it seems, to be particularly troubling to biblical scholars. A great deal of biblical interpretation rests upon the reconstruction of ancient Israelite social settings solely on the basis of mythical texts. For example, it was popular a half century ago and again is so today to assert that the Israel of the Tribal League (premonarchical) era was fairly egalitarian, and much more egalitarian than would later be the case. This assertion is founded essentially upon data obtained from myths about the Tribal League period, for example, in the Books of Judges or Samuel. A more uncertain foundation is difficult to imagine. Given the conclusions of researchers who can compare myths with empirical social settings, it is quite possible that an egalitarian myth can come out of a highly stratified social formation.

The Unconscious in Myth

A psychological equivalent to the social functionalist model for the genesis and preservation of myth is the theory that affirms that myths are produced by the human unconscious. Both theories

have it that myths respond to human needs. The social functionalist theory locates these needs in a group setting: Humans need
myths to create and preserve social bonds that might otherwise
disappear. The psychological theory locates these needs on the
individual level: Any human being has psychological needs that
are met best or solely by the production and repetition of myths.
That which prompts these needs is the unconscious, whose existence this particular theory obviously begins by positing. For various reasons, the unconscious needs expressing. Myths perform
this task, as do dreams and other mechanisms.

In the case of each of the theories described in this chapter, there
are some slight differences in the ways in which each theory's
advocates will state and then apply the theory, but these differences remain slight and are not of central importance in the present context. This is not true for the theory of the unconscious and
myth. Here, there are two distinct versions, each associated with
the name of a different thinker: Sigmund Freud (1856–1939) and
Carl Jung (1875–1961). These versions differ significantly enough
to demand separate treatment, though no claim is voiced here to
offer anything like a comprehensive survey of the thought of these
two founders of modern psychology. First, the theory presented
by Freud: Freud views the human unconscious, a notion that he
himself can fairly be said to have discovered, as the repository of
various instinctive drives. Of these drives, the most widely or
perhaps notoriously known is that of sexuality. But the unconscious contains more than sexuality alone for Freud; other instinctive and aggressive impulses are also present. If, however, the
unconscious is the location of these drives, the unconscious also
demands that they be given more open expression. And that is
plainly impossible. To act with complete freedom and upon all
occasions on the basis of one's instinctive drives would be to create
chaos. Society simply could not survive such constant and un-
modified chaos. Just here is where myths and dreams step in to
perform their functions. Myths express imaginatively those instinctive drives that cannot be expressed in everyday life. So described, perhaps the similarity of this theory to that we have called

the social functionalist theory is now clear. For the social functionalist theory, myths function to create social stability. For the psychological model, myths function to release the tension created by
the unconscious' need for expression, a need whose satisfaction in
more direct fashion might destroy human society.

Jung, of course, was for some years closely associated with
Freud. He too begins by positing the existence of an unconscious.
For Jung, however, the unconscious is both differently located and
produces different drives than for Freud. The unconscious in
Jung's works is chiefly a collective phenomenon, and the drive it
produces is less an aggressive drive than it is a kind of "spiritual
desire" for meaning.[56] Jung granted to dreams an importance like
that which is found in Freud's research. He claimed to find in
dreams and in myths a similar set of symbolic representations.
This similarity he accounted for by suggesting the existence of
" 'autochthonous' " and " 'myth-forming' structural elements"
within the collected unconscious, elements that he went on to
label "archetypes."[57] For Jung as for Freud, the unconscious is not
a rational phenomenon. Hence, he considers the attempt to explain
myths, themselves the products of the collective unconscious, by
recourse to rationality or logic as misguided and impossible.
Myths' function is primarily expressive, as it was for the mythopoeic theory. To say more would be to grant to myth an intellectual significance that myths simply do not possess.

One of the great and tantalizing questions behind the study of
myth since antiquity has been that of accounting at once for the
universality of mythical motifs and yet the specificity of individual myths. Why is it that myths the world around seem so similar
and yet so dissimilar? Why is it that some motifs recur (that of the
flood or of some elements in a hero pattern) in myths from widely
disparate sources? Were myths all quite similar or all clearly dissimilar, these questions might disappear. But myths are neither
entirely alike nor entirely distinct. How might we explain this
demonstrable fact? One of the chief strengths of the psychological
theories under consideration here is that they can provide an answer to these questions. Myths are not all alike because no two

cultures are precisely the same. Many of the individual details in a myth are a product of this cultural specificity. And yet myths are in broad outlines quite similar precisely because of the operation of the human unconscious, whether this be individual or unconscious. The human unconscious produces myths, and the human unconscious operates at all times and in all places.

A second set of intriguing questions is handled with equal ease by that theory of myth that views myth as the product of the unconscious. These questions all revolve around the perception that the emotions that surround myths seem remarkably strong. Why do people feel so strongly about traditional narratives like these? What is the source of the passion that can accompany the transmission and the defense of mythology? The answer from the psychological school is that the drive that produces myths is located in the unconscious and is therefore instinctual. It is instinct, whose forcefulness few will want to question, that explains the strength of the emotions that can accompany myth.

Despite these apparent strengths, this theory, too, is hardly without deep problems. Initially, the very strength of the position can be seen as a weakness. The model that links myths to the unconscious is so quick to answer apparent objections that we have to wonder whether the model is in any way falsifiable. What kind of evidence would it take either to falsify or to prove the correctness of this model? Most of the evidence that might be offered belongs to a most uncertain realm. This is true fundamentally of the recourse that this theory has to the notion of the unconscious. As a posited realm, the unconscious is a difficult construct to falsify and one for which it is equally difficult to provide empirical evidence to support. For example, if one were strenuously to deny the reality of the Oedipal complex, an advocate of this theory might argue that the strength of the denial of this complex demonstrates the reality of its existence. Hence, potentially negative evidence is neatly turned into positive evidence, and there seem to be no grounds for falsifying the position. Such arguments belong, it would seem, more to the sphere of dogma than to that of scientific discussion, a key to which has long been found in the criterion of falsifiability.

A second critique to which the psychological theory is open is one that applies perhaps more to the thought of Jung than to that of Freud. Jung wrote that it was the universal nature of certain symbols and motifs in both dreams and myths that first suggested to him the reality of collective archetypes. Various of his followers, Joseph Campbell, for example, have then extended this claim. However, other investigators have found it difficult to demonstrate that the symbols and motifs about which Jung and others speak are in fact anything like universal. To these investigators, Jung's universalizing of various motifs appears to be another example of the wider tendency to force a certain restricted set of symbols, drawn from the West, upon materials where they cannot natively be found. To put this somewhat differently, twentieth-century ethnography has discovered at least a fair amount of cultural relativity across the globe. The view of Jung leaves precious little play for such cultural relativity, so little that one wonders if a particular group of Western ideas has not been illegitimately extended.[58] Here, too, then, an apparent strength of the psychological theory becomes upon further reflection a weakness. The tendency of this theory to deal in universals does mean it can offer a ready answer to the question of why many myths share similar themes. But this same tendency can appear to deny otherwise strong evidence for variety within the human community.

STRUCTURAL ANALYSIS

The final theory of myth to be covered here is one of such recent vintage that the tasks of description and assessment are considerably more difficult. Further, and at least in its purest form, this theory remains that above all of but a single scholar, the French thinker Claude Lévi-Strauss.[59] Even locating Lévi-Strauss within a single discipline is not easy. Although he is part anthropologist, part linguist, part philosopher, some representatives from each of these disciplines will want to deny with vigor that he is "one of them." Some scholars find Lévi-Strauss's structural analysis difficult to understand and impossible to apply. Others claim to understand structural analysis but then wish to disagree dramatically with what they understand its chief claims to be. Perhaps the most that can be said at the outset is that which Kirk says, that Lévi-Strauss's structural analysis "contains the one important new idea in this field since Freud."[60]

About every one of the theories of myth surveyed thus far one might say that it searches for the most appropriate analogy with which to discuss myth. Myth then becomes a phenomenon like science or like ritual or like dreams, and so forth. Those analogies that show up most often in Lévi-Strauss's writings are music and language. Music is a suggestive analogy for this scholar because myth operates on several "horizontal" levels at once, much like a musical score. The study of language is another such analogy because Lévi-Strauss wishes to claim that modern linguistics proves that meaning is a result not of essences but of relationships —that is, there is no inherent meaning in any given sound, and meaning is never anything essential. Phonemes, the names that linguists give to the basic sound units in language, are meaningless in and of themselves. But these meaningless units produce meaning through their relationship with other phonemes. A structural relationship of sounds, not the sounds themselves, yields meaning. It is the same, Lévi-Strauss suggests, with the separate elements in a myth. Any element in a myth—the sun, a piece of fruit, long hair, a body of water that must be crossed, wine, and so forth —is itself meaningless. These elements rather produce meaning, just as do phonemes, only through their relationship with other equally meaningless elements. In myths, as in language generally, meaning is a purely relational phenomenon. Structural analysis thus insists that one cannot usefully ask the kind of question that students of myth have asked for centuries. One cannot, for example, ask what the fruit represents in the story of Adam and Eve or what Samson's long hair symbolizes. One can only ask the following kind of questions: How are the separate elements in a myth related to one another? In what other contexts do these elements appear in the totality of any culture's myths? Where in the same culture but outside the domain of myth—in the culture's kinship system, or economic structure, for example—do we find the same kinds, or opposite kinds, of relationships? Lévi-Strauss's asking of these sorts of questions, with their consistent concentration upon structures of relationship, gives this theory its title.

Some of the theories described in this chapter (the intellectualist, for example) grant significance to the literal, narrative level of myth. Others (the mythopoeic, for example) deny any significance to this level. Structural analysis belongs emphatically to this latter group. For Lévi-Strauss, a myth's narrative level offers another instance of what is so often true in other areas of inquiry within the natural, social, and human sciences—an instance of the fact that appearances can deceive. In making this point, Lévi-Strauss often appeals to another of his favored analogies, that of geology. Here, obviously, apparent reality can never be mistaken for true reality. The surface appearance of many geological phenomena would give a geologist a misleading story of the earth's surface, if "read" literally. Myths are thus like that part of the earth's surface that is visible. Myths possess an attractive surface appearance— that of the narrative line—but myths are never most truly "about" this narrative line. Rather, myths, like rocks, need "decoding." The process of decoding is one that demands of the student of myth that he or she be familiar with the entire corpus of myths produced by the culture that yielded the myth in question. As a single mythical element is meaningless in and of itself, so too any single myth can never produce an adequate meaning. Lévi-Strauss's study of the story of Asdiwal, to which reference has already been made, illustrates this with particular clarity. He devotes about half of this study to describing both this myth and the economic and social organization of the British Columbian culture that produced it. This part of the study he concludes with the statement, "having separated out the codes [economic, geographical, sociological, culinary, etc.], we have analyzed the structure of the message. It now remains to decipher the meaning."[61] To accomplish this final and most significant task, Lévi-Strauss turns to a group of additional myths from the same culture. Only when he can place the structure of these myths alongside that of the story of Asdiwal does he reach any conclusions about the myth's meaning.

Some of the statements Lévi-Strauss makes about the tasks myths perform might be taken to imply that structural analysis is a special sort of functional analysis. Probably the most frequently cited such statement is one from his essay "The Structural Study of Myth," originally published in 1955: "The purpose of myth is to provide a logical model capable of over-coming a contradiction (an impossible achievement if, as it happens, the contradiction is real)."[62] Though Lévi-Strauss's more recent work never returns to so directly functionalist formulations, that which is most significant in this early statement is the phrase *logical model*. The phrase suggests what the rest of Lévi-Strauss's work amply demonstrates: that the function that myths perform is not so much a social or a psychological function as it is an intellectual function. Thus, even though structural analysis rejects the significance that Tylor granted to a myth's narrative level as explanatory, and even though Lévi-Strauss insists throughout that the "savage mind" is every bit as advanced and logical as is the modern mind, structural analysis does share with Tylor an emphasis upon the human mind.

As they manifest themselves in myths, the contradictions that Lévi-Strauss finds articulated in any corpus of myths are often variations upon the theme of nature versus culture. The opposition of nature to culture then becomes a kind of symbolic summary of a host of other oppositions. Just as human beings are both of nature, like all other animals, and yet of culture, since they speak and thus create a world apart from nature, so, too, the elements within any group of myths are often seen to arrange themselves according to a long series of paired oppositions: natural, raw food versus cooked food; youth versus old age; woman versus man; north versus south or east versus west; terrestrial versus marine life; and so forth. It is again important to remember that such oppositions are never taken literally or granted absolute significance in themselves for structural analysis. They are rather the products of what the human mind, in an extraordinarily crea-

tive and systematic fashion, does to more basic contradictions that
appear in life itself.

A growing number of quite recent studies within biblical scholarship have gone by the name of "structural" or "structuralist"
inquiries.[63] Though there is nothing to be gained by any attempt
to determine who has the best claim to a title like structural analysis, a most important and often overlooked difference exists between the majority of these biblical studies and the kind of analysis practiced by Lévi-Strauss. Most structural studies within
biblical scholarship belong to a category of literary criticism that
is greatly removed from the structural analysis created by Lévi-
Strauss and then applied by him and other anthropologists. The
key distinction is that anthropological structuralism attempts,
with varying degrees of success, to relate the structures discerned
in a corpus of myths to a host of other structures that occur in the
society that produced these myths; literary structuralism usually
does not. Hence, a structural study by Lévi-Strauss will refer to
kinship, economic, social, and other arenas as the locations of
structural relationships that can also be found in direct or inverted
form in myths. Like Marx, Lévi-Strauss does wish in the end to
grant a kind of primacy to the economic and social level rather
than to the imaginative or literary level. This much seems clear
from statements of his, such as the following: "I do not at all mean
to suggest that ideological transformations give rise to social ones.
Only the reverse is in fact true. Men's conception of the relations
between nature and culture is a function of modifications of their
own social relations."[64] Whether or not the founder of structural
analysis is entirely consistent on this point, Lévi-Strauss' studies
of myth almost always make some reference to relational structures beyond the textual level; and it is this which separates these
studies most dramatically from literary structuralism.

The relative novelty of structural analysis means that assessing
its strengths and weaknesses can be done with less sureness than
is the case for the other theories of myth described here. For each
of those other theories, sufficient time has passed for reflection to
have occurred and a consensus, or at least a majority of opinion,

to have emerged. There is, for example, a consensus that the notion of mythopoeic thought is an artificial construct with little or no empirical foundation. Such is not true for structural analsyis, where wide disagreement exists between advocates and critics. No signs of this disagreement's abating exist at present. Therefore, any assessment of the work of Lévi-Strauss and of its potential usefulness for biblical scholarship must remain provisional.

The very controversy sparked by the works of Lévi-Strauss must be counted as an initial advantage of this theory. These works' novelty and their open departure from previous models for the study of myth have kindled an interest in the meanings and functions of mythology unmatched for nearly a century. In the absence of this interest and the theoretical and empirical studies it has prompted, scholars might never have turned to the Hebrew Bible with a new appreciation of the potential risks and gains that accompany studying biblical myths. Secondly, whatever the faults in Lévi-Strauss's analyses of myth, these analyses do possess the virtue of comprehensiveness. Lévi-Strauss has stressed repeatedly the necessity for any adequate analysis of a myth to deal in some fashion with *all* of a myth's details. Hence, a most useful criterion has been created for adjudicating between two competing studies of the same myth: That study is the more valuable that can account meaningfully for a greater number of the myth's separate elements. In this instance, structural analysis may prove to have formulated an assessment mechanism that will lead to the eventual modification or discarding of structural analysis itself, should another theory of myth offer a more adequate explanation of the many details in a given myth.

Thirdly, structural analysis takes with utmost seriousness and regards with utmost respect the thought processes of so-called primitives. It is thus that theory of myth that breaks most fundamentally with all evolutionary models. The latter always make a distinction between the mental processes of traditional peoples and those of modern peoples. Lévi-Strauss has argued for over forty years now that though humans in traditional societies may think about different phenomena than do we, such humans think

88 / BIBLE WITHOUT THEOLOGY

equally well. This conclusion accords nicely with twentieth-century ethnographic research. A fourth potential gain from structural analysis comes as a result of Lévi-Strauss's suggestion that all of a culture's myths must be studied before any one of these myths can be said to have received adequate analysis. The gain here is that scholars have now begun to look seriously at myths long regarded as minor and of peripheral importance. If Lévi-Strauss is at all correct in this regard, then biblical scholars can no longer dismiss as without central significance such problematic passages as that relating the marriage of deities to women just before the Flood account (Gen. 6: 1–4) or that telling of the attack upon Moses as he returned to Egypt after his encounter with Yahweh (Exod. 4: 24–26). For structural analysis, there simply are no myths without central significance, since it is any culture's entire corpus of myths that alone may reveal the structural relationships that can then be compared with kinship, economic, social, and other relationships. Finally, those for whom the proof of any theory's value comes only with the results achieved might point with approval to the results of Lévi-Strauss's four-volume study of South and North American myths. Myths that for decades seemed nonsensical and utterly without order no longer appear so.[65] The tradition within biblical scholarship of distrusting theory and of respecting alone the interpretive consequences of any theory might mean that only a long string of successes in applying structural analysis to biblical myths will persuade biblical scholars of the potential benefits of this theory. If such successes are not forthcoming, then anthropological structuralism may takes its place with other discarded theories of myth.

In most quarters, structural analysis was greeted with initial skepticism. Still today the majority judgment is probably negative, founded upon some or all of the following observations. First, radically different as is structural analysis from the psychological theories of Freud or Jung, it may well share with these theories of myth one major problem, that of the difficulty of either proving true or falsifying the assumptions that lie behind each. Though Lévi-Strauss most often compares mythic structures with structures observable elsewhere in a culture, he also wrote near the end of his first volume on American myths that myths in the end "signify the mind that evolves them."[66] Such reference to the mind seems at present as slippery and as difficult to test empirically as does the psychological notion of the unconscious. Secondly, among the analogies to myth of which Lévi-Strauss is so fond, primacy probably belongs to the linguistic analogy. The linguistic research to which Lévi-Strauss chiefly appeals is work done before and during the period of the Second World War. Some critics have argued that more recent work in linguistics demonstrates that Lévi-Strauss's use of this particular analogy does not prove anything like what he thinks it proves.

A third criticism of structural analysis might focus on that level of myth that Lévi-Strauss chooses largely to ignore. We remember that Lévi-Strauss argues that the narrative, surface level of a myth is a deceptive region and that the interpretor of myth pays chief heed to this level only at great peril. However, the discussion of how best to define myth has revealed that the single criterion in defining myth upon which there is the widest agreement is precisely here: However they may disagree otherwise, scholars are agreed that myths are stories. If, then, the narrative serves to define myth, can one offer an adequate analysis of myth that begins by rejecting narrative as secondary and deceptive? Fourthly, biblical scholars in particular have missed in structural analysis any concentration upon an area to which they have long given the most attention, the historical. While biblical scholarship focuses upon the changes that long transmission has introduced into a body of myths, Lévi-Strauss is persuaded that a myth's structure is preserved despite historical changes. It has become a cliché of late to criticize biblical study for too exclusive a concentration upon the historical, but the remedy here may not be that of ignoring history. Possibly, the attempt of Walter Burkert to combine structural analysis with a concern for myths' history of transmission may recommend itself especially to biblical scholars.[67] Finally, there remain some difficulties in the area of applying structural analysis. One of these in particular may prove troublesome for the analysis of biblical myths, especially the earliest of these myths. If a student of myth must compare mythical structures with structures found elsewhere in the culture that produced the myth, as Lévi-Strauss argues, then is there sufficient information about early Israel to permit a structural analysis of all biblical myths? Some scholars might argue there is. However, as we have said previously, much of the economic, social, and political "data" about ancient Israel comes at present from myths themselves, and myths are notoriously unreliable sources of ethnographic data. Perhaps, then, a fair assessment of structural analysis' potential contribution to biblical myths must await the collection, by archaeology above all, of far more information about ancient Israel, independent of biblical sources.

5. CONCLUSIONS

The most general impression that results from a summary account and assessment of some theories of myth is a negative one. All of the theories in use during the past century are heir to some flaws. Some, for example, the mythopoeic model, are plainly flawed beyond repair and ought to be abandoned. Others, however, might still be applied with validity, if an account is taken of their limitations or of the further work required to render them useful. For example, the myth-ritual theory may yet prove of great value, but only if we can (1) demonstrate that a particular body of myths did indeed accompany rituals and (2) appeal to a comprehensive theory for the meaning of ritual itself. The structural model requires further testing on both theoretical and empirical levels. For now, it would seem fair to insist that any structural analysis of a biblical myth must make reference to another, extranarrative level in which structures can be found that have generated or are parallel to those in the myth.

The chief conclusion here remains that with which we began. There is a wide body of scholarly inquiry into myths and into the theories that might be used to explain their origins and functions. This inquiry has concluded that some theories formerly in fashion are too faulty to permit their continued utilization, at least in the absence of new evidence, and that other theories are radically limited in their applications. However, and coincident with our conclusions with regard to a particular model of historical understanding in Chapter 1, biblical research for too long demonstrated a lack of awareness of the wider inquiry into the meaning of myth and hence, too, an apparent blindness to the dangers of the continued uncritical utilization of many theories of myth.

The two chapters that follow attempt, through analyses of some myths in the Book of Genesis, further to document how the theological setting of biblical scholarship is partly responsible for the utilization of arguments that would not and could not be utilized outside of this setting. These analyses will seek to heed the conclusions reached in the present chapter. Thus, no reference will be made to any such construct as the mythopoeic mind, nor will biblical myths be presumed to bear witness to a sort of thinking less logical or less fully developed than our own. So, too, the myth-ritual model will be largely avoided on the grounds that little evidence survives from antiquity on the basis of which we might know of the existence and form of rituals that accompanied the myths in question. A historically contextualized and broadly comparative form of structural analysis is perhaps the fairest description of the particular method of mythical analysis that the following studies will apply to some myths in the Book of Genesis.

3. Grace or Status? Yahweh's Clothing of the First Humans

1. MYTHS IN THE BIBLICAL PRIMEVAL HISTORY (GEN. 1–11)

Perhaps most biblical scholars are archaeologists in the etymological sense of this term. Most are students, to a greater or lesser extent, of humanity's most ancient historical remains: the oldest poems in the Hebrew Bible, the first Israelite prophets, the initial responses to the Exile, and so forth. This observation, along with the general intrigue that accompanies any report from remotest antiquity, goes a long way toward explaining the great attention that has been granted to the Book of Genesis, especially the first eleven chapters. These chapters, which represent the Primeval History, are in some sense the beginning of the beginning. To this section both literature (from long before to long after *Paradise Lost*) and scientific inquiry have granted a primacy of place.

Further, Genesis 1–11 was recognized as a collection of partial or even complete myths long before such recognition was granted to other sections of the Hebrew Bible. It was precisely here that the long tradition of denying the presence of myths in the Bible began first to erode, for several reasons. First, the biblical Primeval History speaks of times and events that are obviously mythical when compared with other tales from antiquity, tales that had long been regarded as myths. In this first section of Genesis, we read of the creation of the ordered cosmos, of the creation of the first humans, of a group of divine beings who mate with women (Gen. 6:1–4), and of much else that corresponds to the cosmogonic myths of the ancient Greeks and many others. If this latter group of tales were to be labeled myths, then the conclusion seemed inescapable that the analogous tales in Genesis 1–11 must also receive this label. Secondly, given the presence here of various divine or semidivine beings, it became increasingly obvious that one could not exile the category myth from the Primeval History even if utilizing the long regnant definition of *myth* as a story about the gods. And finally, it was just here that the longest and most certain parallels to extrabiblical Near Eastern myths were discovered. The flood story in the Eleventh Tablet of the Epic of Gilgamesh and the Tale of Adapa were both fairly widely known by the end of the nineteenth century. The latter was in some ways parallel to the Eden story in Genesis—indeed, we will seek later to demonstrate that a particular motif from the Tale of Adapa coincides with a motif in the Eden story in a way that has not been sufficiently noted. And the former (Gilgamesh, Tablet Eleven) was in plot structure and in detail strikingly similar to the biblical account of the flood. It was also noted that the cosmology from Hermopolis in Egypt shared many of the elements now present in Genesis 1–2, and that other stories in the Primeval History overlapped with additional myths from the ancient Near East.

The forcefulness of all these pieces of evidence combined to produce an early, sustained willingness to regard Genesis 1–11 as different in character and genre from the remainder of the Hebrew Bible, and with this a willingness to begin to speak of this section as mythological. Hermann Gunkel, for example, became persuaded that age-old mythical fragments and mythical structures were clearly present in the Primeval History, even as Gunkel still clung to the older definition of myths as stories about the gods. Of course, and as we have seen, Gunkel continued to insist that these myths were only borrowed fragments, the brightness of whose original colors had faded under the power of Israelite thought.[1] Much more recently, the first thoroughgoing structuralist analysis of biblical material also predictably concentrated upon the first few chapters in the Book of Genesis.[2]

However, even given the sanction that treating the Primeval

History as partly mythic in character has received, most studies of the material here remain fully within the theological tradition. Such studies are therefore largely of a "historical" (in the sense outlined in Chapter 1) character and seek answers to questions like: What are the antecedent, ancient Near Eastern myths upon which the Primeval History is based? How has Israelite thought transformed (usually, this was assumed to mean "demythologized") the sources here? Such studies are also largely after conclusions of an overtly theological sort: What do the stories in Genesis 1–11 teach us about the character of Yahweh, the god of Israel? How ought humans to behave in light of the lessons implicit in these tales? The investigation of the material here is thus a good place to begin specifying in detail the contrasts between a theological approach to biblical narratives on the one hand and an approach founded more on comparative religion (or the history of religions) on the other. The present chapter seeks to accomplish just this task by focusing upon a single incident, even a single verse, near the end of the story of Adam and Eve.

2. THE CLOTHING INCIDENT (GEN. 3:21) IN THE THEOLOGICAL TRADITION

We choose this single verse near the conclusion of the Paradise story partly because Genesis 3:21 is one of the few verses in the entire Primeval History upon whose meaning general agreement has existed for centuries. Such agreement begins on the level of the Hebrew text and its appropriate English translation. Genesis 3:21, nearly all scholars argue, is to be read and translated as follows: *wayya'aś yhwh 'ělōhîm lĕ'ādām ulĕ'ištô kotnôt 'ôr wayyalbišēm,* "And Yahweh God made for man and his wife garments of skin; and he clothed them."[3] Within the theological tradition broadly, this incident in the Paradise Tale is read quite literally. The meaning of the brief account, it is widely agreed, is this: Yahweh's act here in providing the primal pair with garments prior to their expulsion from the garden is a divine concession to human frailty. It is an act of grace, an act of extraordinary and unmerited solicitude. In between the curse and the blessing, the argument runs, the Yahwist inserts a notice about God's generosity; Yahweh knows that the man and the woman need clothing to cover their recently discerned nakedness. Further, the standard reading of Genesis 3:21 sees the act of clothing here as a response not only to a psychological need but also as a response to the more overtly practical need of protection from the rigors of the world beyond the garden.

The context of the clothing incident in Genesis 3:21 is as follows. The verse appears immediately after that in which the man indicates that his spouse is to be the mother of all humanity (Gen. 3:20). The brief narratives in these two verses follow the "judgment sentence" in Genesis 3:14–19.[4] Directly after the statement that Yahweh provided clothing for Adam and Eve, the primal pair are expelled from the garden (Gen. 3:22–24). Like all of Genesis 3, verse 21 is commonly ascribed to the Yahwist ("J"), though usually to a Yahwistic redactor ("Y^a" or the like) or to a different stage in the tradition.[5]

As a supplement to the regnant interpretation of the clothing incident, which will soon be documented at length, biblical scholars in the nineteenth century especially began with a search for the origin of the brief story recorded in Genesis 3:21. This they found in an etiological tradition about the history of culture and the beginnings of animal sacrifice. Thus, Robertson Smith, whom we have cited repeatedly as a superb exemplar of late nineteenth-century thinking, found in J a tradition in which, immediately after the Fall, humanity's "war with hurtful creatures (the serpent) began and domestic animals began to be slain sacrificially, and their skins used for clothing." The biblical tale was then, for Robertson Smith, in agreement "with Greek legend in connecting the sacrifice of domestic animals with a fall from the state of pristine innocence."[6] Both Driver and Skinner, in commentaries that appeared in roughly this same era, follow Robertson Smith in offering similar etiological explanations.[7] In addition to the Greek analogy noted by Robertson Smith, other cosmogonic materials do provide some support for the presence of traditions about the advancement of culture in narratives like the biblical paradise tale.

The *Phoenician History* preserved by Philo of Byblos, for example, mentions that Ousoos, who also initially dared to sail on the sea, "first discovered how to gather a covering for the body from hides of animals which he captured."[8]

Such comments on the origin of Genesis 3:21, however, come from a fairly limited era within biblical scholarship and are not in the main exegetical tradition that I want now to document. This tradition, it will be recalled, finds in the clothing incident an instance of divine graciousness and generosity toward humanity, perhaps the first such in the Hebrew Bible. This reading of Genesis 3:21 is at least as old as the Talmud: "R. Simlai expounded: Torah begins with an act of benevolence [*gĕmîlût ḥăsādîm*] and ends with an act of benevolence. It begins with an act of benevolence, for it is written, 'And the Lord God made for Adam and for his wife coats of skin, and clothed them'; and it ends with an act of benevolence, for it is written, 'And He buried him in the valley [Deut. 34:6a].' "[9] As dominant as this interpretation will become, it does not appear in Christian tradition, as far as I can determine, until after the Reformation. From the period of the early church until the sixteenth century, the clothes Yahweh provides Adam and Eve are seen not as signs of protective care but rather as badges of shame. This is the interpretation of Genesis 3:21, for example, in both Augustine and Bede.[10] It is also the interpretation given vivid expression by Luther: "Whenever they looked at their garments, these were to serve as a reminder to them to give thought to their wretched fall from supreme happiness."[11]

With Calvin, however, we begin to see hints of the particular theological tradition that will come to dominate. Though Calvin begins as did Augustine, Luther, and others ("God therefore designed that our first parents should, in such dress, behold their own vileness"), he goes on to reach the following conclusion about the ending to the paradise story: "God mercifully softens the exile of Adam, by still providing for him. . . . Adam thence infers that the Lord has some care for him, which is proof of paternal love."[12] Not surprisingly, Milton reads the biblical incident in the same way: "pitying how they stood / Before him naked to the air, . . . / As father of his family he clad / Their nakedness with skins of beasts, . . . / [robing] inward nakedness, much more / Opprobrious, with his robe of righteousness."[13] Indeed, it is quite conceivable that the powerful expression given to this particular interpretation in *Paradise Lost* is partly responsible, however unconsciously, for its continued hold upon subsequent students of Genesis.

By the time we arrive at the modern critical period, so readily is Genesis 3:21 interpreted as an indication of Yahweh's generous grace that it becomes difficult to find exceptions to this reading. If only to demonstrate the extent to which biblical scholarship has remained fundamentally theological in nature, I cite here a sampling of the frequency with which this increasingly dominant interpretation is expressed. The author of a widely influential nineteenth-century commentary, Franz Delitzsch, describes Genesis 3:20 (Adam's naming of his wife) as an "act of faith" that is then followed "by an act of grace on the part of God" in 3:21.[14] Skinner's Genesis commentary in the International Critical Commentary series begins by repeating the standard interpretation of this verse (the incident "exhibits God's continued care for man even after the fall") and then goes on to conclude that "the real *Protevangelium* which lies in the passage" is "the fact that God tempers judgment with mercy."[15] Benno Jacob, though he comes much closer in the end to a reading of Genesis 3:21 to be proposed later in this chapter, also sees the clothing incident as "a supplement to creation" demonstrative of Yahweh's protective care.[16] Bonhoeffer's brief homily on Genesis 1–3 finds the verse to be the first instance in which "the Creator is now the Preserver. . . . God's new action toward man is that he preserves him in his fallen world."[17] Cassuto discovers a two-part structure of divine activity in Genesis 3, such that the chapter includes both *punishments* . . . [and] also, and chiefly, *measures taken for the good of the human species* in its new situation"; the clothing incident, clearly among the latter kinds of activity for Cassuto, is an "ameliorative measure" in response to "the *cold* and all other natural phenomena that are injurious to human beings."[18]

As did Delitzsch, von Rad reads the naming episode in verse 20 as "an act of faith" that is then matched by the divine response in verse 21 where "for the first time we see the Creator as the preserver."[19] Westermann, both in his comprehensive commentary and in a more popular study, gives expression to the same tradition we are following here. Yahweh's activity in clothing the primal pair is, for Westermann, "a solicitous act" in which "the Creator shelters his creature";[20] Genesis 3:21 thus exhibits a "concern for man" that "precedes the expulsion from the garden."[21] For Davidson, the act of providing garments for Adam and Eve proves that "God's hand is still stretched out to meet their immediate need."[22] Vawter's commentary on Genesis argues that Genesis 3:21 demonstrates "God's continued solicitude for his creatures" as here "even when on the point of banishing the man and the woman from his presence in the garden, God manifests his care for their progress and well-being."[23] In a study largely devoted to the previous verse, A. J. Williams notes that "in Genesis 3:21 it is God who supplies the humans with clothes and the verse may suggest, in its present context, that it is still a merciful God who provides proper clothes for the humans prior to their expulsion from Eden."[24] B. D. Naidoff's "new interpretation" of the paradise story still finds in the clothing incident an "expression of Yahweh's grace."[25] Brueggeman's recent commentary views Genesis 3:21 as an expression of Yahweh's "graciousness" where "the one who *tests* is the one who finally *provides.*"[26] And finally, E. Fox's recent notes on Genesis concur completely with the tradition traced here as he views the clothing episode to be proof that "God cares for the man and the woman" who "are provided with protection (clothing)."[27]

3. AN ALTERNATIVE TO THEOLOGY: CLOTHING AS AN EMBLEM OF STATUS

Though the elaborate documentation we offered for the exegesis of Genesis 3:21 has perhaps been completed at the cost of some redundancy, it may serve to prove that what was labeled the regnant interpretation of this incident is just that.[28] Why take issue with it? Partly because this reading is so thoroughly theological, and the present volume has as its aim the presentation of alternatives to the theological tradition. And partly because a different reading seems suggested by the force of other texts, both biblical and extrabiblical. To these we will turn directly. But initially, we might take issue with the conventional reading of Genesis 3:21 because, despite the frequency with which this reading is offered, its understanding of the clothing incident is odd within the context of the Paradise story. Preceding the episode, we read of the sentence passed upon Adam and Eve. Following the episode, the pair is expelled from the garden. The link between Genesis 3:21 and especially what follows is so strong that Davidson is quite right when he argues that we view the clothing incident as the "prelude to the story of the expulsion from the garden."[29] Apart from the force of later developments, especially in Christian and Jewish theological thinking, why should there be a radical softening of the sentence between its pronouncement and its initial delivery? Where else in the Hebrew Bible do we find, in the midst of a narrative that includes a judgment sentence and that sentence's execution, such a "gracious accommodation"? The answers to these questions already point to a quite different meaning for the clothing incident.

Further textual study lends strength to our doubts about the conventional reading of Genesis 3:21. These doubts are strengthened initially by brief word studies of the significant terms used in this verse. Of these, 'ôr ("skin") provides the least help. The occurrences of 'ôr in the Hebrew Bible are about evenly divided between those that refer to human skin and those that refer to the skin of animals. It is perhaps worth noting in passing that, of the latter, most refer clearly to the skin of domestic animals.[30] This already casts doubt upon the interpretation of Genesis 3:21 as an etiological explanation for the origin of hunting wild animals, an explanation that was often offered as an addition to the central view of the verse as an instance of divine grace. Much more helpful are the results of some investigation into the uses of *kuttōnet/kĕtōnet* ("garments") and *lābēš* ("to clothe"). With regard to the former, whatever sort of garment is meant by *kuttōnet*/*kĕtōnet,* the word is rarely if ever used in a strictly utilitarian context, as the conventional interpretation of Genesis 3:21 would have it. Rather, the word appears chiefly in one of the following general contexts: (1) to indicate favored status (e.g., Gen. 37:3, of Joseph's garment); (2) to indicate sacred status (very often, especially in Exodus and Leviticus, of the clothes presented to Aaron and his sons); (3) to mark a ritual occasion (e.g., 2 Sam. 13:18–19, where Tamar is said to wear a *kĕtōnet passîm* ["a long robe with sleeves," or the like], as do all the king's maiden daughters, which she rends in addition to placing ashes on her head); or (4) in contexts establishing the dominance of a given person or office (e.g., Isa. 22:15–23, where Shebna is removed from his office and station, as a token of which his garment [*kuttonĕtekā*] is given to Eliakim as a sign of the latter's authority). All of these, of course, are markers of status, and not responses to pragmatic considerations of physical need.

Similarly useful is an investigation into the uses of *lābēš* ("to clothe") in the causative (Hiphil) conjugation. The results of such a study are readily summarized: The causative of *lābēš* is regularly employed in the context of a presentation of a gift from a social, religious, or kinship superior to that person's subordinate. Thus, when pharaoh confers upon Joseph the office of his special representative, he gives to Joseph his ring and a chain, and clothes him (Gen. 41:42). When priests are invested with sacred garments, the investiture is accomplished by Moses to Aaron and his sons at the direct behest of Yahweh (e.g., Exod. 28:40–41; Lev. 8:7, 8:13; Num. 20:26; and so on). Often, it is Yahweh himself who clothes an official (as in Isa. 22:21) or all of Israel (as in Ezek. 16:10). The one apparent exception to this is an exception that in the end proves the rule. In 1 Sam. 17:38, Saul clothes *(wayyalbēš)* David with armor, yet Saul's decline is already well in motion. Therefore, the reason why David removes the armor immediately afterwards is not simply due to the folklore requirement that David fight the enemy representative unarmed but also because it is not fitting that David be clothed by Saul.

In the Hebrew Bible then, both the verb for the act of clothing and the garment mentioned in Genesis 3:21 are words used in significant contexts. These contexts are those of status marking. The garment and the act of investiture are symbolic indications of the status both of the one presenting the clothing and of the one receiving it. This in no way conflicts with the anthropological study of the use of garments in traditional societies (or, for that matter, in not-so-traditional societies). Such study in a systematic fashion was largely inaugurated by the Russian scholar Petr Bogatyrev, whose volume *The Functions of Folk Costume in Moravian Slovakia* is of greater general interest than its title might indicate.[31] Bogatyrev's central conclusion is that clothing is "as universal, constant, and consequently as natural a means of communication as is language."[32] Other studies support the conclusion that garments are among the most obvious and the most frequently utilized of status markers.[33] This conclusion is perhaps intuitively acceptable to almost everyone who observes clothing conventions in many different social settings. In specifically religious or liturgical settings, garments often serve to "protect the religious individual in his encounter with the supernatural."[34]

THE SIGNIFICANCE OF CLOTHING IN THE STORIES OF GILGAMESH AND ADAPA

More chronologically and geographically proximate to the story told in Genesis 2–3 than recent anthropological research are those Near Eastern myths in which the investiture of clothing plays a significant role. Although the evidence of these texts is complex and in some instances contradictory, that clothing plays in some Near Eastern myths chiefly a status-marking, rather than a utilitarian, function is an unavoidable conclusion. Among these myths, the Epic of Gilgamesh and the Tale of Adapa are especially significant in our attempt to understand Genesis 3:21.

The Epic of Gilgamesh in particular, because of its length and its intrinsic interest, is often seen as comparable in many ways to much of the biblical Primeval History. However, the frequent and precise significance of clothing in this epic has perhaps been insufficiently noted. A few examples may serve to call attention to this. Enkidu's original status is indicated as follows:[šu´]ur šārta kalu *zumrisu* ("all of his body was hairy with fur"; I.ii.36).[35] Enkidu thus arrives in the world as do animals, equipped with his own clothing. The harlot's first account of the world of civilization to Enkidu is an account that notes that there, in Uruk, "people" *(nišê)* wear "clothes" *(ṣubātu;* I.v.7). After the harlot mates with Enkidu, and just before the latter eats, drinks, and anoints himself as is the "custom of the land" *(šimti māti,* II.iii.14), we read the following: "She removed (her) garment; / With one (garment) she clothed him, / With the second garment / She clothed herself *(išḫuṭ libšam / ištēnam ulabbiššu / libšam šaniam / ši iltalbaš;* II.ii.27–30). That is, their preparations for an entrance into urban, civilized life are signalled by various customs, including the donning of clothing. The statement "she clothed him" *(ulabbiššu)* here is perhaps the closest semantic parallel to the Yahwist's "and he [Yahweh] clothed them" *(wayyalbišēm)* in Genesis 3:21. When Enkidu later curses the civilized setting responsible for his mortality, Shamash notes that the harlot whom Enkidu includes in the curse is the one who "clothed you with a great garment" *(ulabbišuka lubši rabâ;* VII.iii.38). Shamash predicts that after Enkidu's death, Gilgamesh's altered state will be indicated by his shaggy appearance, with a "lion's skin" *(maški labimma)* for a covering (VII.iii.47–48), another instance of dress signalling status. Enkidu's description of "the place of darkness" *(É ikleti),* the dwelling of Irkalla, includes an account of the garments worn by the unfortunate inhabitants: They "are clothed like birds, a garment of plumage" *(labšama kīma iṣṣūri ṣubāt kappi;* VII.iv.38, cf. Descent of Ishtar, 10). Again, their animallike appearance marks the status of those below. Siduri's account of the mortal lot is an account that mentions that humans as humans are those who wear garments (X.iii.10). Finally, and significantly, Utnapishtim asks that Gilgamesh return to civilization, to his city, wearing a "garment" *(tēdīqi),* "his finest garment" *(ṣubāt baltišu;* XI.243–244, cf. 252–253).

The cumulative effect of all these references to clothing in the Gilgamesh Epic is impressive. The human state—and that, among many other things, is partly what Gilgamesh is all about—is a state symbolized by the donning of manufactured garments. Animals, like the dead and like Enkidu in his precivilized and preurbanized state, have feathers or fur. Humans are those who live most properly in cities (the social setting *par excellence*), are mortal, have obligations to one another—and wear clothing.

The Tale of Adapa is equally revealing for a reconsideration of the clothing episode in Genesis. This is true not simply because the story of Adapa is about the conditions surrounding a human's loss of a chance for immortality but also because both this story and the Paradise Tale in Genesis 2–3 characterize the realm of the gods similarly (the gods are those who possess both wisdom and immortality). Also, in both tales the human protagonist or protagonists gain(s) the former characteristic (wisdom) while failing to gain the latter (immortality). In addition, if Beattie is right in arguing that in Genesis 2–3 the serpent tells the truth about the fruit while God does not,[36] then another theme is shared by the two stories, since in Adapa Ea lies to Adapa in asserting that the food and drink he will be offered above are the food and drink not of life but of death.

Clothing figures at least twice in the Adapa tale. The first occurrence, which is less telling for the present argument, is that when Ea "clothed him [Adapa] with mourning apparel" (*karra ušalbassuma;* EA 356.15, 43).[37] This episode is a part of the flattering strategem that allows Adapa access to Anu, the acknowledged leader of the pantheon. When Adapa is before Anu, he refuses Anu's offer of the "food of life" *(akal balaṭi),* which Ea had told him was the "food of death" *(akala šu mūti).* Adapa refuses as well the offer of the "drink of life" *(mê balāṭi),* which Ea had told him was the "drink of death" *(mê mūti).* Adapa's refusals mean that he is mortal. Adapa then, and this is the point of immediate significance in our investigation, anoints himself with oil and "puts on clothing" *(lubāra . . . ittalbaš;* EA 356.61–64). The clothing, of course, comes from Anu.[38] And the significance of the incident is clear. Now mortal, Adapa is forever marked as such partly by Anu's investing him with a garment.

When an anthropologist investigating the many functions of clothing recently asked an East African why he wore clothes, the latter replied, "Because it shows we are human beings."[39] This response is precisely what I am suggesting is the meaning of Genesis 3:21. The investiture of the man and the woman with a garment here is not an act prompted by generosity or by a grace that is concerned lest humans become ashamed or cold[40] or both. This investiture is rather a significant symbolic act that firmly distinguishes humans from the divine. Genesis 3:21 is, then, another instance of an issue that shows up repeatedly in the Primeval History. What is the status of humanity, of the "all flesh" *(kol-ḥay)* mentioned in the preceding verse? It is not a divine status, and Yahweh's clothing the first humans further indicates just this.

Thus interpreted, Genesis 3:21 may well make more sense in its immediate and wider contexts. With regard to the immediate context, Westermann well summarizes the central meaning of the Paradise story as follows: "The aim is the banishment of humanity from the Garden and with this the separation from God."[41] With regard to the wider context, Patrick Miller's comment on Genesis 3:22 serves also as a succinct statement of the meaning of much of the Primeval History: "The text clearly has in mind the relation between the divine world and the human world. . . . The danger that Yahweh sees in the disobedient actions of the human couple is a threat *not only to Yahweh but to the divine world.*"[42] Yahweh's act in presenting clothing to the man and the woman is not a gracious concession. It is an authoritative marking of the pair as beings who belong to a sphere distinct from that of the divine.

4. CONCLUSION

At one point in Thomas Carlyle's *Sartor Resartus,* a representative of the world of scholarship makes with studied profundity the following comments: "Clothes, as despicable as we think them, are so unspeakably significant. Clothes, from the King's mantle downwards, are Emblematic. . . . The essence of all Science lies in the *Philosophy of Clothes.* "[43] I would no more wish than does Carlyle himself to press into service any such argument as a key to interpret all of mythology. But that the particular clothing incident in

Genesis 3:21 can fruitfully be read as symbolic and "Emblematic" seems clear. This reading is a dramatic departure from the conventional theological view that the incident that immediately precedes the expulsion from Eden provides evidence for the early graciousness of Yahweh's behavior toward humanity. At the same time, it would not be fair to claim that this "novel"[44] interpretation of Genesis 3:21 can carry with it no implications useful for theological discussion. Indeed, the opposite may be the case, since the theme of the radical division between Yahweh and humanity appears to play an important role in the larger theological scheme of the Yahwist. We thus have here to do with at least one instance where nontheological and theological analyses can be mutually helpful one to another.

4. The Patriarchal Narratives as Myth: The Case of Jacob

The repeated focus upon the Primeval History noted at the beginning of Chapter 3 has produced many important results, sometimes at the expense of the stories that ensue in Genesis 12 and the following chapters. These stories, too, have occasionally been treated as myth. This treatment reached an early peak beginning with the era of the "solar mythology" associated with Max Müller and then continuing into the period of intense mythological study at the turn from the nineteenth to the twentieth century. During this period, a few scholars dared to view the biblical patriarchs as "faded" deities. But, in general, the patriarchal narratives, from the call of Abraham in Genesis 12 through the stories of Jacob and his children, have been viewed as dramatically different from the material in the Primeval History. The patriarchal narratives, it has often been said, are less international and less cosmogonic in character. They are more often called sagas or legends than myths. These labels usually imply that in the patriarchal narratives the chief actors are families or clans and the chief chronological setting is less remote antiquity.

However, it seems impossible any longer to deny that the patriarchal narratives are myths if we utilize any of the definitions of myth most widely accepted today. This is true even if we grant that the scope and the setting of the stories that begin in Genesis 12 are different from those of the stories in the Primeval History. The patriarchal narratives are traditional stories; they treat characters who act at the behest of a divine being and who themselves do things that ordinary human beings cannot do. If a myth is a traditional story that recounts the activities of at least one superhuman being, then the patriarchal narratives are beyond question myths.[1]

It is in this context that the present chapter offers an analysis of the patriarchal narratives as myths, attempting to heed the conclusions reached about mythical study in Chapter 2. Since even a sketchy study of all of this material, which runs from Genesis 12 through at least Genesis 36, would be impossible here, the concentration is upon the Jacob traditions in Genesis 25:19–35:29. This emphasis is no accident. Jacob is the patriarch who is renamed Israel and who is thus the eponymous ancestor of Israel. Stories about Jacob might then be expected to be the locations of material defining, directly and indirectly, the people Israel. At least two of the theories of myth available to us (the social-functionalist and the structuralist) speak of the function of myth as one of defining a particular group in opposition to other groups. This is a hypothesis we might begin to test with the Jacob narratives. Finally and perhaps most importantly, these same narratives offer us another clear example of the differences between a theological approach to biblical stories and an approach from outside the theological setting.

A question that any adequate interpretation of the patriarchal narratives might be expected to answer is that of the reasons for the narrowing definition of the group to whom Yahweh will eventually reveal his divine instructions. Though the full revelation of this instruction does not occur until the Sinai pericope that begins in the Book of Exodus (Exod. 19ff.), this question already begins in the Book of Genesis. It reaches a particularly pointed stage with the patriarch Jacob, *all* of whose sons become incorporated into the definition of Israel. Thus, a pattern that biblical scholars have long noted begins to emerge: More and more is revealed to a group that is defined through a series of "narrowings." Thus, if the group to whom the promise of Genesis 12 is made originally includes the entire family of Abraham, this group is quickly and permanently narrowed. Abraham's nephew Lot is excluded. Lot subsequently becomes the ancestor of the Moabites and the Ammonites (Gen. 19:30–38), two nations in close proximity to, and sharing many aspects of social and religious life with, Israel. Ishmael, who is born to Abraham and Hagar, is excluded, as are the many sons born to Abraham and Keturah (Gen. 25: 1–6). Only Isaac, the son of

Abraham and Sarah, and then Isaac's direct descendants are encompassed within the promised group that the patriarchal narratives seek in part to define. Nor, of course, does the narrowing stop here. Isaac's firstborn son is Esau. He, too, like Ishmael, is excluded and becomes the ancestor of one of the other nations of the earth (Gen. 25:21–26). The promised group is thus narrowed to encompass Isaac's second son, Jacob, alone. But at this point, as is well known, the narrowing pattern notable thus far changes. Jacob, now renamed Israel, becomes the father of twelve sons. All twelve sons are included within the definition of Israel. Each becomes the ancestor of one of the twelve tribes of the traditional portrait of Israel.

There are several questions we will ask about this pattern, which reaches a kind of architectural completion with the Jacob stories. Why does the pattern begin as it does and run consistently through the Abraham and Isaac narratives? Why does the pattern conclude where it does and with whom it does—in the stories about Jacob and with Jacob's sons? The answers to these and similar questions from the theological tradition of biblical criticism on the one hand and from a perspective outside this tradition on the other differ dramatically. These widely divergent answers thus become a clear demonstration of the fundamental differences between two different ways of interpreting the same material.

1. THE THEOLOGICAL TRADITION

More than once in the course of the present study we have had occasion to remark that however much biblical research in the present and the future may wish to part company with the theological mainstream in which biblical study was born and matured, it would be imprudent, even callously ungrateful, to fail to note the contributions that have come from this main tradition. This is nowhere more the case than it is with the patriarchal narratives. Archaeology, form criticism, tradition history, literary criticism, and a host of other subdisciplines within biblical study have allowed us to view the growth and the meaning of the stories that begin in Genesis 12 far more clearly than was possible a century ago.[2] That much granted, it remains true that the questions asked of Genesis by most biblical scholars are those that might have been predicted given the position of biblical scholarship within the particular stream of theological historiography surveyed in Chapter 1. Thus, the single issue of greatest concern can fairly be said to have been the origin and development of the separate traditions evident beneath the text of Genesis. The studies of Noth, for example, are brilliant testimony to a sustained effort at separating traditions now fused, at reaching conclusions about the relative date of each tradition, and at identifying the mechanisms and motives for fusing these traditions.[3] Similarly creative and influential have been von Rad's conclusions, which emphasize the development of larger complexes of tradition but which share with Noth and many others the larger concern for tracing the tendencies within the historical development of Israel's religious traditions.[4]

Such an emphasis upon religious and national development is, of course, completely coincident with the fundamental aims and assumptions of the larger tradition of historiographic understanding described in Chapter 1. If this tradition and its impact upon the theological study of the Hebrew Bible is responsible for great advances, the tradition, like any tradition of scholarly understanding, is not without its limitations. One of these is evident in the answers to the questions we are attempting to pose of the patriarchal narratives. These questions, again, have chiefly to do with the manner in which Genesis 12–36 utilizes kinship and lineage structures to define the people Israel. Why is it that the patriarchs enter into the kinds of kinship relations they do? How do the resulting kinship alliances shape both the narratives before us and the issue of who is included and who is excluded within Israel?

The answers from the theological tradition of biblical study, the answers of Gunkel, Noth, von Rad, and many others, are chiefly answers prompted by an over-riding concern for historical development. When an impasse is reached on almost any issue, it is history that comes to the rescue. Perhaps an example or two will make this clear. Several of the patriarchs enter into marriages that seem prohibited by legislation elsewhere in the Hebrew Bible. Thus, and we will return to these examples in detail later in this chapter, Abraham is said to have married his half sister Sarah (Gen. 20:12) and Jacob marries both Leah and Rachel, who are sisters (Gen. 29:21–30). Both marrying one's half sister and two sisters are forbidden by material now to be found elsewhere in the Hebrew Bible. Deuteronomy 27:22 forbids the former alliance, and Leviticus 18:18 prohibits a man from marrying the sister of a woman to whom he is already married. Rather than asking whether these prohibited alliances play some role in structuring the Genesis narratives and hence in further defining Israel, biblical scholars generally have asked if perhaps the answer is not to be found in the date of the traditions in Genesis on the one hand and the date of those in Deuteronomy and in Leviticus on the other. And the usual answer is that heeding the historical growth of the biblical traditions does indeed solve the problem here: The stories of Abraham's marriage with Sarah and of Jacob's marriage with Leah and Rachel are standardly said to be dependent upon traditions that precede the legislation that forbids such alliances.[5]

Though this conclusion about the relative dates of the materials in Genesis and in Leviticus may be quite correct, it is important to realize how such ready and sole resort to the model of historical development can prevent other questions from being posed. That is, it is quite possible that other reasons can be found for the so-called incorrect marriages in Genesis and that these reasons may provide a clue for understanding the function of the Genesis myths in defining Israel. These other reasons are not typically sought within biblical scholarship simply, but importantly, because questions of historical development are seen to outweigh all other considerations.

There is a more pointed example of the way in which an adherence to the dominating theological tradition of biblical study can lead us to be satisfied too easily with a ready answer to a puzzle within the patriarchal narratives. This is the example of Jacob and his sons, the example to which we will return when we turn away from the theological tradition. Why is *Jacob* renamed Israel? Why not Abraham or Isaac? Why are *all* of Jacob's sons included within Israel, while all the sons of Abraham and Isaac are not? Two of the answers to such questions that have been forthcoming from the main tradition of biblical study are quite revealing. The first is that of Gunkel. His answer is, essentially, that Jacob (rather than Abraham or Isaac) receives the name Israel and that all of Jacob's sons (unlike those of Abraham and Isaac) are included because of a kind of accident in the history of the tradition's transmission. Thus, Gunkel argues that at an advanced stage in the history of the Jacob tradition, "someone" identified Jacob with Israel, with the result that "a new meaning was given to the older tales."[6] This answer may seem initially satisfactory. It may even be historically correct, though how we might test it is not obvious. But the answer can also be viewed as the (doubtless unconscious: How else might one proceed?) employment of the power of historical understanding to block further inquiry. Might there not be other motives within the story itself that suggested the identification of Jacob with Israel? Gunkel's immediate appeal to a model of historical development, and such appeal is anything but atypical, prevents this question from being raised.

A second answer to these questions (Why *Jacob?* and Why *all* of Jacob's sons?) is both far more frequently voiced and far more revealing of the limits of the theological tradition. This is an answer that was offered already by Saint Paul in the New Testament (Rom. 9). The answer, Saint Paul affirms, is to be found in the mystery of divine freedom and mercy. That is, Isaac is chosen and Ishmael rejected, Jacob is chosen and Esau rejected, Jacob is renamed Israel and all of Jacob's sons included within the group also called Israel for reasons that we cannot truly fathom. But the fact that we cannot arrive at an answer, Saint Paul and then many others within this tradition argue, is itself significant. We are to learn from this that Yahweh is free and that Yahweh chooses whom he will choose and has mercy upon whom he will have mercy. This answer is then taken up and formulated anew by the plain majority of modern commentators on Genesis. Von Rad's formulation is representative. The answer to all the puzzling questions posed here, argues von Rad, is that the P source, which is in the end responsible for the literary structure here, "knew about the riddle of divine election and wanted to make its harshness theologically vivid in his history."[7]

This may be as clear a case as can be cited of the aims and the limitations of the theological tradition. Within this tradition, reference to such notions as the mystery of divine freedom or the secret of divine election are legitimate and make sense. But where, outside such a narrowed tradition, would appeal to the "mysterious" be mistaken for explanation? It is precisely this point that the anthropologist Mary Douglas makes when she assesses one of the common and unambiguously theological answers to the question of the apparent randomness of the Hebrew Bible's dietary laws— the answer that the apparent randomness of these laws demonstrates the mystery of divine freedom. This answer, Douglas sharply concludes, is an expression of "bafflement in a learned way."[8] Douglas's answer is not so much uncharitable as it is, in its own way, an expression of bafflement. How could any scholar possibly conclude that the absence of an explanation is itself an explanation? Few scholars would so conclude, and the only scholarly tradition of which I am aware where the mysterious becomes a mode of explanation is that of biblical study and of other areas of concentration within the larger theological context. Moreover, theology here not only provides an avenue whereby a difficult issue is too neatly bypassed. Theology is also served by the very failure to provide an answer acceptable within any kind of scientific tradition: In the end, there is no explanation for the puzzles in Genesis because the explanation lies with the designs of the deity. Hence, argument is ended and confessional aims are served. And this is at once the task and the limitation of theological inquiry.

2. KINSHIP AND LINEAGE IN THE JACOB STORIES

There are alternatives to the historical and theological explanation of the workings of the Jacob narratives, despite what one might conclude from reading any number of commentaries on Genesis. Those that are available at present may also prove in the end inadequate and may well require radical recasting in the future. But our chief concern at present is not so much the ultimate satisfactoriness of one such alternative as it is to define sharply how far this alternative departs from theological explanation.

Since the key questions to which the theological tradition might fairly be said to offer only limited answers are those about the kinship networks in the patriarchal narratives, we might concentrate upon the issues of kinship and lineage. Let us begin with some generally accepted definitions of these terms. "Kinship," according to a widely used textbook devoted to this topic, "is simply the relations between 'kin', i.e., persons related by real, putative or fictive consanguinity."[9] And lineage, in the formation of a similarly useful introduction to this issue, is "a unilineal descent group whose members trace their descent from a known ancestor and know the genealogical connection to that ancestor."[10] Thus defined, it is particularly clear that kinship and lineage play a constant and central role throughout the patriarchal narratives. First, the entire cycle of stories about Abraham and his family is "framed" by the genealogy that precedes these tales in Genesis 11:27–32 and by that which concludes them in Genesis 25:1–18.[11] Secondly, the promises to the patriarchs, promises that have figured so largely in the recent discussion of the patriarchal narratives, typically include the promise of the descendants who will make up the lineage of the particular patriarch in question.[12] These promises from Yahweh then play a vital role in the stories that follow, partly because a theme in each of the stories is that of the lineage in danger. Thus, Sarah (Gen. 11:30, and elsewhere), Rebekah (Gen. 25:21), and Rachel (Gen. 29:31) all are barren for some time. Both Sarah and Rebekah are themselves in danger of becoming incorporated into foreign kin groups in the three "jeopardizing of an ancestress" stories (Gen. 12:10–20; ch. 21; and 26:1–11). These stories, and the dramatic question of whether or not Yahweh's promise will be fulfilled, are of great significance to the plot of the patriarchal narratives. All emphasize again the issue of a lineage's survival. Again, a concern that appears in the tales

of Abraham, Isaac, and Jacob is that of correct and incorrect marriages. This issue is perhaps most clearly portrayed in the long
narrative in Genesis 24 about Isaac's search for the correct wife
with whom to continue the lineage. Finally, if one might fairly
summarize the Abraham tradition as in part about the rivalry
between wives, so, too, one might with justice summarize the
Jacob tradition as in part about both wife and sibling rivalry.

KINSHIP AND MYTH

Concentrating as they do upon issues of kinship and lineage, the
patriarchal narratives demonstrate their typical nature in any kind
of comparative perspective. That is, these same issues are precisely
those to which so much traditional literature, from a wide variety
of eras and areas, is devoted. Why? How do we explain the recur-
rence of such emphasis upon kinship and lineage in myths? One
answer that many scholars have found satisfactory and that seems
pointedly appropriate in the particular case of the patriarchal narratives is this: Kinship and lineage provide the central focus or
structure in many myths because both myths and kinship systems
can be viewed as systems of communication. Which ever, if any,
of the theories of myth outlined in Chapter 2 proves most satisfactory in the end, it cannot escape our attention that several of these
theories share the conclusion that myths function in part to communicate. According to the social functionalist model, for example, myths are among the ways the members of any social group
communicate to themselves and to outsiders who they are. Group
identity is thus the chief object of communication. According to
the psychological model, myths, like dreams, communicate to an
individual in symbolic form the deepest tensions generated from
within the unconscious. And the structuralist model is founded
perhaps most firmly of all upon the same conclusion: Myths communicate to a social group the structures that can be found embedded in a host of additional relationships (economic, social, political, and so on) within that same social group.

But if myths are in some sense communicative, it is among the
firmest conclusions of modern study that so, too, are kinship sys-

tems. That Lévi-Strauss, the founder of structural analysis, argues this is hardly surprising. For this scholar, "marriage regulations and kinship systems" represent "a kind of language, a set of processes permitting the establishment between individuals and groups, of a certain type of communication."[13] More importantly, many other contemporary students of kinship phenomena, whatever their assessment of anthropological structuralism, concur in this conclusion. Thus, Fredrik Barth observes as a kind of truism that "people everywhere seem to see 'who they are' in terms of the whole kinship network, i.e., both with reference to relations of descent (or filiation) and marriage."[14] And Robin Fox, whose textbook on kinship has been cited earlier, offers a similar conclusion: "In many societies, both primitive and sophisticated, relationships to ancestors and kin have been the key relationships in the social structure; they have been the pivots on which most interaction, most claims and obligations, most loyalties and sentiments, turned."[15]

THE STUDY OF KINSHIP

If myth and kinship share a communicative function, this is not the sole characteristic these two aspects of culture share. The study of kinship is, unfortunately, at least as difficult and fraught with potential pitfalls as is the study of myths. Hence, one might offer for kinship studies the same kind of theoretical overview as Chapter 2 attempted to provide for the study of myths. Since space prohibits this, we will rest content with a few indications of the direction kinship studies has taken of late.[16]

Perhaps what needs to be said first in this context is that the past forty or fifty years have witnessed a shift away from looking at kinship in terms of the empirical relationships that might exist in any given society and toward looking at kinship in systematic terms. That is to say, recent inquiry in this area is directed primarily at descriptions of *conventionalized* relationships, not at accounts of *actual* relationships. It is kinship as system, not kinship as a study of how any particular individual in fact "feels" about, for example, his uncles or cousins, which has come to be seen as the object of most importance. Almost all traditional societies have

established norms of behavior that describe the appropriate relationship between, say, a man and his maternal uncle. It is these
established norms, not whether or not a chosen individual adheres
to or departs from the convention, that make up the kinship system. Just this highly theoretical and antiempirical characteristic of
recent kinship study creates the greatest difficulty for anyone new
to this discipline. This is especially true for biblical scholars who
are traditionally skeptical (for reasons explored in Chapter 1) of
the theoretical. Upon further reflection, however, the concentration by contemporary students of kinship upon systems of conventional behavior can readily be seen as offering a distinct advantage for biblical study. This advantage is the following: The
kinship data with which biblical scholarship deals is chiefly that
of data embedded in traditional narratives, i.e., myths; it is not raw
data of an empirical nature. The biblical scholar's material represents a series of traditional accounts of conventionalized relationships rather than anything like demographic accounts of actual
relationships. Hence, and in the end, what we see in the Hebrew
Bible corresponds neatly with the focus of recent kinship study.

Secondly, we might note about kinship study that here too, as
with myth, the works of Lévi-Strauss have been at the forefront
of a kind of scholarly revolution. However, a major difference
exists between the assessment of Lévi-Strauss's contribution to
myth on the one hand and to kinship on the other. While this
scholar's inauguration of the structural analysis of myths has been
greeted with the widest extremes of enthusiastic approval and
deeply skeptical disapproval, his work on kinship has received a
more uniformly positive evaluation. This work "is more generally
accepted by contemporary sociologists and anthropologists" than
are his comments on myth, as Mara Donaldson has correctly observed.[17] Lévi-Strauss's particular contribution to kinship studies
can be seen most clearly in his *The Elementary Structures of Kinship.*[18]
Here, Lévi-Strauss seeks the clues to the essential structures of
kinship systems not in the shape of descent groups but rather in
the marriage rules that characterize any social group. It is these
rules, he argues, that in fact create the alliances upon which kin-

ship systems are most fundamentally based. The significant re-orientation of kinship study that marks this volume and many others by different scholars to follow is just this move toward the investigation of marriage alliances, of "systems of affinal exchange or prescriptive marriage."[19] This reorientation is, therefore, some-times called the focus upon kinship as alliance. What marriage alliances does a given social group define as proper? What marriage alliances does the same group prohibit? These questions, and others in a similar vein, are those to which the study of kinship has increasingly moved. Again, it must be remembered in light of what has been stated, the object of study remains prescribed and prohibited marriage alliances according to the conventions of the kinship system, not the statistical study of what kind of marriage alliances a given group of individuals actually enter into.

The force of both of these recent emphases within kinship study has been to yield a noteworthy concentration upon two particular areas of kin relationship. These two relationships are, first, the avunculate relationship, and, second, cross-cousin marriage. The avunculate relationship refers to that between a man and his ma-ternal uncle (Latin *avunculus*). Cross-cousin marriage refers to the marriage between the offspring of siblings of the opposite (hence, "cross") sex. Its opposite is parallel-cousin marriage: marriage be-tween the offspring of siblings of the same (hence, "parallel") sex. In both cases, we are dealing with the marriage of cousins A marriage between the offspring of two brothers or two sisters is a parallel-cousin marriage, while a marriage between the offspring of a sister and a brother is a cross-cousin marriage. Since both the avunculate and cross-cousin marriage appear as significant rela-tionships in the Jacob narratives, a ready opportunity exists to apply the results of recent kinship study to this set of stories.

KINSHIP SYSTEM IN THE JACOB NARRATIVES

Approaching the patriarchal narratives, and especially those in which Jacob figures, from the viewpoint of kinship studies can produce initial bafflement. These stories appear as puzzling and daunting as is the study of kinship itself. Indeed, it almost appears as if the actors in these narratives are systematically exploring every possible variety of marriage alliance. This, however, is not quite true, for every marriage here is to an extent endogamous. That is, each approved marriage adheres to "the obligation to marry within an objectively defined group."[20] Thus, and as we have observed, Abraham marries Sarah, who is his half sister according to at least one of the traditional sources of the Pentateuch.[21] Isaac marries Rebekah, who is either his cousin or his second cousin, depending upon whether Rebekah's father is Bethuel or Nahor.[22] Jacob, of course, marries Leah and Rachel, both of whom are his cousins. Indeed, and to this we shall return, Leah and Rachel are more precisely Jacob's cross-cousins, since they are the daughters of his mother's brother rather than (any) daughters of his mother's sister or of his father's brother who would be his parallel cousins.

In the attempt to answer the questions posed earlier in this discussion (Why is *Jacob* renamed Israel? Why are *all* of Jacob's sons included within the definition of Israel?), it is interesting to note initially that Jacob's relationship to his spouses is defined without any ambiguity. If there is some uncertainty surrounding both Abraham's kin relationship to Sarah and Isaac's kin relationship to Rebekah, there is none in the case of Jacob. In marrying Leah and Rachel, he is plainly marrying his two cross-cousins. The difference between Jacob on the one hand and Abraham and Isaac on the other hand in this regard corresponds to another obvious difference that many have noted before. This is the difference that has prompted one of our key questions: From Abraham through Jacob, we are concerned with a linear genealogy, while after Jacob we are concerned with a segmented genealogy. When Isaac is chosen, while Abraham's other offspring are excluded, and when Jacob is chosen, while Isaac's firstborn son Esau is excluded, these choices and exclusions define a linear genealogy, a genealogy in which the lineage is continued only through a single offspring. But when all twelve of Jacob's sons are included within the lineage of Israel, a segmented genealogy is inaugurated, one in which all the offspring of an ancestor become inheritors of the lineage.

Why is it that the patriarchal narratives in Genesis 12–36 describe a linear genealogy through Jacob but a segmented genealogy thereafter?[23] The answer from the theological tradition, it will be recalled, is that the choice of Isaac alone of the sons of Abraham and of Jacob alone of the sons of Isaac but the inclusion of all of Jacob's sons is a part of the mystery of the divine plan. We have noted the possible limitations in such an answer. Another answer is offered by Edmund Leach. This answer is that "a rank order is established which places the tribal neighbors of the Israelites in varying degrees of inferior status depending upon the nature of the defect in their original ancestry as compared with the pure descent of Jacob (Israel)."[24] This statement does not, to be sure, require any appeal to the mysterious. But Leach's answer is not completely accurate and it stops short. It is not wholly accurate because Esau's ancestry is surely as pure as is Jacob's, and it stops short because it fails to deal with the switch to a segmented genealogy that begins with Jacob's children.

In search of a more adequate answer, we might begin by noting that among the more obvious functions of the patriarchal narratives is that of defining Israel. The task of definition (here as generally) is a contrastive or a relational task. That is, Israel must always be defined in contrast and in relation to something else. But that "something else" in the case of Israel as the recipients of Yahweh's blessings is not a simple issue and it is never a constant· It varies as it must when dealing with something as complex as a religious and social group. And this complexity provides a possible answer to the quandary that arises from the presence of both linear and segmented genealogies here. Externally—that is, in relation to the other nations of the earth—Israel is defined as the descendants of Abraham and not of Haran, and then as the descendants of Isaac and not of Ishmael or of the sons of Keturah. But internally—that is, from a perspective inside this group—all Israelites are not identical. The segmented genealogy that begins when all twelve of Jacob's sons are included within the definition of Israel addresses this issue. Hence, *externally,* Israel is defined as the particular line descended solely from Abraham and solely from Isaac. But, *inter-*

nally, Israel is defined as the various descendants of the various sons of Jacob. We can even rephrase this in the fashion of an algebraic formula, though so doing will confirm the suspicions of those skeptical of any concentration upon structure: the difference between Israel *(x),* as distinct from the other nations of the earth, and individual Israelites *(y),* as distinct one from another, is the reason for the difference between the linear genealogy *(x¹)* and the segmented genealogy *(y¹).*

THE CROSS-COUSIN RELATIONSHIP

This is but a beginning of the potential answers to be offered from carefully heeding the kinship relationships articulated in the Jacob narratives. Again, let us look with especial care at the role played by Jacob, who is to become the eponymous ancestor of Israel. Thus far, we have concentrated upon Jacob's role as father, and hence upon the difference between his offspring, who inaugurate a segmented genealogy, and those of Abraham and Isaac, who make up a linear genealogy. Let us turn now to concentrating rather upon Jacob's kinship roles as nephew and as husband. This means, of course, looking to the web of relationships that is inherent within Jacob's relationships to Laban and then to Leah and Rachel. To begin with the latter, we have noted that Jacob's relationship with his wives is defined without ambiguity in the stories here. This absence of ambiguity is distinctive. While the various traditions lying behind the patriarchal narratives present some uncertainty in the cases of the marriage alliances of Abraham (Is Sarah Abraham's half sister or not?) and of Isaac (Is Rebekah Isaac's first or second cousin?), there is certainty in the case of Jacob's marriage alliance: Leah and Rachel are defined without variation in the Jacob stories as the daughters of Jacob's mother's brother Laban (Gen. 28:2; 29:10). The distinctive clarity with which this particular marriage alliance is defined suggests already that this alliance is of great significance. The suggestion is one that receives great support from recent studies of kinship. In marrying his mother's brother's daughters (Leah and Rachel), Jacob creates two kinship relationships of special significance: a cross-cousin relationship and an avuncular relationship. Each of these kinship relationships has been singled out as of particular importance in recent scholarship. Here, we will look first at the cross-cousin relationship, the relationship created when Jacob marries his mother's brother's daughters.

Perhaps somewhat surprisingly to those unacquainted with kinship studies, cross-cousin marriage turns out to be a frequent norm in many traditional societies. Any such surprise quickly fades when one consults the standard literature on marriage between the offspring of opposite-sex siblings.[25] George Murdock's statistical study of kinship cites cross-cousin marriage as the initial example in his discussion of "preferential mating" because of the great frequency of this particular marriage alliance. In the 250 societies that provide the data for Murdock's study, cross-cousin marriage is allowed or preferred in fifty-six cases.[26] Murdock was hardly the first scholar to have noted the special status of cross-cousin marriage. In 1940, Radcliffe-Brown wrote that "in many societies it is regarded as preferable that a man should marry the daughter of his mother's brother."[27] Nor is the preference for this alliance limited to any particular geographical area. Cross-cousin marriage was regarded as the ideal marriage among the African Ashanti as recently as the middle of the twentieth century, and the custom was also widespread among the Chin of western Burma and the Murngin of Australia.[28] It was thus clear to scholars by the period shortly after the Second World War that the phenomenon of cross-cousin marriage represented "a regularity of such high order that it . . . demanded functional explanations."[29]

Among Lévi-Strauss's ambitions in his *The Elementary Structures of Kinship* was to offer an explanation for just this intriguing phenomenon. This volume opens with a repetition of the observations of many others: "Cross-cousin marriage, despite the very close degree of consanguinity between the spouses, is regarded as an ideal."[30] Why? Because, concluded Lévi-Strauss, "whether descent is matrilineal or patrilineal, the children of the father's brother and of the mother's sister [that is, parallel cousins] are found in the same moiety as Ego, while those of the father's sister and of the mother's brother [that is, cross-cousins] always belong to the other moiety."[31] The same conclusion is repeated in Fox's recent textbook on kinship: "Cross-cousins have the advantage of being outside ego's lineage/clan under either unilineal descent system. They are therefore ideal mates if ego wants to marry a close relative."[32] In other words, cross-cousin marriage is a most elegant solution to the typical problem of marriage that is at once neither too exogamous nor too endogamous. A cross-cousin is one's close relative. But because he or she is the son or daughter of one's mother's brother or of one's father's sister, a cross-cousin is also outside one's own tribal division. Parallel-cousin marriage would not solve this problem, since the offspring of one's mother's sister or of one's father's brother are in one's own moiety or "exchange" division. Though this is somewhat incidental to our primary argument here, it is interesting to note that the sharp distinction often drawn between cross-cousin marriage and parallel-cousin marriage demonstrates aptly the cultural, rather than biological, nature of kinship systems. Biologically, a cross-cousin is identical with a parallel cousin; culturally, they are defined as anything but identical.

A recent study that does grant significance to the kinship relationships in the Jacob stories is Donaldson's "Kinship Theory in the Patriarchal Narratives." As we have just attempted to do, Donaldson also notes the potential significance of the relationships established when Jacob marries his cross-cousins Leah and Rachel. Donaldson argues as well that a similar alliance occurs in the generation before Jacob, where Rebekah can be seen as "Isaac's matrilateral cross-cousin since Nahor is also Sarah's half-brother."[33] However, only once, and only in one of the traditional sources of the Tetrateuch, is Sarah identified as Abraham's (and hence Nahor's) half sister. Thus, the marriage alliance in the generation before Jacob is defined with less specificity, clarity, and unanimity than is Jacob's marriage alliance. Donaldson finds the greatest significance in Jacob's cross-cousin marriages with Leah and Rachel to be the role these marriages play in the scheme of increasingly "correct" marriages that Donaldson acutely discerns behind the patriarchal narratives. This scheme begins with the dangerously incestuous alliance of Abraham with Sarah (if Sarah is indeed to be seen as Abraham's half sister) and then concludes triumphantly with the perfect alliance of Jacob with Leah and Rachel.[34] This alliance is "correct," again, precisely because cross-cousin marriage is a logical solution to the problematic extremes of marriages that are either too endogamous or too exogamous.

The central conclusion of the present analysis is quite in keeping with Donaldson's investigation, even if the implications of Jacob's kinship relations are pressed a bit further. This conclusion can be summarized as follows: That marriage alliance (cross-cousin marriage) that Lévi-Strauss and other scholars discovered to be a key to elementary structures of kinship generally is precisely the same alliance that is recapitulated in the marriages of the man who would be renamed Israel. Jacob's (Israel's) marriage alliance is a highly and demonstrably *conventional* alliance. It is arguably *the* conventional alliance most often used by traditional societies the world around as a means to fulfill a kinship system's function of cultural self-definition. The author of a recent account of the post–World War II revolution in kinship studies, John Barnes, has gone so far as to argue that cross-cousin marriage is "the most universal of all institutions except the prohibition of incest."[35] Therefore, the relationship that creates and defines the descendants of Jacob (Israel) in the patriarchal narratives is the same relationship by which a great number of societies first define themselves culturally, both through their kinship systems and also through myths in which these kinship systems are recounted.

The Avunculate Relationship

A second set of important conclusions are also to be drawn from Jacob's marriage alliances. For these, our focus will be upon Jacob's relationship with his mother's brother—that is, the avunculate relationship between Jacob and Laban. The latter, of course, is Jacob's mother's brother as well as being the father of Jacob's wives Leah and Rachel. A major theme in the Jacob narratives is the deceit and animosity generated by this particular relationship.

As with Jacob's relationship to Leah and Rachel, so, too, here his relationship to Laban is articulated with precision and without ambiguity. For example, three times in a single verse (Gen. 29:10) Laban is introduced as Jacob's mother's brother: "And when Jacob saw Rachel, the daughter of Laban, *the brother of his mother,* and the flock of Laban, *the brother of his mother,* Jacob approached and rolled away the rock from the well, and watered the flock of Laban, *the brother of his mother."* Again, as with the cross-cousin relationship, so too the avunculate relationship is one of pointed significance in many traditional narratives.

Lévi-Strauss followed up his work on cross-cousin marriage and the ensuing alliances thus created with additional study of just this second relationship. Why is it, he asked, that the relationship between nephew and maternal uncle is "the focus of significant elaboration in a great many primitive societies?"[36] Already much earlier in the present century, Radcliffe-Brown had begun to provide an answer to this question by collecting material relating to the curiously significant avunculate relationship.[37] His comments and those of other anthropologists who have extended this particular inquiry read almost as if they were a direct commentary upon the Jacob-Laban relationship, even though they are in fact based upon completely independent evidence. Radcliffe-Brown began his initial study with the observation that "among primitive peoples in many parts of the world a good deal of importance is attached to the relationship of mother's brother and sister's son."[38] He then documents several instances of the conventional behavior entailed within the avunculate. The modes of behavior he cites cannot fail to remind us of the narratives in Genesis 29–31. For example, Radcliffe-Brown notes that frequently and in disparate settings "the sister's son has certain special rights over the property of his mother's brother."[39] Such rights may entail the nephew's taking his maternal uncle's property, or the maternal uncle his nephew's property, though any such seizures are often followed by a set of conventionalized protests. Thus, among the Hottentot, "the mother's brother may take from his nephew's herd any beast that is deformed or decrepit," while among the inhabitants of Fiji and Tonga, "the sister's son is permitted to take many liberties with his mother's brother and to take any of his uncle's possessions that he may desire."[40] Beyond such highly conventionalized "thefts," the avunculate relationship often entails special verbal freedoms that a nephew is permitted to take with his mother's brother or an uncle with his sister's son. Examples of this include many cultural settings in which "a sister's son teases and otherwise behaves disrespectfully toward his mother's brother" and thus engages in behavior that is nowhere else expected or sanctioned.[41]

Were Radcliffe-Brown and Lévi-Strauss the only students of kinship systems to have observed the pointed significance granted to the avunculate, any implications of this relationship for the Jacob-Laban narratives would rest on uncertain ground. However, these two scholars are far from solo voices. There is instead a chorus of agreement on this issue. Homans and Schneider, for instance, directly contrast the father-son relationship with the nephew–maternal uncle relationship in order to conclude that the latter relationship often entails as many freedoms as does the former relationship demand constraints. Examples of the "considerable freedom" that is the convention in the avunculate relationship include that according to which "either ego or mother's brother is free to use the other's possessions without asking permission."[42] In the same vein, Fortes documents the frequency in many settings of the rule that allows the nephew to expect gifts from his mother's brother.[43] Very recently, Keesing has again observed that "characteristically, in patriarchal systems, a young man has special and close ties to his mother's brother," ties that usually mean that there is a "separate 'uncle' term for M[other's] B[rother]."[44] Indeed, English is rather the exception here in not making such a distinction. More typical is Latin, where *avunculus* refers, of course, to "mother's brother" and *patruus* to "father's brother."

In the absence of a full awareness of the status and conventions of the avunculate relationship in traditional societies and in the myths of such societies, the story of Jacob's dealings with Laban has long seemed curious. Why is it that these two characters meet one another with such initial warmth (Gen. 29:13–14) and yet then systematically engage in plots and counterplots to deceive one another (e.g., Gen. 29:22–25)? Against the background of the material just cited, the apparent contradictions in this story are anything but unusual. Rather, the complex turns of the plot here might best be seen as providing a kind of set script that adumbrates fully the contradictory nature of the avunculate relationship. The plot's tensions extend to the arena of avunculocal versus patrilocal residency, which is again an altogether expected controversy.[45] While Laban regards Jacob's departure as a flight, an abandonment of Jacob's family's proper home, Jacob on the contrary regards his time spent with Laban as time away from his proper home in the land of his father.

Other elements in this same narrative may receive their explanations from our awareness that Jacob's relationship with his maternal uncle Laban completes a scheme that Lévi-Strauss has called the basic unit, or "atom," of kinship. For a long time, anthropologists were tempted to find in the nuclear or conjugal family the basic unit of kinship. But in most societies, as Fox observes, "the nuclear family is a derivative and secondary unit," so that "taking our own rather peculiar system as the norm leads only to confusion" since our system "is decidedly odd if we simply count heads."[46] The reason why it is instead the avunculate relationship that might best be seen as the basic unit is the comprehensiveness of the kinship relations inherent within the avunculate. That is, "in order for a kinship structure to exist, three types of family relations must always be present: a relation of consanguinity, a relation of affinity, and a relation of descent."[47] These three needs are met most economically by the total web of relationships that center upon the nephew–maternal uncle relationship.

If it is the case that the avunculate serves as the defining hub around which circle the other key kinship relations, then it is no surprise that the nephew–maternal uncle relationship has been the recipient of such obvious elaboration in traditional stories generally. Hence, too, we have discovered an explanation for that which has resisted adequate explanation for many years—the complexity and apparent duplicity in the Jacob narratives. Only in the generation of Jacob, and only in the tales of his dealings with his maternal uncle Laban, is a complete system of kinship relationships fully present. Precisely because of the loaded significance of the avunculate relationship for the kinship system in its entirety, Jacob's interactions with Laban merit, indeed demand, a long and complex series of stories. Further, an investigation of the widespread nature of the conventions surrounding the avunculate demonstrates that the "thefts" and the "animosity" in the Jacob-Laban stories are nothing like instances of true theft or spontaneous animosity. Rather, here, too, we are dealing with the performance, as it were, of a kind of script: a script that elaborates the conventions of the avunculate relationship.

KINSHIP STUDIES AND HISTORICAL RECONSTRUCTION

Given the sustained concern within biblical study for historical reconstruction that has been responsible both for some of this discipline's greatest advances and also for some potential problems (as noted in Chapter 1), we might close this inquiry into the Jacob narratives by asking if kinship studies provide a foundation for any historical conclusions. The frankest answer to this question is: perhaps in the future, but probably not at present. A particular example may clarify the tentativeness of such an answer. We have noted that a tension between patrilocal and avunculocal residence rules is found quite commonly in the kinship systems behind a variety of traditional literature. Just this tension may well help us to explain some of the "strife" between Laban and Jacob: Laban acts on the assumption that Jacob and his family will reside with him, that is, avunculocally, while Jacob himself appears to assume that a rule of patrilocal residence compels him to return to the land of his father. Interestingly, a conflict between two residence rules seems often related to broad and lasting social change. For example, Murdock's statistical study of kinship over a great many different societies demonstrated to him that "the rule of residence is normally the first aspect of a social system to undergo modification in the process of change from one relatively stable equilibrium to another."[48] The best documented such change is, more interestingly still, just that which might have played a role in the composition and transmission of the patriarchal narratives—the change from some form of unsettled existence to the social context that exists within a settled agricultural life. The conditions of such a new mode of existence will normally give rise, over time, to a revised kinship system, including perhaps first a change in the rules of residence.

Provisionally, we might then conclude that an analysis of the Jacob narratives based upon an awareness of kinship studies provides further support for a conclusion drawn on the basis of more traditional methods. Both kinship study and more traditional inquiry might be taken to be in agreement in suggesting that the patriarchal narratives were composed in an era when the inhabitants of the land that would become Israel first abandoned a wandering existence and adopted a settled agricultural life.

Such a conclusion, however, must remain quite provisional for a specific reason mentioned in Chapter 2. Any such conclusion assumes that there is complete coincidence between: (1) kinship systems as these appear in a society's myths and (2) the actual social formation, including the kinship relationships that existed at the time of the myths' composition. This assumption, we noted in Chapter 2, is deeply problematic because of the evidence that clearly points to frequent divergences between a myth's social background and the empirical social setting in which the myth was composed and transmitted. Problems such as this have prompted anthropologists throughout much of the present century to warn us of the dangers of composing "conjectural history" based upon the knowledge of kinship systems as these are related in a society's myths.[49] There is, of course, *some* relationship between any people's empirical social formation and the social background that appears in that people's myths. But this relationship need not be, and demonstrably *is* not in many cases, a relationship of coincidence. For example, societies whose myths speak of, say, patrilocal residence and cross-cousin marriage may well be societies for which there is no evidence for the actual practice of patrilocal residence and cross-cousin marriage in any era—and least of all in the remote past. Biblical studies in particular, unfortunately, have repeatedly assumed just such a perfect correspondence between the social background of biblical myths and the social setting of Israel in various epochs. These same studies have further often taken the step, more dangerous still, of appealing to the remote past as the presumed locus of practices and systems whose existence cannot be established in any era for which we have sufficient historical and ethnographic data.

Hence, we are not in a position to conclude that the kinship tensions within the Jacob narratives offer proof that these narratives were composed against the background of changing residence and settlement patterns. Attractive as such a historical deduction might be, any such deduction must remain highly hypothetical and perhaps even deeply misleading. Lamentably, the study of kinship networks does not provide us with a firm foundation for the building of history, and we ought not repeat the errors of the past in proceeding hastily to such historical reconstruction.

3. CONCLUSIONS

The apparent symmetry between the roles played by the stories about the Jacob-Laban relationship on the one hand and by those about Jacob's marriages with Leah and Rachel on the other hand is itself support for the application of kinship study to biblical narratives. In both these sets of narratives, the recounting of Jacob's kinship relations completes a system that is basic to the social nature of kinship itself. That is, when Jacob marries his mother's brother's daughters, and when he is through this alliance forced to confront a series of relationships with his maternal uncle, a complete kinship system is described. Israel is thus "born" as an adequate descriptive unit with Jacob's cross-cousin and avunculate relationships. This conclusion, in turn, coincides with that reached in this chapter through an investigation of the alteration from a linear to a segmented genealogy. Again, with the birth of Jacob's sons, Israel is first adequately defined, externally as well as internally. In every case under consideration, the decisive relationships are those established by Jacob, the man who is to be renamed Israel.

All of this, then, suggests a ready and novel answer to a question we posed of the theological tradition at the outset of this chapter. The question, again, is this: Why is it Jacob, rather than someone else, who is renamed Israel? The answer from the theological tradition, as we noted, is that the choice of Jacob to be Israel's eponymous ancestor is either an accidental result of the transmission of the patriarchal narratives or remains a mystery in the realm of the divine. The answer that results from our attempt to describe a web of kinship relations embedded within the biblical text is quite the opposite of this. Jacob is renamed Israel not because of the haphazard transmission of these stories or because of a divine motive forever beyond the reach of human reason. Rather, because the decisive relationships that culturally define the people Israel are those that are recounted in the stories of Jacob, it is something of an inevitability that it is he who receives the name Israel.

5. Religious Identity and the Sacred Prostitution Accusation

Readers of most translations of the Hebrew Bible or of almost any summary treatment of the religion of Israel will be familiar with the accusation that various neighbors of Israel practiced a form of sacred prostitution. The accusation, many of whose ancient and modern sources will be cited, is usually formulated like this: Part of the religion of the Canaanites/Phoenicians, the Babylonians, and perhaps others involved a series of rites in which sacred personnel performed various sexual acts, largely to ensure the fertility of the land and its inhabitants. In the Hebrew Bible itself, this theme figures especially prominently in the Book of Deuteronomy and in materials that shaped and that were then influenced by Deuteronomism. For example, among the many materials collected in Deuteronomy and presented as originating in the Sinai revelation to Moses we read the following: "There shall be no cult prostitute of the daughters of Israel, neither shall there be a cult prostitute of the sons of Israel" (Deut. 23:17).[1] So too, within the block of material that extends from Deuteronomy through 2 Kings that is usually viewed today as having undergone editing from one or more Deuteronomistic editors, various kings' reigns are assessed with some mention of the same cultic institution. Thus, Rehoboam's reign is said to have witnessed the practice of cult prostitution (1 Kings 14:24), while Asa, Jehoshaphat, and Josiah are all praised for having made efforts toward ridding the land of cult prostitutes (1 Kings 15:12, 15:46; 2 Kings 23:7). Most modern scholars have also found documentation of this practice in the Book of Hosea (chs. 1–3, with regard to Hosea's marriage, and 4:14) and in Elihu's speech in Job (Job 36:14).

If, however, the existence of sacred prostitution as an element in the liturgical life of several ancient Near Eastern religions and as a continuing temptation for Israelites has achieved the status of a kind of given, it remains true that discovering unambiguous evidence for any such rites among these religions remains quite difficult. This difficulty too is an issue to which much of the present chapter will be devoted. For now, we might note that an article on sacred prostitution in a modern biblical dictionary concludes, somewhat surprisingly following the article's repetition of the standard accounts of this rite, that "the meagerness of the data regarding the practice of cult prostitution is in contrast to the considerable amount of material of a denunciatory nature."[2] Precisely this contrast between meager evidence and repeated condemnation provides the framework for the discussion which follows.

Clearly, denunciations of sacred prostitution play a key role in various theological statements within the Hebrew Bible. Within Deuteronomic literature, for example, this theme is part of this literature's "intensified . . . nationalistic views," views that led to the requirement that "the Canaanite be slain, exterminated, and annihilated."[3] Clearly too, denunciations of sacred prostitution also play a similarly key role in modern summaries of biblical thought written from within the theological tradition. An approach to the issue of sacred prostitution from outside the theological tradition, however, might begin, not with expressions of condemnation for this rite but rather by accenting the very contrast between elaborate and even passionate denunciation on the one hand and slight and ambiguous evidence on the other hand.

This contrast immediately suggests a direction of inquiry quite apart from that pursued from within the theological tradition. Perhaps sacred prostitution ought to be investigated as an *accusation* rather than as a *reality*. Perhaps, then, this alleged practice belongs in the same category with cannibalism, sodomy, and abhorrent dietary and sexual practices generally—that is to say, in the category of charges that one society levels against others as a part of that society's process of self-definition. Such charges play a well-

known role in the heresiographic traditions of a great many religions. Viewed in this way, the accusation that other societies
utilize religious personnel as a part of sacred sexual rites surely
tells us something about those who formulate and repeat the accusation. In the present case, it tells us something about ancient
Israel, ancient Greece and Rome, early Christian tradition, and the
modern theological tradition. But the accusation may tell us little
or nothing about those religions against which the charge is leveled.

Speaking in this fashion about the charge of sacred prostitution
means we are investigating this particular issue under the more
general heading of the symbolic use that various societies make of
accusations against their neighbors by way of marking clearly the
boundaries of their own sense of self. Though this issue has
figured prominently in much of the present century's anthropological research, a single volume edited by the Norwegian scholar
Fredrik Barth provides a convenient recent summary of the symbolism of ethnic boundary marking.[4] Barth begins with a definition of *ethnic group* that depends directly upon the opposition between self and others: "To the extent that actors use ethnic
identities to categorize themselves and others for the purposes of
interaction, they form ethnic groups."[5] Such categorizations, Barth
continues, fall largely into two sorts of material. There are, first,
"overt signals or signs," such as dress, language, kinship, eating
habits, and so forth; and there are, secondly, "basic value orientations," that is, "the standards of morality and excellency by which
performance is judged."[6] The use to which a given group puts both
these overt signs and these basic orientations means that ethnic
boundaries are marked less by any "objective" criteria than they
are by the kinds of conduct and standards to which a group says
it holds firm and from which the group charges its neighbors
depart. Especially relevant to the present discussion is the observation that those areas of conduct upon which a group focuses in
making these distinctions form a quite limited set. The set includes
above all sexual and eating habits. And given the perhaps more
fundamental use of these same habits to distinguish the human

from the nonhuman, such focus upon diet and sex suggests that there is a sense in which any society using these symbols to define itself is also proclaiming that "we" are human and "they" are less than human. "We," as humans, do not practice sodomy, do not mate indiscriminately, do not eat each other; "they," as less than humans, encourage indiscriminate mating as a religiously sanctioned rite and are sodomites and cannibals. The British anthropologist Rodney Needham puts this perhaps more pointedly. Why, Needham asks, do the charges of cannibalism, sodomy, and the like figure so largely in traditional literatures if there is little or no evidence for the actual practice of such things among those groups alleged to practice them? Because, answers Needham, "any group can appreciate their own existence more meaningfully by conjuring up others as categorical opposites."[7]

That particular accusation utilized as a part of ethnic boundary marking that has received the most contemporary attention is probably that of cannibalism. This is the case partly because of the controversy sparked by W. Arens's recent volume entitled *The Man-Eating Myth.*[8] Arens here asks us to entertain the thesis that cannibalism is nowhere an institution that can be established beyond a doubt. Though most scholars seem less than fully persuaded by this thesis and suggest that there are a few cases in which the evidence speaks clearly for the practice of cannibalism, Arens has demonstrated the flawed and tendentious nature of some of the data standardly cited to prove the widespread nature of this practice. Most intriguingly, Arens begins his debunking attempt just where we will concentrate, with the Greek historian Herodotus. About the evidence offered by Herodotus and a host of others, Arens concludes: "All cultures, subcultures, religions, sects, secret societies and every other possible human association have been labeled anthropophagic by someone. . . . The idea of 'others' as cannibals, rather than the act, is the universal phenomenon. The significant question is not why people eat human flesh, but why one group invariably assumes that others do."[9] Hence the use of the term *myth* (as ideological fiction) in the title of Arens's volume: "The idea of the cannibalistic nature of others is a myth in the sense of, first, having an independent existence bearing no relationship to historical reality, and second, containing and transmitting significant cultural messages for those who maintain it."[10]

For our purposes, a discussion of any evidence supporting or questioning the existence of this particular practice is less significant than is the observation that cannibalism is "but one item in a whole battery of moral obloquy."[11] The larger battery includes sacred prostitution as well. Almost everyone who discusses ancient Near Eastern religions, as will be documented in part, assumes that sacred prostitution was an established practice in this era and area. And almost everyone then goes on to join the Deuteronomistic editors and others within the Hebrew Bible in denouncing this practice. But is there sufficient evidence for this assumption? Or, is sacred prostitution rather the extension of a cultural and theological accusation of chief service in distinguishing and thus absolutizing the religions on whose behalf ancient and modern thinkers are campaigning?

1. SACRED PROSTITUTION IN MODERN STUDY

Although accounts of the religiously sanctioned practice of various sexual acts begin in antiquity, the growth of historical-critical biblical study within the past century coincides with a perceptible increase in the rehearsing of such accounts. The reasons for this increase are not difficult to understand: The more Israel's religion appeared to be related closely to the religions of her neighbors, the more intently scholars from within the theological tradition sought grounds to establish the distinctiveness and superiority of this religion. Within the last decades of the nineteenth century, Robertson Smith would argue both for the necessity of comparative research and for the conclusion that this research demonstrated Israel's uniquely high standing among the religions of antiquity. This conclusion was bolstered in part by Robertson Smith's statement that "the temples of the Semitic deities were thronged with sacred prostitutes."[12] This statement is not supported by any evidence, nor was this thought necessary. Robertson Smith was in good company in assuming that the existence of crowds of cultic prostitutes within the temples of the ancient Near East was something not requiring documentation. Within a few years of the initial appearance of Robertson Smith's *The Religion of the Semites,* the Continental scholar Karl Budde offered a summary of Israelite religion that similarly utilized sacred prostitution as a means of contrasting Israelite cultic rites with those of her neighbors. The religion of Canaan, Budde begins, "brought with it its dangers" to early Israel: "It was voluptuous and dissolute; debauchery and sexual excesses went with it hand in hand. . . . [However] the healthy and austere moralty of the [Israelite] nomad revolted against these excrescences of over-civilization, and so gradually prepared the way for the defeat of the gods of Canaan by the God of Israel."[13] Both Budde's assumption that such statements required no documentation and his use of extreme language in denunciation of sexual practicies in religious rites are far from atypical. Listen, for example, to the account first written in 1906 by the Belgian historian of religion Franz Cumont: "Immorality was nowhere so flagrant as in the temple of Astarte, whose female servants honored the goddess with untiring ardor. . . . These aberrations, that were kept up until the end of paganism, probably have their explanation in the primitive constitution of the Semitic tribe. . . . [Sacred prostitution constitutes] a blemish . . . [which] transformed the temples of Astarte into houses of debauchery."[14]

However, from the period of the beginning of the twentieth century, no single scholar can quite compete on this particular field of magnetically attractive polemic with the claims of Sir James George Frazer. Because Frazer's statements and assumptions are both so typical and so influential, his comments on sacred prostitution merit full citation:

In Cyprus it appears that before marriage all women were formerly obliged by custom to prostitute themselves to strangers at the sanctuary of the goddess, whether she went by the name of Aphrodite, Astarte, or what not. Similar customs prevailed in many parts of western Asia. Whatever its motive, the practice was clearly regarded, not as an orgy of lust, but as a solemn religious duty performed in the service of the great Mother Goddess of western Asia. . . . Thus at Babylon every woman, whether rich or poor, had once in her life to submit to the embraces of a stranger at the temple of Mylitta, that is, of Ishtar or Astarte, and to dedicate to the goddess the wages earned by this sanctified harlotry. . . . At Heliopolis or Baalbec in Syria, . . . the custom of the country required that every maiden should prostitute herself to a stranger at the temple of Astarte. . . . At Byblus, . . . women who refused to sacrifice their hair had to give themselves up to strangers on a certain day of the festival and the money which they thus earned was devoted to the goddess. . . . In Lydia all girls were obliged to prostitute themselves in order to earn a dowry. . . . In Armenia the noblest families dedicated their daughters to the service of the goddess Anaitis in her temple at Acilisena, where the damsels acted as prostitutes for a long time before they were given in marriage. . . .

We may conclude that a great Mother Goddess, the personification of all the reproductive energies of nature, was worshipped under different names but with a substantial similarity of myth and ritual by many peoples of western Asia; that associated with her was a lover, or rather a series of lovers, divine yet mortal, with whom she mated year by year, their commerce being deemed essential to the propagation of animals and plants, each in their several kinds; and further, that the fabulous union of the divine pair was simulated and, as it were, multiplied on earth by the real, though temporary, union of the human sexes at the sanctuary of the goddess for the sake of thereby ensuring the fruitfulness of the ground and the increase of man and beast.[15]

Of course, behind these elaborate claims by Frazer lies his own reconstruction of the history of human society, a portrait Frazer shared with many others in the late nineteenth century. Briefly, this reconstruction has it that in the history of humanity's social development: (1) Marriage was originally communal; (2) subsequently, when marriage ceased to be communal, its earlier form was commemorated by every woman's engaging in ritual sexual intercourse once in her life; and (3) later still, when even this practice was abandoned, the earliest stage of marriage was kept alive ritually by those whose profession it was to act as sacred prostitutes.[16] This particular reconstruction, like so many of the theoretical foundations of Frazer's work (see Chapter 2), has been quite completely abandoned by twentieth-century ethnographic historians. But the statements Frazer made about sacred prostitution continue to be repeated in slightly (sometimes, very slightly) different form, as if these were beyond rebuttal.

Though the years between the first decades of this century and the end of World War II witnessed a host of similar accounts attributing ritual sexual practices to ancient Near Eastern religions,[17] in the interest of establishing the contemporary currency of such accounts let us advance to more recent scholarship and conclude this section with a survey of some descriptions of these rites in the years since the Second World War. The great American archaeologist and philologist William F. Albright rarely summarized the religion of Israel without offering accounts of abhorrent and religiously approved prostitution in the societies surrounding Israel. Typical are his comments in his frequently reprinted *Archaeology and the Religion of Israel*. Here, Albright writes that "sacred prostitution was apparently an almost invariable concomitant of the cult of the Phoenician and Syrian goddess, whatever her personal name, as we know from many allusions in classical literature, especially in Herodotus, Strabo, and Lucian. . . . the erotic aspect of their cult must have sunk to extremely sordid depths of social degradation."[18] Nor, in Albright's view, was this the worst of it. Israel's neighbors also knew of male cult prostitutes. These "sodomites," whose existence is "confirmed by the Deuteronomic passage in 1 Kings 14:24," are "known to classical writers as *cinaedi* or *galli,*" and are "familiar to cuneiformists under such names as *kulu'u, asinnu, kurgarrū;*" "modern nomadic Arab ethos and Israelite religious tradition agree in their loathing for the practice of male prostitution."[19] A commentary on a collection of legal materials, chiefly the laws of Hammurabi, concludes that "in the Laws there is nothing definite to show whether the various priestesses named in them were temple-prostitutes, but there can be little doubt that sacral prostitutions existed in connexion with the temples, especially with that of Ishtar, if only because of the widespread testimony of antiquity."[20] The article "Prostitution" in *The Interpreter's Dictionary of the Bible,* a tool to be found in almost every theological library, is primarily devoted to cult prostitution. According to this popularizing summary, "the prostitute who was an official of the cult in ancient Palestine and nearby lands of biblical times exercised an important function." These officials' "chief service was sexual in nature—the offering of their bodies for ritual purposes."[21]

Perhaps the most frequently used Old Testament theology of the past several decades, that of Gerhard von Rad, readily identified the woman of harlotry whom the prophet Hosea marries with "a woman who took part in the Canaanite fertility rites," so that the prophet here expressed an "abhorrence of the fertility rites and sacred prostitution of the cult of Baal."[22] So, too, recent commentaries on the Book of Hosea repeat the same charge. Thus, in his comment on Hosea 4:14, James Mays presents as established fact the view that "sacred prostitutes *(qĕdēšōt)* are professionals who served as cultic personnel at the shrines where fertility rites were practiced. Sacrifice accompanied by ritual intercourse with them was meant to stimulate the sexual activity of the gods for the sake of the land's fertility. The custom of using both male and female sacred prostitutes was widespread in the ancient Near East."[23] The commentary of H. W. Wolff observes in like manner that the "Canaanite sexual rite" was one "in which young virgins offered themselves to the divinity and expected fertility in return. They surrendered themselves to strangers inside the holy precincts."[24] Most revealingly, a long and careful critique of Wolff's reconstruction of the "sex cult" argues that the evidence Wolff cites does not support his reconstruction and yet goes on to conclude that we must still assume on the basis of the widespread nature of the charge in antiquity that some such rites did in fact exist.[25]

Recent portraits of the religion of Israel throughout the biblical period repeat these same accusations. According to Helmer Ringgren, "the cultic drama of the dying and rising fertility god clearly played an essential role in the cultus [of the Canaanites]. There was, in addition, sacral prostitution, considered very impor-

tant because it was felt to promote fertility."²⁶ And for Georg
Fohrer, "Canaanite religion, being a fertility cult, was familiar
with the sacral prostitution that was widespread throughout the
ancient Near East."²⁷ Studies even from the most recent years
repeat the identical charges. This is true, for example, of an article
by Yamauchi, in which he assumes the existence of sexual rites
among Israel's neighbors, partly in reliance upon research as dated
as that of Frazer and even Westermarck, though Yamauchi does
note that "there are no explicit texts which can prove this" for
Ugaritic religion and that "the most explicit references to sacred
prostitution in Syria and Phoenicia are to be found in later texts,"
e.g., Lucian and a collection of Patristic sources.²⁸ It is also true of
any number of additional studies that have appeared of late.²⁹

Little, then, has changed in the past century. There is, to be sure,
a mounting hesitancy to claim clear, unambiguous testimony for
the existence of sacred prostitution among several Near Eastern
religions. But this hesitancy hardly prevents scholars from asserting repeatedly that the rite must have existed. Surely, the reasoning seems to run, the evidence of the Hebrew Bible and of a host
of classical and Patristic sources cannot be ignored. Surely, this
reasoning continues, the weight of this evidence is enough to
counterbalance the paucity of textual attestation from Canaan or
Mesopotamia for such rites. Perhaps. But let us turn now to a brief
assessment of this evidence's weight.

2. SACRED PROSTITUTION ACCORDING TO CLASSICAL AND PATRISTIC SOURCES

Scholars seeking to establish the existence of sexual rites in the
religions of the ancient Near East most often cite the Hebrew
Bible, especially the Deuteronomic literature (Hosea, the Book of
Deuteronomy, and the Deuteronomistic History), in support of
this. But since the status of the biblical testimony is partly what
is at issue here, let us look instead at that body of material cited
next in frequency by modern scholars—the material in Greek and
Latin from Herodotus in the fifth century B.C. to Saint Augustine

and others in the fifth century A.D. As in the preceding section, it is perhaps best to survey the most important pieces of this testimony in roughly chronological order.[30]

SACRED PROSTITUTION AND SIMILAR PRACTICES: HERODOTUS TO SOZOMON

The most extensive and most frequently utilized such testimony comes from the Greek historian Herodotus.[31] Herodotus refers in passing to the Lydian custom by which parents turn their daughters into prostitutes who thereby earn dowries for themselves (I. 93–94). His comments on what he claims to have learned about Babylon and about Cyprus are much fuller:

The foulest Babylonian custom is that which compels every woman of the land once in her life to sit in the temple of Aphrodite and have intercourse with some stranger. Many women who are rich and proud and disdain to consort with the rest, drive to the temple in covered carriages drawn by teams, and there stand with a great retinue of attendants. But most sit down in the sacred plot of Aphrodite, with crowns of cord on their heads; there is a great multitude of women coming and going; passages marked by line run every way through the crowd, by which the stranger men pass and make their choice. When a woman has once taken her place there she goes not away to her home before some stranger has cast money into her lap and had intercourse with her outside the temple; but while he casts the money, he must say, 'I demand thee in the name of Mylitta' (that is the Assyrian name for Aphrodite). It matters not what be the sum of money; the woman will never refuse, for that were a sin, the money being by this act made sacred. So she follows the first man who casts it and rejects none. After their intercourse she has made herself holy in the goddess's sight and goes away to her home; and thereafter there is no bribe however great that will get her. So then the women that are fair and tall are soon free to depart, but the uncomely have long to wait because they cannot fulfil the law; for some of them remain for three years, or four. There is a custom like to this in some parts of Cyprus. (I. 199)

I have cited in full Herodotus's comments on the Babylonian custom partly so that the extraordinary extent to which later writers rely directly upon Herodotus will be clear. This is demonstrable already in what Strabo reports about the custom. Strabo's *Geography,* written at some time very close to the beginning of the Christian era, is beyond doubt the classical source cited next in frequency after Herodotus.[32] Strabo reports the following: "And in accordance with a certain oracle all the Babylonian women have a custom of having intercourse with a foreigner, the women going to a temple of Aphrodite with a great retinue and crowd; and each woman is wreathed with a cord round her head. The man who approaches a woman takes her far away from the sacred precinct, places a fair amount of money upon her lap, and then has intercourse with her; and the money is considered sacred to Aphrodite." (16.1.20) Strabo also reports that elsewhere in western Asia nobles consecrate their daughters "to be prostitutes in the temple of the goddess for a long time" (11.14.16) and that the Thebans in Egypt dedicate an especially beautiful maiden to be a prostitute in honor of Zeus (17.1.46).

In general, comments made by other classical and Patristic sources are less elaborate than are those of Herodotus and Strabo. Valerius Maximus, who was active during the reign of Tiberius, reports that Punic women engage in sexual rites in honor of the goddess Venus.[33] In the *Syrian Goddess,* a second-century A.D. text attributed to the satirist Lucian of Samosata and descriptive of the religious rites at the city of Hierapolis near the Euphrates River, we read that the women of the city "shave their heads, as do the Egyptians when Apis dies. The women who refuse to shave pay this penalty: For a single day they stand offering their beauty for sale. The market, however, is open to foreigners only and the payment becomes an offering to Aphrodite."[34] Later in the second century, Clement of Alexandria mentions the "orgies" celebrated in honor of Aphrodite on Cyprus.[35] A piece of symposium literature by the late second-century author Athenaeus repeats the charge that the Lydians and the Cyprians both give up their daughters to prostitution as a part of a sacred rite, and the accusation is made again of the Lydians by Aelian some years later.[36] In the third century A.D., Justinus' Latin abbreviation of the work of one Pompeius Trogus cites Cyprus, once more, as the site where maidens "earn a great deal of money" by practicing prostitution in honor of Venus.[37] From the following century comes a report by Arnobius, the teacher of Lactantius. Arnobius's *Adversus Nationes,* an extended exposé of all non-Christian cults, speaks briefly of the mysteries practiced on Cyprus, rites that Arnobius describes as including sacred prostitution in honor of Venus.[38] Lactantius himself, in his lengthy defense of Christianity that appeared during the first decades of the fourth century, describes this alleged rite in somewhat greater detail: Venus "was the first . . . who instituted the prostitute's art, and she was the authority for the women in Cyprus to make profit by prostituting their bodies. She authorized this so that she would not seem alone, different from other women, in her unchaste pursuit of men."[39] *The Life of Constantine,* by the prolific fourth-century Church historian Eusebius of Caesarea, purports to describe the rites celebrated at the Syrian city of Heliopolis. In this city, Eusebius writes, "those who dignify licentious pleasure with a distinguishing title of honor, had permitted their wives and daughters to commit shameless fornication."[40] At about the same time of Eusebius's work, Athanasius, the opponent of Arianism, wrote another *Against the Nations* that returns to the familiar theme of pagan sexual excess and unnaturalness: "In time past women displayed themselves in front of idols in Phoenicia, offering the price of their bodies to the local gods, and believing that by prostitution they conciliated their goddess and incurred her favour through these practices. And men, denying their own nature and no longer wishing to be male, assume a female nature, as if thereby they pleased and honoured the mother of those they call gods. . . . For from Zeus they learned pederasty and adultery, from Aphrodite fornication, from Rhea lasciviousness, from Ares murder, and from other gods other similar things, which the law punishes and which every decent man avoids."[41]

The mid-fourth century A.D. plea by Firmicus Maternus that the power of Rome be exercised to destroy paganism rehearses the standard accusations against the island of Cyprus: "I hear that Cinyras of Cyprus gave a temple to his harlot friend Venus, and even initiated many in the rites of the Cyprian Venus, and devoted them to her by senseless consecrations—yes, even stipulated that whoever wanted to be initiated, with Venus' secret confided to him, should give the goddess one penny as pay. What sort of secret it was we all must understand without telling, because its shameful character is such that we cannot explain it in clearer detail. The lover Cinyras observed well the laws of whoredom: he bade the priests of the consecrated Venus give her a piece of money, as if to a whore."[42] In the early fifth century, Augustine's *City of God* makes brief reference to the Phoenician custom of devoting their daughters to prostitution before the time of their marriage.[43] Finally come reports from two Church historians, both near contemporaries of Augustine. The first of these, Socrates, cites again Heliopolis in Phoenicia as a site whose laws "ordered the women among them to be common, and therefore the children born there were of doubtful descent, so that there was no distinction of fathers and their offspring. Their virgins also were presented for prostitution to the strangers who resorted thither."[44] A second Church historian, Sozomon, speaks again of Heliopolis and of the custom there of killing virgins and feeding their remains to pigs: "I am convinced that the citizens of Heliopolis perpetrated this barbarity against the holy virgins on account of the prohibition of the ancient custom of yielding up virgins to prostitution with any chance comer before being united in marriage to their betrothed."[45]

EVALUATING THE CLASSICAL AND PATRISTIC SOURCES

Though few modern scholars cite anything like all of the material just mentioned, it is the custom to make reference to at least a number of these texts. Any such reference lends a tone of certainty to the assumption that sacred prostitution was a regular part of various religions in antiquity. A full list of these sources appears impressively long—at least fifteen authors from antiquity. The list seems equally impressive with regard to the era covered—the better part of a thousand years. However, once we cease to rest content with merely counting heads and begin rather to evaluate critically these sources, the documentary edifice supporting the existence of sacred prostitution leans heavily and perhaps altogether collapses.

First, given the assumption that sacred prostitution flourished during the period before the existence of Israel and during parts of the biblical era, most of the sources cited are remarkable for their late date. This is true already for Herodotus, who will have been a near contemporary of Ezra and Nehemiah, and for Strabo, who wrote close to the beginning of the Christian era. It is all the more true for those who wrote in the second through the fifth centuries A.D. Most of the sources mentioned belong in this latter category. The great length of time between the era when this custom was purported to have existed and the eras from which the reports come is already problematic for anyone wishing to establish the existence of the custom. A prevalent convention in a great many societies, both ancient and modern, is that which labels the "ancestors" as less civilized and less fully human than contemporaries. This convention alone could account for Herodotus and others reporting what was told to them about the behavior of their sources' ancestors.

Second, none of these sources is noteworthy for its disinterested, objective character. Herodotus, to whom we will turn again in a moment, composed his *History* in part for the greater glory of Greece, and the contrast between civilized Greece and the bizarre East is everywhere apparent in this work. And that we might expect an accurate and fair account of non-Christian religious practices from Clement of Alexandria or Arnobius, from Lactantius or Eusebius is of course out of the question. All the Patristic sources are deeply apologetic. The great majority were written in the interest of demonstrating the cruelty, impiety, and primitiveness of the pagan religions of Syria, Mesopotamia, and elsewhere. Modern scholars do not accord much credit to those pagan sources that label all Christians as incestuous cannibals who feast upon human flesh and blood. Why, then, should they accept at face value the Christian accusation that pagans sanctify prostitution?

Third, the approximately fifteen sources listed is in fact nothing like a catalogue of fifteen separate and independent sources. Rather, the geographers, historians, ethnographers, and others cited are interdependent. Socrates and Sozomon were both deeply dependent upon Eusebius, and Eusebius's work is a pastiche of earlier reports. Lactantius was the student of Arnobius, and Arnobius's *Adversus Nationes* is an uncritical amalgam of earlier reports. All the non-Christian evidence and most, if not all, of the Christian evidence is dependent, directly or indirectly, upon Herodotus. We could continue with such literary genealogies, but to do so is unnecessary since even in English translation the interdependency of the materials cited is immediately obvious. What appears to be a list of more than a dozen sources may in fact be a list of a couple of sources, perhaps even and ultimately a single source: Herodotus.

Fourth, what about Herodotus? The history of scholarship investigating the reliability of Herodotus is a classic case study of the vicissitudes of academic inquiry. Briefly, the presumed accuracy of Herodotus's tales about Egypt, Syria-Palestine, and Mesopotamia has risen and fallen as frequently as does the temperature in the course of a year in any untemperate climate. As long ago as the eighteenth century, Voltaire found it incredible that we might actually place any trust in Herodotus's tales. Many scholars at the beginning of the twentieth century concluded that Herodotus could never have visited the lands he alleged to have visited, while others later concluded that Herodotus was a markedly accurate reporter. A detailed study, first published in 1950, of the reliability of Herodotus's information about Mesopotamia suggested that the truth lay somewhere between such extremes. This study determined: (1) that Herodotus's knowledge of Mesopotamian topography was quite reliable, though accompanied by fanciful explanations; (2) that his cultural observations were at best superficial and largely dependent upon his source, Hecataeus; and (3) that Herodotus's knowledge of Mesopotamia was much less accurate and complete than was his knowledge of Egypt.[46] Particularly in light of the third conclusion, it is instructive to turn to the most recent assessments of the reliability of Herodotus's accounts of

Egyptian practices.[47] These assessments do not encourage confidence in what Herodotus "reports" about Babylonian customs. The conclusions of one of these most recent studies are worth citing here: "Herodotus may indeed have gone to Egypt, but his narrative bears little or no relation to whatever his travels may have been on the basis of archaeological evidence now in hand. . . . It is the frequent absence of even superficial knowledge that tries our belief in the veracity of Herodotus. . . . We can find reasons for all these stories among the Greeks at home, regaled as they were with the legend of soldiers and traders. . . . Ionian tradition rather than Herodotus' own experience was decisive in shaping his story. . . . Herodotus drew heavily on previous Greek traditions of the country when he came to build his narrative, and we must look to those traditions to account for it."[48] This, of course, is hardly the last word on this issue. But given that previous research had concluded that Herodotus's Mesopotamian information—from which comes the all-important account of sacred prostitution in Babylon—was of mixed accuracy and was less reliable than his Egyptian information, we cannot but conclude that our chief source for the existence of cultic prostitution in Mesopotamia cannot be used with any confidence. And if Herodotus's account in this regard is of questionable value, then *a fortiori* so, too, are all of the later classical and Patristic sources.

3. THE EVIDENCE FROM MESOPOTAMIA

We have seen that even the most ardent supporters of the reality of sacred prostitution in Near Eastern antiquity admit that very meager or no primary evidence for this practice comes from the Canaanites in ancient Syria. The case is somewhat different for Mesopotamia. Here, a number of terms for sacred personnel have been understood from time to time as terms descriptive of the office of sacred prostitute. Even here, however, many investigations, especially the most recent, have concluded that these sacred personnel can only doubtfully be identified as cult prostitutes.[49] A brief and fairly untechnical survey of five of the titles that have sometimes been translated as "sacred prostitute" or the like may demonstrate the state of our uncertainty.

(1) *ēntu.* The office of the *ēntum,* conventionally translated "high priestess," is now thought to have entailed a vow of chastity.[50] Understanding the vow that those accepting this office took may well help us to understand a part of the Legend of Sargon. Since Sargon's mother is called an *ēnetu* (=*ēntu*), and since "a principal condition for holding the office was to avoid pregnancy," the reason why the baby Sargon had to be exposed may perhaps be clear.[51] Understood thusly, the *ēntu* is no longer a very strong candidate for a term describing a sacred prostitute.

(2) *nadītu.*[52] The older view was that the *nadītu* was a sacred prostitute and that the area associated with this term and called the *gagû* was a kind of brothel. Driver and Miles, for example, suggest that "it is likely that she was in some temples, as for instance those of Ishtar, a sacred prostitute."[53] However, B. Landsberger argued at length that chastity was required as well of the *nadītu,* and this view seems generally accepted today.[54] About the *nadītu* (usually translated "dedicated woman") we know only that they usually came from the nobility, that many were the daughters of royalty, and that they were forbidden to bear children. More about their possible cultic role cannot be said at present.

It is possible that the *ugbabtu* priestess, for whose office no satisfactory translation has been offered, is to be identified with the *nadītu.* J. Finkelstein, for example, concluded that there was perhaps little distinction between the the *nadītu* and the *ugbabtu,* and that "it may even be that the titles are in some circumstances interchangeable."[55] The *ugbabtu* perhaps stood below the *ēntu* in rank, usually (though not necessarily) lived within a *gagû,* and remained unmarried and childless.[56]

(3) *qadištu.* The office that *qadištu* designates has been the subject of especially careful inquiry because the title is so closely related to the biblical words *qĕdēšâ/qādēš*, standardly translated "female/male cult prostitute." *Qadištu* is often translated "hierodule" or the like, but Driver and Miles already observed that "there is nothing to show the nature of her service nor whether she may or may not have been devoted to sacred prostitution."[57] The *qadištu* could marry and bear children, and apparently often acted as wet nurse or midwife. It frequently used to be said that the holders of this office played some role in the Ishtar cult. However, Renger has recently shown that there is no evidence for any particular link of the *qadištu* with the Ishtar cult or for the assertion that she functioned as a cult prostitute.[58]

(4) *ištarītu.* The translation of *ištarītu* in the *CAD* as "a woman of special status" is a token of how little is known about this class of priestess.[59] Beyond our knowledge that the *ištarītu* could not marry, too little is known to make any meaningful statements about this class of personnel, much less to conclude that the office involved ritual sexual activity.

(5) *kezertu.* This class of priestess is mentioned together with the *harīmtu,* a word usually associated with harlotry, and hence the term is often translated "prostitute."[60] Still, Renger's survey of the terminology of the Mesopotamian priesthood concludes that "about her [the *kezertu's*] functions we know little."[61] In a quite recent study, M. Gallery argued that a group of women mentioned in a series of Babylonian texts from the middle of the second millennium B.C. are to be identified with the class of *kezertu* and are to be seen as serving in some sort of sexual function. As such, these Old Babylonian texts may be the first to give "explicit indication that certain Babylonian wives engaged in some sexual activity as part of their services rendered to a goddess, for which heretofor [sic] the only native evidence was the post–Old Babylonian literary tra-

dition."[62] This study is doubly interesting. First, if this evidence does indeed demonstrate what Gallery argues it does, it is surely noteworthy that this would then be the first and thus far the only Old Babylonian testimony to support the common conviction that the services of temple priestesses included cultic sexual activity. Secondly, the texts in question do not explicitly identify the women performing these services by their office. The evidence that these women are to be identified with the office of *kezertu* is, as Gallery readily admits, at best "circumstantial."[63]

Our brief survey of some of the terms for female temple personnel from Mesopotamia demonstrates what we have found elsewhere when surveying other bodies of evidence. The testimony in this case is complex, is such that certainty in many areas is impossible at present, and surely does not offer unambiguous clues for the widespread existence of sacred prostitution in ancient Mesopotamia. There are, however, other Mesopotamian literary remains that require some treatment here. Of chief significance are omens and related literature such as the following: "The *ēntu*-priestess will die of a venereal disease" (NIN.DINGER *muruṣ nīkti imāt*); "the high priest will repeatedly have intercourse with the *ēnu* priestess" *(šagûm ēnam itanayak);* "the *ēntu* priestess will have illicit intercourse" *(ēntu innak);* and "the *ēntu* priestess will permit intercourse per anum in order to avoid pregnancy" *(ēntu aššum la eriša qinnassa ušnâk).*[64] All these texts might be, and thus have been, used to support the existence of sexual activity as a part of the office of various Babylonian cultic personnel. However, it is significant that all these references are contained within omen literature. This observation means that it is risky to assume that the texts are a commentary on normal or approved behavior. With regard to the last text just cited, Lewis argues precisely this: "The significance of the omen, however, is in doubt, for it is not clear from the protasis whether the apodasis is favorable or unfavorable; and in addition, one could argue that by its very nature, the omen does not reflect the normal behavior of the priestess.

SACRED PROSTITUTION / 151

Whether the *entu* would permit natural sex or any sex at all is unclear as is the identity of her partner in the omen."[65] This same argument could be applied to the remainder of the texts. When read in context, none of these omens provides anything like transparent testimony for cultic prostitution.

Textual evidence, of course, can be supplemented by other kinds of material. Are there, perhaps, some extratextual, archaeological remains from ancient Mesopotamia that support the existence of the practice of sacred prostitution? Though scholars have claimed to have found some such evidence, a recent summary article on Sacred Marriage in the chief Assyriological encyclopedia provides a wise corrective to these claims. The author of this article, J. S. Cooper, introduces the issue of archaeology and the alleged Sacred Marriage ceremony with the warning, to which too few have paid heed, that "there are no artifacts bearing inscriptions to support any such relationship [between the artifacts and the Sacred Marriage ceremony], nor are there representations that can be unambiguously related to contemporary textual evidence."[66] There are objects from ancient Mesopotamia, to be sure, that can be viewed as portraying scenes from some such ceremony. But the conclusion of Cooper after evaluating all such material is that "the very nature of the evidence makes any degree of certainty unattainable. Cuneiform has many allusions, mostly vague, to ritual sexual activity."[67]

Finally, in this account of the native Mesopotamian materials bearing upon the issue of sacred prostitution, we might take note of two collections of texts published quite recently. Each of these makes it yet more obvious that we are far from attaining a fair portrait of the functions of Babylonian and Assyrian cultic personnel. The first of these is the Epic of Atrahasis, the Old Babylonian creation story whose account of the deluge and the reasons for it is the fullest yet from Mesopotamia.[68] The final lines of this Epic establish three classes of female cultic personnel (*ugbabtu-*, *ēntu-*, and *igiṣītu-*women) for whom childbearing is prohibited. Of course, the conclusion that because these priestesses were not allowed to bear children they were therefore chaste is not a necessary one. Finkelstein has maintained that there is a "wide gulf between a ban on bearing children and a vow of chastity" and hence that these priestesses may still have had some cultic role involving sexual activity if one presumes that the Mesopotamians "had by trial and error come upon some drug" that functioned as a contraceptive.[69] This argument is, of course, highly speculative. In the absence of any firm evidence from Mesopotamia on behalf of either readily performed abortions or effective contraceptive drugs, it is surely safer to assume that the priestesses whose offices are listed at the conclusion of Atrahasis were expected to remain chaste. This is potentially important testimony, since two of these offices (the *ēntu* and the *ugbabtu*) have in the past been cited as those whose holders engaged in sexual activity as a part of the official cult.

Finkelstein has also recently edited a series of Old Babylonian texts from Kish that may have some bearing upon this issue. These texts suggest to their editor that the roles of the *nadītu* as a midwife and of the *qadištu* as a wet nurse that are attested in later texts may also have been the roles performed by these priestesses in the Old Babylonian period.[70] The same texts mention the *kezertu-* women, and offer no testimony to support the view that these personnel were cultic prostitutes. Once again, we meet the phenomenon of an increase in our knowledge casting doubt upon earlier assumptions about the widespread utilization of sexual activities in the religion of Mesopotamia. And we are left very much where we were following our summary of classical and Patristic sources. We are left in both cases with no unambiguous proof that sacred prostitution was practiced in the religions of Israel's neighbors.

4. CONCLUSION

It would be imprudent to claim on the basis of our, quite preliminary summary that there can have been no such institution as that of sacred prostitution anywhere in the ancient Near East. In this case as in others we might well pay heed to a kind of maxim formulated by the anthropologist Rodney Needham. This maxim goes as follows: "Whatever conduct can be imagined will, if it is socially feasible, be put into practice by some people somewhere and for some time."[71] Since sacred prostitution, crystal clearly, has put no strain on the imaginations of peoples ancient and modern, this institution probably did exist somewhere and at some time. However, that it existed in ancient Syria-Palestine or Mesopotamia is not demonstrated in any of the evidence to which appeal is so frequently made.

This issue, then, is another final example of the distinction between theological inquiry and other ways of approaching the religion of Israel. Comments on sacred prostitution in scholarship within the theological tradition are essentially extensions of the biblical view. Since the practice of sacred prostitution is claimed for Israel's neighbors and then denounced in the Hebrew Bible, biblical scholars have generally extended precisely this view. They have assumed the existence of the institution and then, in very Deuteronomic-like fashion, condemned it. An approach to the same issue from a wider, more comparative vision seeks to analyze rather than to extend the biblical testimony. The chief issue from this viewpoint is one in which biblical denunciation is an object of study in itself. Biblical denunciation thus ceases to be an apologetic position to be continued.

The conclusion here is similar to that reached earlier through our inquiry into the function of various biblical myths. Sacred prostitution *as accusation* played an important role in defining Israel and Israelite religion as something distinctive. So, too, similar accusations played the same role for Herodotus and other Greeks, and then for the early Church Fathers and other Christians. Whether or not sacred prostitution was ever a reality in the ancient Near East, accusations about the practice turn out to be very much the norm. Accusations that functioned to demonstrate to the adherents of a religion their religion's distinctiveness thus turn out to prove that the religion is anything but distinctive.

Epilogue. The Persistence of Theology in Biblical Study

At once the alluring power and the limitations of biblical study's long alliance with theology have been themes upon which each of the preceding studies have touched. With regard to the power, the theological tradition's notable forcefulness has resulted largely from its insistence both that fully historical and comparative work can be done within a theological framework and that such work will in the end demonstrate the truth of a set of confessedly apologetic themes. Historical and comparative work, the claim is made, will demonstrate (indeed—has already demonstrated) that the religion of Israel is more ethically motivated or more historically grounded than are the religions of any of Israel's near or far neighbors. Israel, we hear repeatedly, is "unique," and unique in this theological context consistently implies not just discernibly different but also ultimately superior.

At the same time, however, such claims reveal the limits of the lengthy alliance between biblical study and theology. For in the end theologically governed biblical scholarship wishes to imply that what makes Israel's religion unique is not simply a nonrepeatable set of historical circumstances. That which is responsible for this religion's essential character is also the presence of revelation —of divine guidance that is subtle, complex, and often almost hidden but that remains unexampled elsewhere. And this means that this religion's history is wholly different from that of any other religion. Hence, comparative religion in the instance of the religion of the Hebrew Bible is strictly speaking impossible. Hence, too, a whole range of potential historical and comparative questions is at the outset so removed by the theological tradition that questions at the center of a variety of academic disciplines throughout the course of the present century here go unasked.

Just what these questions have been for other disciplines and what they might be for biblical study has been of major concern in each of the chapters of this volume. This concern has achieved formulation, especially in the initial chapters, chiefly through historical sketches of biblical study's place in the wider intellectual world of the nineteenth and earlier twentieth centuries. Documenting the force of this era's abiding conclusions has perhaps been the least problematic in the case of methods of analyzing myths. Here, the gap between mythical study generally and the theologically prompted study of biblical myths is as patent as it is unfortunate. But a similar, if subtler, division exists between comparative religion or the history of religions as applied to "primitive" or non-Western religions and what passes for comparative religion in biblical scholarship. Perhaps a summary review of more recent extensions of some older historiographic principles will clarify this.

We recall that the nineteenth-century historiographic tradition seemed unable in the end to reconcile its insistent claims to objectivity on the basis of empirical investigations with its foundations in a set of radically contextualized value judgments. Yet the central principles of this tradition appeared with uncomfortable frequency in all but the most recent inquiries into the religion of Israel. This exists most clearly and least surprisingly in Old Testament theologies of the past several generations. The frequently reprinted theologies of both Walther Eichrodt and Gerhard von Rad are in many ways textbook applications of the central emphases of that nineteenth-century historiographic tradition described in Chapter 1. Eichrodt, for example, distinguishes sharply between the Mesopotamian or the Egyptian notions of the divine word and that understanding of Yahweh's "Word" that lies behind the religion of Israel. While in Mesopotamia, "of conscious understanding of the moral function of the divine word there is none," and while in Egypt the divine word "is a potent medium

of magic, a word within which the power of the divine enchanter
is concealed," in Israel on the other hand "the word was understood as the cosmic power of the Creator God, but there is no
instance of its being conceived as a medium of magic concealed
from Man." In Israel, Eichrodt continues, Yahweh's word "is a
clear declaration of the will of the divine sovereign, . . . an expression of the free self-direction of a will conscious of its goal." So,
too, the surrounding world in Egyptian and Mesopotamian religions belongs to "the sphere of naturalistic determinism or magical
caprice," whereas in Israel "the processes of Nature also fall into
the category of the free moral activity of a purposeful will."[1]
These sorts of distinctions Eichrodt makes between Israel on the
one hand and all other ancient cultures on the other have passed
for truisms for much of the present century, but it is worth recall-
ing that they are but another application of the twin themes of the
vital individuality of cultures and the superiority of moral choice
over determinism so stressed by nineteenth-century historiography.

So, too, von Rad's *Old Testament Theology* is an elegant, comprehensive extension of these and other themes from the same tradition of historical understanding. For von Rad, "one of the most
momentous advances in man's understanding of himself" was
Israel's discovery of the subtle, hidden nature of Yahweh's intervention in history. In Israel, "people were beginning to see that,
in addition to activity by means of miracles or dramatic, catas-
trophic events, Jahweh had another quite different field in which
he worked, one which was much more hidden from men's view
and lay rather in their daily lives." Narratives such as that of the
wooing of Rebecca, of Abimelech's fate in the Book of Judges, or
of the rise of David demonstrate to von Rad that Israelite "story-
tellers have no need of wonders or the appearance of charismatic
leaders—events develop apparently in complete accord with their
own inherent nature. . . . And yet the reader is made aware that,
in order to direct history, Jahweh is using them, their hearts and
their resolutions."[2] What von Rad here sees as the hidden intervention of Yahweh is of course precisely what historians like

Droysen or von Ranke came to label the "hand of God" in and behind history. Indeed, it might fairly be said that for von Rad, as for others, the modern discovery of the significance of history is only a rediscovery of what was divinely revealed first to Israel: "This idea of history which Israel developed theologically in various directions over a period of centuries is one of this people's greatest achievements."[3] Further, in von Rad's formulation Israel's development here distinguishes her religion absolutely from those of her neighbors: "Looked at from the point of view of comparative religion, this idea of history made a radical division between Israel and her environment. . . . With her idea of saving history she completely parted company with these religions. Not one of them understood the dimension of history in the way that Israel did!"[4] Nor are our expectations upset when von Rad extends this argument to include a demarcation between mythical and nonmythical, a demarcation traced in Chapter 2: "The ancient east's view of the world bears to a greater or lesser degree the clear impress of cyclical thinking in terms of myth. . . . This sacral understanding of the world is essentially non-historical; at least, it leaves absolutely no place for the very thing which Israel regarded as the constitutive element in her faith, the once-for-all quality of divine savings acts within her history."[5] And the conclusion of all this is something historians from Herder through von Ranke would warmly have applauded: "What we see," von Rad concludes, "is that it was in the earliest period of her [Israel's] life that, with a great and unconscious assurance, she rested in her own peculiar religious ideas, and grew stronger and stronger in them."[6] For von Rad, as for the older tradition in which he still so plainly stands, the essence of historical investigation is the proof that Israel is a unique, and uniquely superior, individual organism.

That such judgments appear in theological works of this century accords with our expectations, though their appearance does aid in the demonstration of the fundamentally theological and apologetic nature of nineteenth-century history writing. Less expected and more indicative of the limits of the theological tradition is the appearance of similar conclusions in works that purport to be histories of the religion of Israel, not theologies of the Old Testament. This is again true of a pair of widely utilized textbooks, those of Helmer Ringgren and Georg Fohrer. The former begins his volume with the assertion that "the reader will not find in this book a theology of the Old Testament, but a history of the Israelite religion." However, Ringgren quickly adds his "hope that theologians will find some value in the comparative approach, which is extremely important for determining, among other things, the uniqueness of the Old Testament religion."[7] As before, we note that "uniqueness" here implies not just difference; rather, and as the remainder of the volume makes clear, uniqueness implies superiority and is a result of a kind of evaluative comparison far removed from what comparative religion means outside the biblical camp. In a markedly similar vein, Fohrer inaugurates his *History of Israelite Religion* with the statement that his purpose is "to depict the course of this religion's development as the history of one normal religion among many others, without undertaking theological value judgments or giving weight to apologetic considerations."[8] Still, Fohrer, too, goes on to note that his comparative approach "must of course be careful to observe and maintain the unique features of Israelite religion."[9] Such observance leads Fohrer to frankly apologetic comments on the "central," "organic" (note!) ideas of Israel as opposed to those of her Canaanite neighbors. In Fohrer's reconstruction, contact with Canaan and especially with the Canaanite cult "marked the first dangerous steps toward degrading the nucleus of Yahwism and an aberrant development."[10] Here again we might be listening to a summary of the older theological and historiographic school: Real history is constituted by the tracing of a nation's organic individuality and of the dangers that beset this individuality from alien influences. In any such history will be found the hand of the divine.

Such is the power of the theological tradition that a restricted understanding of comparative religion as it might be applied to Israel exists even beyond biblical study, though the genesis of course comes from this discipline. For example, when Mircea Eliade, perhaps this generation's most prolific historian of religion, treats Judaism and Christianity, he seems to display a curious hesitancy to speak here as boldly and as comparatively as he does elsewhere. In a wide-ranging and suggestive article called "The Prestige of the Cosmogonic Myth," Eliade pulls the reader up short near the end with an unexpected and unsupported distinction between pre- and extra-Judaic religions on the one hand and all others on the other. "In all the *pre-Judaic religions,*" Eliade writes, "sacred time was the time of myth."[11] He then goes on to conclude that "thanks to the cosmogonic myth, religious man from the *pre- and extra-Mosaic societies* attempts to live in continuous imitation of the gods."[12] Such a conclusion cannot but undercut any confidence we may have in Eliade's attempts to free himself from apologetic constraints. Moreover, Eliade's conventional statements about the unique value accorded history in Judaism and Christianity again must be traced to the continued power of the theological character of biblical study. Even this historian of religion can conclude another essay by asserting, "from the standpoint of the history of religions, Judaeo-Christianity presents us with the supreme hierophany: the transfiguration of the historical event into hierophany."[13] Equally the labeling of the incarnation as "the transfiguration of the historical event into hierophany" and the evaluating of this as "the supreme hierophany" are moves with which a host of nineteenth-century theologians and historians would have rested quite comfortably.

Anything but atypical, Eliade's isolation of biblical religion from all other religions serves to demonstrate that even well beyond the traditional confessional setting of biblical study its fundamentally theological direction is heeded. As has been stressed with some frequency throughout the present volume, theology undeniably has a role to play in biblical study in certain contexts. But other contexts exist. Among these pride of place belongs to the study of religion in the modern university. Here, dramatically different alternatives to the theological tradition are more at home. It has been the concern of each of the present volume's studies to describe and exemplify these alternatives. Whatever we call the approach that incorporates such departures from theology, and

8

"comparative religion" or "the anthropology of religion" are each good candidates for an appropriate title, this approach consists both of a systematic shunning of some elements of theological argumentation and also of the application of comparisons drawn from the entire bank of religious data. With regard to the former, the approach suggested in this volume ought never to rest satisfied with any incomplete explanations that make appeal to such notions as the ultimately inexplicable workings of divine election. To do so would be to sever the study of religion from all other academic disciplines. In every academic inquiry worthy of the name, the apparently inexplicable presents a challenge and not a solution. Though in a quite different context, Lévi-Strauss has formulated this argument as clearly as has anyone: "If it is maintained that religion constitutes an autonomous order, requiring a special kind of investigation, it has to be removed from the common fate of objects of science. Religion having thus been defined by contrast, it will inevitably appear . . . to be distinguished as no more than a sphere of confused ideas." On the other hand, Lévi-Strauss concludes, "if religious ideas are accorded the same value as any other conceptual system," then "the procedures of religious anthropology will acquire validity, but it will lose its autonomy and its specific character."[14] It is precisely the loss of biblical study's theologically prompted autonomy upon which its future survival beyond a narrowly apologetic context depends.

With regard to the second element in the approach suggested in this volume, I have argued implicitly throughout that comparison has long been radically limited in its extent and applications. Within the mainstream of biblical study, comparative religion has been understood chiefly as both evaluative and as restricted to the religions of ancient Israel's nearest neighbors. Typically, the religion of Israel is contrasted with the religions of Egypt, Canaan, or Mesopotamia, almost always to the benefit of Israel. There are historical reasons for so restricted an understanding of comparative religion, for example, the diffusionist excesses of the turn-of-the-century "Pan-Babylonian" school. But it is theology's apologetic concerns that bear a greater responsibility for these limitations. The approach advocated in the studies within the current volume neither substitutes evaluation for comparison nor restricts comparison to those cultures temporally and geographically most proximate to ancient Israel. This, too, is in keeping with the new intellectual and institutional setting of the study of religion. In a recent and quite brilliant essay on this issue of the limits of comparison, Jonathan Z. Smith observes that most of his readers will agree with the "stricture that comparison be limited to cultural artifacts contiguous in space and time—the method of 'limited' or 'controlled' comparison." "Unfortunately," Smith continues, just this stricture has been "used as the smug excuse for jettisoning the comparative enterprise and for purging scholarship of all but the most limited comparisons."[15] Smith concludes, as does the present book, that any such limited understanding of religious comparison removes Judaism, for example, from the list of issues addressable in our present and wider setting: "No matter how intrinsically interesting and worthwhile the study of the complex histories and varieties of the several Judaisms may be, they gain academic significance primarily by their capacity to illuminate the work of other scholars of other religious traditions, and by the concomitant desire of students of Judaism to be illuminated by the labors of these other scholars."[16] Examples of the benefits that accrue when the comparative net is stretched more widely may perhaps be found in some of the conclusions to Chapters 3–5 of this volume. An undeniable instance of these same benefits is Susan Niditch's study of the final nine chapters in the Book of Ezekiel, a study that boldly and persuasively compares this prophet's linking together of visions and architecture with the same linkage in the Buddhist mandala tradition.[17]

Plainly, then, a thoroughly comparative and anthropological approach offers us a clear set of alternatives to the theological tradition. Further, these departures from the long dominant tradition are more in keeping with methods employed elsewhere in the modern university, a setting to which the study of religion has only recently been invited and in which it still sits somewhat unsurely. And here it is that these alternatives merit an extended trial coincident in depth to that long granted the theological tradition.

Table of Abbreviations

AA	*American Anthropologist*
AB	Anchor Bible
AE	*American Ethnologist*
ACW	Ancient Christian Writers
AHW	W. von Soden, *Akkadisches Handwörterbuch*
AJSL	*American Journal of Semitic Languages and Literature*
ANET	J. B. Pritchard (ed.), *Ancient Near Eastern Texts* (3d ed.)
ANF	The Ante-Nicene Fathers
AOAT	Alter Orient und Altes Testament
APOT	R. H. Charles (ed.), *Apocrypha and Pseudepigrapha of the Old Testament*
AQ	*Anthropology Quarterly*
ArOr	*Archiv orientální*
ASOR	American Schools of Oriental Research
ATD	Das Alte Testament Deutsch
BJRL	*Bulletin of the John Rylands University Library of Manchester*
BKAT	Biblischer Kommentar: Altes Testament
BZAW	Beihefte zur *ZAW*
CAD	*The Assyrian Dictionary of the Oriental Institute of the University of Chicago*

CBQ	*Catholic Biblical Quarterly*
CBQMS	Catholic Biblical Quarterly—Monograph Series
CChr	Corpus Christianorum
Exp Tim	*Expository Times*
FOTL	The Forms of the Old Testament Literature
FRLANT	Forschungen zur Religion und Literatur des Alten und Neuen Testaments
HAT	Handbuch zum Alten Testament
HKAT	Handkommentar zum Alten Testament
HR	*History of Religions*
HSM	Harvard Semitic Monographs
HT	*History and Theory*
HZ	*Historische Zeitschrift*
ICC	International Critical Commentary
IDB	G. A. Buttrick (ed.), *Interpreter's Dictionary of the Bible*
JAF	*Journal of American Folklore*
JAAR	*Journal of the American Academy of Religion*
JARCE	*Journal of the American Research Center in Egypt*
JAOS	*Journal of the American Oriental Society*
JBL	*Journal of Biblical Literature*
JHI	*Journal of the History of Ideas*
JSOT	*Journal for the Study of the Old Testament*
KAT	E. Sellin (ed.), Kommentar zum A.T.
LCL	Loeb Classical Library

Maarav	*Maarav: A Journal for the Study of the Northwest Semitic Languages and Literatures*
Man	*Man: The Journal of the Royal Anthropological Institute*
NPNF	Nicene and Post-Nicene Fathers
Numen	*Numen: International Review for the History of Religion*
Or	*Orientalia* (Rome)
OTL	Old Testament Library
PEQ	*Palestine Exploration Quarterly*
RSV	*Revised Standard Version*
SAJS	*South African Journal of Science*
SBL	Society of Biblical Literature
SBLTT	SBL Texts and Translations
SBT	Studies in Biblical Theology
SC	Sources chrétiennes
SJA	*Southwestern Journal of Anthropology*
TLS	*The* [London] *Times Literary Supplement*
VT	*Vetus Testamentum*
YOS	Yale Oriental Series
ZA	*Zeitschrift für Assyriologie*
ZAW	*Zeitschrift für die alttestamentliche Wissenschaft*
ZTK	*Zeitschrift für Theologie und Kirche*

Notes

PREFACE

1. Claude Lévi-Strauss, *Totemism* (Harmondsworth: Penguin, 1969 [first published in French in 1962]), p. 140.
2. Chapter 1 grows out of a seminar paper delivered to the Society of Biblical Literature in 1980 entitled "Hermeneutics and Historiography." An earlier version of Chapter 4 appeared in *JBL* 102 (1983): 189–205; I am grateful to the editor of *JBL* for permission to use some of the material from that earlier article. And the central argument in Chapter 5 was first developed in the context of papers delivered on various occasions in the late 1970s and then at the national SBL convention in December 1981.

CHAPTER 1: HISTORICAL UNDERSTANDING AND UNDERSTANDING THE RELIGION OF ISRAEL

1. Thomas S. Kuhn, *The Structure of Scientific Revolutions*, 2d ed. (Chicago: University of Chicago, 1970).
2. Kuhn, *Scientific Revolutions*, pp. 2–3.
3. Kuhn, *Scientific Revolutions*, p. viii.
4. Kuhn, *Scientific Revolutions*, p. 19 or p. 144, for example.
5. Kuhn, *Scientific Revolutions*, pp. 6, 92.
6. For an introduction to the many issues raised by Kuhn and his critics, see the essays by Karl Popper, Paul Feyerabend, Imre Lakatos, and others in Imre Lakatos and Alan Musgrave, eds., *Criticism and the Growth of Knowledge*, Proceedings of the International Colloquium in the Philosophy of Science, London, 1965, vol. 4 (Cambridge: Cambridge University, 1970).
7. Kuhn, *Scientific Revolutions*, p. 208.
8. T. K. Cheyne, *Founders of Old Testament Criticism: Biographical, Descriptive, and Critical Studies* (London: Methuen, 1893). This volume was composed before Cheyne, who was for a time the Oriel Professor of the Interpretation of Scripture at Oxford, began to advocate some of the less sustainable hypotheses for which he was eventually to become notorious.
9. The works of both scholars are of sufficient number and depth that no attempt is made here to list, much less survey, them all. For studies of direct relevance to biblical scholarship, see especially Arnaldo Momigliano, *Quarto Contributo alla storia degli studi classici e del mondo antico* (Rome: Edizioni di storia e letteratura, 1969); *Quinto Contributo alla storia degli studi classici e del mondo antico*,

2 vols. (Rome: Edizioni di storia e letteratura, 1975); and M. I. Finley, *The Use and Abuse of History* (New York: Viking, 1975).

10. For an introduction to the work of F. C. Baur and an assessment of the value of viewing this work against the thought of Hegel, see Peter C. Hodgson, *The Formation of Historical Theology: A Study of Ferdinand Christian Baur* (New York: Harper & Row, 1966), especially pp. 54–70. The issue of Wellhausen's alleged "Hegelianism" will be treated briefly in this chapter; it is the chief focus of Lothar Perlitt's *Vatke und Wellhausen*, BZAW 94 (Berlin: Alfred Töpelmann, 1965). Bultmann's work is treated briefly in Chapter 2.

11. A superb and evenhanded introduction to the contributions of the sociology of knowledge to issues often treated only within intellectual history is Barry Barnes, *Scientific Knowledge and Sociological Theory* (London/Boston: Routledge & Kegan Paul, 1974). Barnes's chief conclusion with regard to scientific research is coincident with the conclusions of the present study with regard to research into the religion of Israel: "Those general beliefs which we are most convinced deserve the status of objective knowledge— scientific beliefs—are readily shown to be overwhelmingly theoretical in character" (p. 10); in the natural sciences, as elsewhere, there is in fact no "clear fact-theory boundary" (p. 21).

12. See Fritz K. Ringer, *Education and Society in Modern Europe* (Bloomington/London: University of Indiana, 1979), pp. 87, 100. Together with other work of Ringer cited in this chapter, this volume is of great and unexpected value for those interested in the course of biblical research.

13. Maurice Mandelbaum, *History, Man, and Reason: A Study in Nineteenth-Century Thought* (Baltimore/London: Johns Hopkins University, 1971), p. 51.

14. Given the rightful emphasis that students of historiography have placed upon this particular tradition, these studies abound. See, for a start, G. P. Gooch, *History and Historians in the Nineteenth Century* 2d ed. (London: Longmans, Green, and Co., 1952); Friedrich Meinecke, *Die Entstehung des Historismus*, ed. Carl Hinrichs (Munich: R. Oldenbourg, 1959); Perlitt, *Vatke und Wellhausen*, pp. 57–85; George Iggers, *The German Conception of History: The National Tradition of Historical Thought from Herder to the Present* (Middletown, Conn.: Wesleyan University, 1968); Fritz K. Ringer, *The Decline of the German Mandarins: The German Academic Community, 1890–1933* (Cambridge, Mass.: Harvard University, 1969), pp. 90–102; and Mandelbaum, *History, Man, and Reason*, pp. 39–138. That the present study is especially indebted to the ground-breaking work of Iggers will be apparent.

15. Iggers, *German Conception of History*, p. 4.

16. Iggers, *German Conception of History*, p. 30.

17. Among contemporary philosophers of history, Mandelbaum has been especially wise in pointing out the inaccuracies and dangers in any wanton periodization of history; see Maurice Mandelbaum, *The Anatomy of Historical Knowledge* (Baltimore/London: Johns Hopkins University, 1977), pp. 22–23, 134–36.

18. This is the central thesis of Peter H. Reill's *The German Enlightenment and the Rise of Historicism* (Berkeley/Los Angeles/London: University of California, 1975).

19. Mandelbaum, *History, Man, and Reason*, p. 57.

20. Studies that accent Herder's role in the shaping of the following century's

historical (including biblical) research include Perlitt, *Vatke und Wellhausen,* pp. 15–24; J. W. Rogerson, *Myth in Old Testament Interpretation,* BZAW 134 (Berlin/New York: Walter de Gruyter, 1974), pp. 9–15; and Hans W. Frei, *The Eclipse of Biblical Narrative: A Study in Eighteenth- and Nineteenth-Century Hermeneutics* (New Haven/London: Yale University, 1974), pp. 183–201.

21. Hayden V. White, "On History and Historicisms," translator's introduction to Carlo Antoni, *From History to Sociology: The Transition in German Historical Thinking* (Detroit, Mich.: Wayne State University, 1959 [originally published in 1940]), p. xviii. The German title of Herder's ground-breaking work is *Auch eine Philosophie der Geschichte zur Bildung der Menschheit.*

22. Perlitt, *Vatke und Wellhausen,* pp. 18–19 (citing Herder). On Herder's plea that we view peoples as individuals, see also Iggers, *German Conception of History,* p. 35.

23. Iggers, *German Conception of History,* p. 46 (citing Herder). The German term for this most important concept is *Eigentümlichkeit.*

24. For the demonstration that Herder's hermeneutic comes from a poetic, rather than a scientific, spirit [*Geist*], see Perlitt, *Vatke und Wellhausen,* pp. 31–32.

25. Frei, *Eclipse of Biblical Narrative,* pp. 184–93.

26. Barthold Georg Niebuhr, *Römische Geschichte,* 3 vols. (Berlin: Realschulbuchhandlung, G. Reimer, for vol. 3, 1811–32).

27. On Humboldt and especially his place in the development of the German historiographic tradition, see Joachim Wach, *Das Verstehen: Grundzüge einer Geschichte der hermeneutischen Theorie im 19 Jahrhundert,* 3 vols. (Tübingen: J. C. B. Mohr, 1926–33), 1:227–66; Iggers, *German Conception of History,* pp. 44–62; and Paul R. Sweet, *Wilhelm von Humboldt: A Biography,* vol. 1, *1767–1808* (Columbia: Ohio State University, 1978).

28. Sweet, *Wilhelm von Humboldt,* pp. ix–xi.

29. Sweet, *Wilhelm von Humboldt,* p. 52.

30. Sweet, *Wilhelm von Humboldt,* pp. 126, 182–85. The term translated by "special individuality" is again *Eigentümlichkeit.*

31. Wilhelm von Humboldt, *"Über die Aufgabe des Geschichtschreibers,"* pp. 35–56 in *Wilhelm von Humboldts Gesammelte Schriften,* ed. Albert Leitzmann, vol. 4, *1820–1822* (Berlin: B. Behr's, 1905). An exceptionally good translation of this essay was published in *HT* 6 (1967):57–71.

32. Humboldt, *"Über die Aufgabe,"* p. 35 *("Die Aufgabe des Geschichtschreibers ist die Darstellung des Geschehenen").*

33. Humboldt, *"Über die Aufgabe,"* pp. 40, 46, 56.

34. Humboldt, *"Über die Aufgabe,"* pp. 36–37 (the historian works *"als der Dichter,"* to create *"einem Ganzem,"* using *"das Ahnden").*

35. Humboldt, *"Über die Aufgabe,"* pp. 51–54.

36. Wach, *Das Verstehen,* 1:239 *("jede Epoche des Menschengeschlechts trage einem eigentümlichen Charakter").*

37. On Ranke's contributions to nineteenth-century historiography, see Heinrich von Sybel, *"Gedächtnisrede auf Leopold von Ranke,"* *HZ* NF20 (1886): 463–81; Wach, *Das Verstehen,* 3: 89–133 (Wach's introduction to Ranke reads: "Ranke—that is the incarnation of the historical sensibility" [*"Ranke—das ist die Inkarnation des historischen Sinnes"*] [3:89]); Theodore Von Laue, *Leopold Ranke: The Formative Years,* Princeton Studies in History, no. 4 (Princeton,

N.J.: Princeton University, 1950); Gooch, *History and Historians*, pp. 72–97; Georg G. Iggers, "The Image of Ranke in American and German Historical Thought," *History and Theory* 2 (1962) pp. 17–40, and *German Conception of History*, pp. 63–89; and Perlitt, *Vatke und Wellhausen*, pp. 61–68.

38. This sentence, which originally appeared in the preface to Ranke's *Geschichten der romanischen und germanischen Völker von 1495 bis 1514* (1824), can be found conveniently in almost any study of Ranke. See, e.g., Gooch, *History and Historians*, p. 74, n. 1 (the historian's aim is to portray *"wie es eigentlich gewesen"*).

39. This definition of empiricism comes from Iggers, *German Conception of History*, p. 76.

40. Von Laue, *Leopold Ranke*, p. 43. See also Iggers, *German Conception of History*, pp. 76–79; Iggers is particularly good on the issue of the "metaphysical forces" that Ranke saw in phenomena, the search for which means that Ranke was anything but a simple empiricist.

41. Leopold von Ranke, *Weltgeschichte: Erster Theil: Die älteste historische Völkergruppe und die Griechen*, 2d ed. (Leipzig: Duncker & Humblot, 1881), p. v *("den Gang der grossen Begebenheiten, welcher alle Völker verbindet und beherrscht")*.

42. For Ranke's insistence that groups of people are to be viewed as individuals, see Von Laue, *Leopold Ranke*, pp. 49, 74–75, 99–100, and 162.

43. von Sybel, *"Gedächtnisrede auf Leopold von Ranke,"* pp. 463–68.

44. Perlitt, *Vatke und Wellhausen*, pp. 67–68.

45. H. Stuart Hughes, *Consciousness and Society: The Reorientation of European Social Thought 1890–1930*, rev. ed. (New York: Vintage Press, 1977), pp. 183–86. On this issue, see also Von Laue, *Leopold Ranke*, pp. 43–44; and Iggers, *German Conception of History*, pp. 63–68.

46. Meinecke, *Die Entstehung des Historismus*, p. 598 *("Verbindung von transzendierender Ehrfurcht vor der Geschichte . . . mit scharf blickender empirisch-kritischer Untersuchung")*.

47. On Droysen, see Hermann Krüger, in John Gustav Droysen, *Outline of the Principles of History*, trans. Benjamin Andrews (Boston: Ginn, 1893), pp. xv–xxxv; Wach, *Das Verstehen*, 3. 134–88; Iggers, *German Conception of History*, pp. 104–115; Jörn Rüsen, *Begriffene Geschichte: Genesis und Begründung der Geschichtstheorie J. G. Droysens* (Paderborn: Schöningh, 1969); Momigliano, "J. G. Droysen Between Greeks and Jews," *Quinto Contributo*, 1:109–126; Robert Southard, "Theology in Droysen's Early Political Historiography: Free Will, Necessity, and the Historian," *HT* 18 (1979): 378–96; Hayden White, review of Johann Gustav Droysen, *Historik*, new edition by Peter Leyh (Stuttgart-Bad Cannstatt: F. Frommann, 1977), *HT* 19 (1980): 73–93; and Michael J. Maclean, "Johann Gustave Droysen and the Development of Historical Hermeneutics," *HT* 21 (1982): 347–65.

48. White, review of *Historik*, p. 73.

49. Johann Gustav Droysen, *Historik: Vorlesungen über Enzyklopädie und Methodologie der Geschichte*, ed. Rudolf Hübner, 5th ed. (Munich: R. Oldenbourg, 1967), p. 384 *("die moderne Zeit des Altertums")*. On Droysen's view of the Hellenistic era, see also Rüsen, *Begriffene Geschichte*, pp. 23–49.

50. Maclean, "Droysen and the Development of Historical Hermeneutics," pp. 352–53.

51. Southard, "Theology in Droysen's Early Historiography," p. 383.

52. See Iggers, *German Conception of History*, p. 105; Rüsen, *Begriffene Geschichte;* and Southard, "Theology in Droysen's Early Historiography," p. 381.

53. Rüsen, *Begriffene Geschichte*, p. 11 *("kritische Geschichtswissenschaft"* and *"idealistische Geschichtsphilosophie")*.

54. All references here to the *Grundriss der Historik* are from the edition of Hübner cited in note 49.

55. Sweet, *Wilhelm von Humboldt*, p. 190. Cf. White's claim that Droysen's *Historik* is "surely the most sustained and systematic defense of the autonomy of historical thought ever set forth—including the attempts of Croce and Collingwood in this century" (review of *Historik*, p. 89).

56. Drosyen, *"Grundriss der Historik,"* pp. 324–26.

57. Droysen, *"Grundriss der Historik,"* pp. 329–35 *("als unmittelbare Intuition")*.

58. Droysen, *"Grundriss der Historik,"* pp. 356–57. The important phrase here is *"die sittliche Welt."*

59. Michael Ermarth, *Wilhelm Dilthey: The Critique of Historical Reason* (Chicago/London: University of Chicago, 1978), p. 56.

60. Iggers, *German Conception of History*, p. 10.

61. Gooch, *History and Historians*, p. 73; and Von Laue, *Leopold Ranke*, p. 44.

62. Mandelbaum, *History, Man, and Reason*, p. 58.

63. This is Mandelbaum's definition of "metaphysical idealism" (*History, Man, and Reason*, p. 6).

64. Maclean, "Johann Gustav Droysen and the Development of Historical Hermeneutics," pp. 363–64. Cf. also Iggers, *German Conception of History*, p. 95.

65. Von Laue, *Leopold Ranke*, p. 93.

66. Mandelbaum, *History, Man, and Reason*, p. 130.

67. Iggers, *German Conception of History*, p. 17.

68. Frei, *Eclipse of Biblical Narrative*, p. 213.

69. Maclean, "Johann Gustav Droysen and the Development of Historical Hermeneutics," p. 362.

70. Reill, *German Enlightenment and the Rise of Historicism*, pp. 190–91.

71. For an introduction to the history of Old Testament scholarship, see the following volumes: Cheyne, *Founders of Old Testament Criticism;* Emil G. Kraeling, *The Old Testament Since the Reformation* (New York: Harper & Brothers, 1955); Hans-Joachim Kraus, *Geschichte der historisch-kritischen Erforschung des Alten Testaments*, 2d ed. (Neukirchen-Vluyn: Neukirchener, 1969); Herbert F. Hahn, *The Old Testament in Modern Research* (Philadelphia, Pa.: Fortress, 1970); and, for the most recent period alone, Ronald E. Clements, *A Century of Old Testament Study* (Guilford/London: Lutterworth, 1976). For the New Testament, see Werner Georg Kümmel, *The New Testament: The History of the Investigation of Its Problems*, trans. S. M. Gilmour and H. C. Kee (Nashville, Tenn./New York: Abingdon, 1972). A truly comprehensive, multivolume history of biblical scholarship, such as exists for classical scholarship, for example, is one of the clear needs in this discipline.

72. On the work of Simon and Astruc, as well as the largely ignored work of Bernard Witter and others, see Kraus, *Geschichte der historisch-kritischen Erforschung*, pp. 85–96.

73. Cited by Kraus, *Geschichte der historisch-kritischen Erforschung*, pp. 185, 176–77.

74. The literature on Wellhausen is, fully appropriately, immense. For a begin-

ning, see the following works and the bibliographies therein: Perlitt, *Vatke und Wellhausen;* Kraus, *Geschichte der historisch-kritischen Erforschung,* pp. 255–74; and all of the essays in Douglas A. Knight, ed., *Julius Wellhausen and His Prolegomena to the History of Israel,* Semeia 25 (Chico, Calif.: Scholars, 1983). The last work contains a piece of great interest by Rudolf Smend, for whose complete biography of Wellhausen the scholarly world awaits with much expectation; for now, see also Smend's "Wellhausen in Greifswald," *ZTK* 78 (1981): 141–76.

75. Rudold Smend, "Julius Wellhausen and His *Prolegomena to the History of Israel,*" in Knight, *Julius Wellhausen,* p. 5.

76. Originally published as *Geschichte Israels. In zwei Bänder: Erster Band* (Berlin: G. Reimer, 1878), the 2d edition was entitled *Prolegomena zur Geschichte Israels, Zweite Ausgabe der Geschichte Israels, Band I* (Berlin: G. Reimer, 1883). Citations here are from this edition of 1883 and from the English translation, *Prolegomena to the History of Ancient Israel,* which was first published in 1885, with a reprint of "Israel" from the *Encyclopaedia Britannica* and a preface by W. Robertson Smith (Gloucester, Mass.: Peter Smith, 1973).

77. Wellhausen's letter of May 4, 1882, to a government minister is cited in Perlitt, *Vatke und Wellhausen,* pp. 153–54, and also in English translation (from which this quote is taken) in Smend, "Julius Wellhausen," p. 6.

78. Wellhausen, *Prolegomena,* p. 4 (English trans., pp. 3–4).

79. The number of Wellhausen's memorable metaphors drawn from the New Testament (e.g., *Prolegoma,* p. 208 or p. 215 [English trans., p. 200 or p. 206]) is revealing, though hardly surprising.

80. William Robertson Smith, *The Religion of the Semites: The Fundamental Institutions* (New York: Schocken, 1972 [originally published in 1889]), p. vii

81. Patrick D. Miller, Jr., "Wellhausen and the History of Israel's Religion," in Knight, *Julius Wellhausen,* p. 63.

82. Wellhausen, *Prolegomena,* p. 107 (English trans., p. 103).

83. Wellhausen, "Israel," in the English edition of the *Prolegomena,* p. 448.

84. Wellhausen, *Prolegomena,* p. 390 (English trans., p. 368).

85. Wellhausen, *Prolegomena,* pp. 422–23 (English trans., pp. 398–99).

86. Cited by Perlitt, *Vatke and Wellhausen,* p. 234 *("die Freiheit der Kinder Gottes").*

87. Wellhausen, "Israel," p. 474.

88. Wellhausen, *Prolegomena,* p. 13 (English trans., p. 12) *("mittelst eines unabhängigen Masses . . . nämlich mittelst des inneren Ganges der israelitischen Geschichte").*

89. Wellhausen, *Prolegomena,* p. 49–50 (English trans., p. 47). It will be remembered that Droysen spoke explicitly of the same movement of "ethical forces."

90. Wellhausen, "Israel," p. 472.

91. Wellhausen, *Prolegomena,* pp. 320–23, 357 (English trans., pp. 304–7, 337).

92. The chief aim of Perlitt, in *Vatke und Wellhausen,* is to refute the charge that Wellhausen was a Hegelian. For an expression of a contrary argument, see Kraus, *Geschichte der historisch-kritischen Erforschung,* pp. 260–68.

93. The letter is cited in Perlitt, *Vatke und Wellhausen,* p. 152 *("Ich habe von keinem Menschen mehr, von kaum Einem so viel gelernt, als von Ihrem Herrn Vater. . . . Hegelianer oder nicht: das ist mir einerlei").*

94. Smend, "Julius Wellhausen," p. 14.

95. Robertson Smith, *Religion of the Semites,* p. 29.

96. Robertson Smith, *Religion of the Semites*, p. 1.
97. Robertson Smith, *Religion of the Semites*, pp. 258–59.
98. Robertson Smith, "Preface" to the English trans. of Wellhausen's *Prolegomena*, p. ix.
99. Robertson Smith, *Religion of the Semites*, p. 415.
100. Robertson Smith, *Religion of the Semites*, pp. v–vi.
101. Robertson Smith, *Religion of the Semites*, p. 215.
102. Frei, *Eclipse of Biblical Narrative*, p. 225.
103. Hughes, *Consciousness and Society*, p. 189.
104. Ringer, *Decline of the German Mandarins*, pp. 220–23, 265.
105. Gooch, *History and Historians*, p. 469.
106. Wach, *Das Verstehen*, 3: 154, citing Droysen's correspondence.
107. On Dilthey, see Richard E. Palmer, *Hermeneutics: Interpretation Theory in Schleiermacher, Dilthey, Heidegger, and Gadamer* (Evanston, Ill.: Northwestern University, 1969), pp. 98–123; Iggers, *German Conception of History*, pp. 133–44; Ringer, *Decline of the German Mandarins*, pp. 316–23; Hughes, *Consciousness and Society*, pp. 192–200; and especially Ermarth, *Wilhelm Dilthey*.
108. Hughes, *Consciousness and Society*, p. 194.
109. Palmer, *Hermeneutics*, p. 99.
110. White ("On History and Historicisms," p. xv) views this as the central problem of all of nineteenth-century German intellectual history.
111. Antoni, *From History to Sociology*, p. 7.
112. Ermarth's volume on Dilthey is largely devoted to correcting what he regards as an incorrect understanding of *Verstehen* and to arguing that it is not, as many have said, "some neo-idealist *gnosis* best left to telepathists and clairvoyants" (p. 241).
113. See Wilhelm Windelband, "History and Natural Science," trans. G. Oakes, *HT* 19 (1980): 169–85; the essay was originally delivered in 1894 as a lecture entitled *"Geschichte und Naturwissenschaft."*
114. Windelband, "History and Natural Science," p. 178.
115. On this School *("die religionsgeschichtliche Schule")*, see Hugo Gressmann, *Albert Eichhorn and die religionsgeschichtliche Schule* (Göttingen: Vandenhoeck und Ruprecht, 1914); Werner Klatt, *Hermann Gunkel, zu seiner Theologie der Religionsgeschichte und zur Entstehung der formgeschichtlichen Methode*, FRLANT 100 (Göttingen: Vandenhoeck und Ruprecht, 1969); Kraus, *Geschichte der historisch-kritischen Erforschung*, pp. 327–40; and Kümmel, *New Testament*, pp. 206–324.
116. Gressmann, *Albert Eichhorn*, p. 25 (*"Kreise"* or *"Bewegung."*).
117. Klatt, *Hermann Gunkel*, pp. 20–21 (*"unbestrittener Wortführer"*).
118. All twenty-four theses may be found in Gressmann, *Albert Eichhorn*, p. 8. (*"Jede Deutung eines Mythus ist falsch, welche nicht die Entstehung und Ausbildung des Mythus berücksichtigt"; "Die Geschichtschreibung ist eine Kunst"*). On the significance for the future of the History-of-Religions School of this event, see also Kraus, *Geschichte der historisch-kritischen Erforschung*, p. 328.
119. Gressmann, *Albert Eichhorn*, pp. 8–14 (*"die Entfaltung des menschlichen Geistesleben"; "seine Vorliebe für Geschichte und geschichtliche Entwicklung"*).
120. Gunkel's letter of June, 1913, is cited by Kraus, *Geschichte der historisch-kritischen Erforschung*, p. 330 (not *"Theorien, sondern Wirklichkeiten"; "Geschichte, aber nicht Philosophie"*).

121. For the life and thought of Gunkel, see Klatt, *Hermann Gunkel;* and Kraus, *Geschichte der historisch-kritischen Erforschung,* pp. 341–67.

122. These three judgments come, respectively, from Kraus (*Geschichte der historisch-kritischen Erforschung,* p. 341), from Kraeling (*Old Testament Since the Reformation,* p. 298), and from James Muilenburg ("Introduction" to Hermann Gunkel, *The Psalms: A Form-Critical Introduction* [Philadelphia, Pa.: Fortress, 1967], p. iii).

123. Klatt, *Hermann Gunkel,* p. 25, n. 39, and p. 74 *("wir am Anfang einer neuen Epoche in der Auffassung der alttestamentlichen Religions-und Literaturgeschichte stehen").*

124. Hermann Gunkel, "The 'Historical Movement' in the Study of Religion," *Expository Times* 38 (1926–27): 533.

125. Hermann Gunkel, "What Is Left of the Old Testament," in *What Remains of the Old Testament and Other Essays* (London: Allen & Unwin, 1928), pp. 52–53.

126. Hermann Gunkel, *"Die israelitischen Literatur,"* in *Die Kultur der Gegenwart: Die orientalischen Literaturen,* ed. Paul Hinneberg (Berlin/Leipzig: Teubner, 1906), p. 78 *("die Entstehung des Individualismus").*

127. Hermann Gunkel, "The Religio-Historical Interpretation of the New Testament," *The Monist* 13 (1902–03): 449. This lengthy essay was also published as *Zum religionsgeschichtlichen Verständnis des Neuen Testaments* (Göttingen: Vandenhoeck und Ruprecht, 1903).

128. Gunkel, "What Is Left of the Old Testament," p. 42.

129. Hermann Gunkel, "Jakob," in *What Remains of the Old Testament,* p. 157.

130. Hermann Gunkel, *"Ziele und Methoden der Erklärung des Alten Testaments,"* in Hermann Gunkel, *Reden and Aufsätze* (Göttingen: Vandenhoeck und Ruprecht, 1913), p. 14 *("Exegese im höchsten Sinne ist mehr eine Kunst als eine Wissenschaft").*

131. Hermann Gunkel, *The Influence of the Holy Spirit: The Popular View of the Apostolic Age and the Teaching of the Apostle Paul,* trans R. A. Harrisville and P. A. Quanbeck, II (Philadelphia, Pa.: Fortress, 1979 [originally published in 1888]), p. 12

132. See Klatt, *Hermann Gunkel,* p. 86.

133. Gunkel, "What Is Left of the Old Testament," p. 31.

134. Gunkel, "Religio-Historical Interpretation," p. 398.

135. Gunkel, " 'Historical Movement,' " p. 533.

136. Gressmann, *Albert Eichhorn,* p. 30 *("Kern der Bewegung"; "die Geschichte der eigenen Religion").*

137. Gressmann, *Albert Eichhorn,* pp. 27–28 *("die allgemeine Zeitströmung . . . die wachsende Verfeinerung des historischen Sinnes"; "Das Aufkommen der religionsgeschichtlichen Schule auf theologischen Gebiet ist demnach nur die Teilerscheinung einer grösseren Gesamtbewegung, die sich überall in der Wissenschaft bemarkbar macht").*

138. Gunkel, " 'Historical Movement,' " p. 533.

139. Gunkel, "What Is Left of the Old Testament," p. 21; and Klatt, *Hermann Gunkel,* p. 269 *("die Offenbarungsmächtigkeit der Geschichte").*

140. Klatt, *Hermann Gunkel,* p. 179 *(" 'ich ein echter Wellhausianer gewesen bin' ");* and Gunkel, " 'Historical Movement,' " p. 533.

141. Gunkel, "Religio-Historical Interpretation," p. 404.

142. Kraus, *Geschichte der historisch-kritischen Erforschung,* p. 251 (citing Kuenen) (*" 'vor allem geistiges Leben und Tätigkeit' "*) and p. 282 (*"'die geistige Sphäre des Ethos"*).

143. See Sweet, *Wilhelm von Humboldt,* p. 38 (citing Humboldt) and p. 61.

144. Edgar Krentz, *The Historical-Critical Method,* Guides to Biblical Scholarship, ed. Gene M. Tucker (Philadelphia, Pa.: Fortress, 1975), p. 30.

145. See Kraus, *Geschichte der historisch-kritischen Erforschung,* p. 397, and the article of Gressman cited there.

146. Krentz, *Historical-Critical Method,* p. 39.

147. Perlitt, *Vatke and Wellhausen,* p. 182; cf. pp. 213–15.

148. Finley, *Use and Abuse of History,* p. 61.

149. Cited by Kümmel, *New Testament,* p. 79.

150. See Hodgson, *Formation of Historical Theology,* p. 161 and 186.

151. Gunkel, "What Is Left of the Old Testament," p. 19; and " 'Historical Movement,' " p. 536.

152. Gressmann, *Albert Eichhorn,* p. 51 (*'"Das letzte Ziel aller unserer Bemühungen ist, das Wesen und die Wahrheit der christlichen Religion zu erhellen"*).

153. The most sophisticated recent discussion of objectivity in historical learning of which I am aware is Mandelbaum's *The Anatomy of Historical Knowledge.* Mandelbaum, it might be noted, concludes that objectivity here is in the end a worthy and attainable goal (pp. 150–51).

154. Iggers, *German Conception of History,* p. 25.

CHAPTER 2: INTERPRETING BIBLICAL MYTHS

1. The flood story known in this era is that which began to be widely discussed by the end of the nineteenth century, the story that we find in the eleventh tablet of the composite Epic of Gilgamesh. One version of the Tale of Adapa has come from the Amarna Tablets, discovered in the late 1880s. These tablets were unearthed in Egypt but are composed in Akkadian, a language that originated in Mesopotamia but was for a time the language of international diplomacy throughout the Near East. For a translation of Gilgamesh, see James B. Pritchard, ed., *ANET,* 3d ed. (Princeton, N.J.: Princeton University, 1969), pp. 72–99; and for Adapa, see the same collection, pp. 101–3. Within recent decades, scholars have had access to a fuller account from the Old Babylonian era of the Flood, the Epic of Atrahasis; on this, see my "Divine Aspirations in Atrahasis and in Genesis 1–11," *ZAW* 93 (1981): 197–216.

2. David Freidrich Strauss, *Das Leben Jesu* (Tübingen: Osiander, 1835). The novelist George Eliot produced an early translation of this work into English. A sympathetic and thoroughly fascinating account of Strauss and the vicissitudes of the various editions of his *Life of Jesus* can be found in Albert Schweitzer's *The Quest of the Historical Jesus* (New York: Macmillan, 1961 [originally published in German in 1906]). Among a great many additional studies, note also Hans W. Frei, *The Eclipse of Biblical Narrative* (New Haven/

London: Yale University, 1974), pp. 233–44, together with the materials cited there.

3. Hermann Gunkel, *The Legends of Genesis: The Biblical Saga and History* (New York: Schocken, 1964 [originally published in 1901]), p. 15. A fine and clear summary of Gunkel's various comments on myth, and on the lack of internal consistency here, can be found in J. W. Rogerson, *Myth in Old Testament Interpretation, BZAW* 134 (New York: Walter de Gruyter, 1974), pp. 59–63.

4. Gunkel, *Legends of Genesis*, pp. 14–15.

5. See Otto Eissfeldt, *The Old Testament: An Introduction* (New York: Harper & Row, 1965 [originally published in 1934]), pp. 35–37; Artur Weiser, *The Old Testament: Its Formation and Development* (New York: Association, 1961 [originally published in 1948]), pp. 57–59; and Georg Fohrer, *Introduction to the Old Testament* (Nashville, Tenn.: Abingdon, 1968 [originally published in 1965]), p. 87.

6. G. E. Wright, *God Who Acts*, SBT 8 (Chicago: Regnery, 1952), pp. 38–48; and Gerhard von Rad, *Old Testament Theology*, 2 vols. (New York: Harper & Row, 1962–65), 1:27–28, 1:136–41, 2:110–11, and 2:349.

7. Rudolf Bultmann, *Jesus Christ and Mythology* (New York: Scribner, 1958), p. 15.

8. G. H. Davies, "An Approach to the Problem of Old Testament Mythology," *PEQ* 88 (1956):88.

9. J. L. McKenzie, "Myth and the Old Testament," *CBQ* 21 (1959):265–82.

10. B. S. Childs, *Myth and Reality in the Old Testament*, SBT 27 (Naperville IL: Allenson, 1960), p. 15.

11. F. M. Cross, *Canaanite Myth and Hebrew Epic* (Cambridge, Mass.: Harvard University, 1973), p. 90.

12. Rogerson, *Myth in Old Testament Interpretation*, p. 173. Among recent attempts to arrive at an adequate definition of myth, the following are especially useful: James Barr, "The Meaning of 'Mythology' in Relation to the Old Testament," *VT* 9 (1959):1–10; W. Bascom, "The Forms of Folklore: Prose Narratives," *JAF* 78 (1965):3–20; J. W. Rogerson, "Slippery Words: V. Myth," *ExpTim* 90 (1978):10–14; L. Honko, "The Problem of Defining Myth," in A. Dundes, ed., *Sacred Narrative: Readings in the Theory of Myth* (Berkeley: University of California, 1984), pp. 41–52; and G. S. Kirk, "On Defining Myths," in Dundes, *Sacred Narrative*, pp. 53–61.

13. Kirk, "On Defining Myths," p. 57.

14. James George Frazer, *The Golden Bough: A Study in Magic and Religion*, 3d ed., 12 vols. (London: Macmillan, 1911–15). The much smaller first edition of this work appeared in 1890.

15. James George Frazer, *Apollodorus: The Library*, LCL (London: Heinemann, 1921), p. xxvii.

16. Bronislaw Malinowski, "Myth in Primitive Psychology," in Robert Redfield, ed., *Magic, Science and Religion, and Other Essays by Bronislaw Malinowski* (Garden City, N.Y.: Doubleday, 1954), p. 101. This essay originally appeared in 1926.

17. E. W. Voegelin, "Myth," in M. Leach, ed., *Funk and Wagnall's Standard Dictionary of Folklore, Mythology and Legend* (New York: Funk & Wagnalls, 1949), p. 778.

18. Mircea Eliade, *Myth and Reality* (New York: Harper & Row, 1963), pp. 5–6.

19. T. H. Gaster, "Myth and Story," *Numen* 1 (1954):185.

20. Paul Ricoeur, "Guilt, Ethics, and Religion," in *Talk of God*, Royal Institute of Philosophy Lectures, vol. 2: 1967–68 (London: Royal Institute of Philosophy, 1969), p. 101.

21. Walter Burkert, *Structure and History in Greek Mythology* (Berkeley: University of California, 1979), p. 23.

22. W. Bascom, "The Forms of Folklore: Prose Narratives," *JAF* 78 (1965):4.

23. Joseph Fontenrose, *The Ritual Theory of Myth*, University of California Folklore Studies no. 18 (Berkeley: University of California, 1966), pp. 54–55.

24. On the issue of the terms *folktale* and *legend*, and their equivalents in other modern European languages, see Bascom, "Forms of Folklore," pp. 16–19. A long (largely inconclusive and fruitless) discussion has occurred within biblical scholarship on just this issue.

25. The matter of whether or not myths differ fundamentally from folktales or legends is treated with especial clarity and skill by G. S. Kirk. See his *Myth: Its Meaning and Functions in Ancient and Other Cultures* (Cambridge: Cambridge University, 1970), pp. 31–41, and "On Defining Myths," p. 55.

26. Burkert, *Structure and History*, p. 24.

27. Several intellectual historians, anthropologists, and others have produced very useful accounts of a number of theories of myths, and these accounts are utilized in various degrees in what follows. See, e.g., Percy S. Cohen, "Theories of Myth," *Man:* NS 4 (1969):337–53; Kirk, *Myth;* Rogerson, *Myth in Old Testament Interpretation*, pp. 175–78; Burkert, *Structure and History;* and especially Robert A. Segal, "In Defense of Mythology: The History of Modern Theories of Myth," *Annals of Scholarship* 1 (1980):3–49. A much abbreviated such overview also appeared in my "Theoretical Assumptions in the Study of Ugaritic Myths," *Maarav* 2 (1979–80):43–63.

28. See F. Max Müller, *Chips from a German Worshop*, 2 vols. (London: Oxford University, 1867); *Anthropological Religion*, Gifford Lectures (London: Longmans, 1892); and *Contributions to the Science of Mythology*, 2 vols. (London: Longmans, 1897).

29. E. B. Tylor, *Primitive Culture*, 2 vols. (London: Murray, 1871).

30. Robin Horton, "African Traditional Thought and Western Science," *Africa* 37 (1967):50–71, 155–87. A version of this essay may be found conveniently in Bryan R. Wilson, ed., *Rationality* (Oxford: Blackwell, 1970), pp. 131–71.

31. Bronislaw Malinowski, "Magic, Science and Religion," in *Magic, Science and Religion*, p. 34.

32. It is Cohen ("Theories of Myth," p. 339) who acutely points to this particular failure of the Tylorean intellectualist model, as well as to the model's chief advantages.

33. William Robertson Smith, *Lectures on the Religion of the Semites*, p. 18.

34. With regard to Frazer, we noted that he adheres more fundamentally to the "intellectualist" position than to the theory under consideration at the moment. On this issue see the excellent study of R. Ackerman, "Frazer on Myth and Ritual," *JHI* 36 (1975):115–34.

35. Jane Harrison, *Themis: A Study of the Social Origins of Greek Religion* (Cambridge: Cambridge University, 1912); *Prolegomena to the Study of Greek Religion* (Cambridge: Cambridge University, 1921).

36. S. H. Hooke, ed., *Myth and Ritual: Essays on the Myth and Ritual of the Hebrews in Relation to the Culture Pattern of the Ancient East* (London: Oxford University, 1933). Note especially Hooke's essay that opens this volume, "The Myth and Ritual Pattern of the Ancient East," pp. 1–14.

37. T. H. Gaster, *Thespis: Ritual, Myth, and Drama in the Ancient Near East* (New York: Norton, 1977) [originally published in 1950]), p. 12.

38. Gaster, "Myth and Story," pp. 185–203.

39. The problems inherent in the myth-ritual theory are discussed briefly by Cross (*Canaante Myth*, pp. 82–83) and at length by Fontenrose *(Ritual Theory of Myth)* and Kirk (*Myth*, pp. 12–31).

40. Frazer, *Apollodorus*, p. xxviii, n. 1.

41. These recent demonstrations can be found most conveniently in Burkert, *Structure and History*, pp. 100–101, with the evidence cited there.

42. Answering this need, however, has proved anything but simple. Almost all students of ritual admit this. For some recent studies of ritual, see the various works of Victor Turner (e.g., *Forest of Symbols* [Ithaca, N.Y.: Cornell University, 1967] or *The Ritual Process* [Ithaca, N.Y.: Cornell University, 1977]); J. H. M. Beatty, "Ritual and Social Change," *Man*, NS 1 (1966): 60–74; "On Understanding Ritual," in Wilson, *Rationality*, pp. 240–68; and H. H. Penner, "Language, Ritual and Meaning," *Numen* 32 (1985):1–16.

43. Lucien Lévy-Bruhl, *Primitive Mentality* (London: Allen & Unwin, 1923) and *How Natives Think* (New York: Knopf, 1925).

44. Particularly good on this point is Segal, "In Defense of Mythology," pp. 24–25.

45. So widespread is this conclusion that elaborate documentation is inappropriate. See the summary arguments and the evidence presented by E. E. Evans-Pritchard, *Theories of Primitive Religion* (Oxford: Clarendon, 1965), pp. 78–99. Evans-Pritchard concludes that "there is no reputable anthropologist who today accepts this theory of two distinct types of mentality" (p. 88).

46. Ernst Cassirer, *Philosophie der symbolischen Formen*, 2 vols (Berlin: B. Cassirer, 1923–31).

47. H. and H. A. Frankfort, "Myth and Reality," in H. Frankfort et al., *The Intellectual Adventure of Ancient Man* (Chicago: University of Chicago, 1946), pp. 3–27.

48. H. and H. A. Frankfort, "Myth and Reality," pp. 4–6, 15.

49. Burkert, *Structure and History*, p. 24.

50. Kirk, "On Defining Myths," pp. 58–59.

51. W. Robertson Smith, *Lectures on the Religion of the Semites*, p. 29.

52. Emile Durkheim, *The Elementary Forms of the Religious Life* (London: Allen & Unwin, 1915) [originally published in French in 1912], p. 420.

53. Malinowski, "Myth in Primitive Psychology," p. 101.

54. Stith Thompson, *Motif-Index of Folk-Literature*, 6 vols, rev. ed. (Bloomington: Indiana University, 1955–58).

55. See my "Theoretical Assumptions in the Study of Ugaritic Myths," pp. 51–55 and the evidence and literature cited there.

56. This formulation is close to that of Segal ("In Defense of Mythology," p. 12) to whom the present section is especially indebted.

57. Carl G. Jung, "The Psychology of the Child Archetype," in Carl G. Jung and C. Kerényi, *Essays on a Science of Mythology*, Bollingen Series 22 (Princeton, N.J.: Princeton University, 1969), pp. 71–72. (This essay was first published in 1941.)

58. This argument is especially well presented by Dundes (*Sacred Narrative*, p. 270).

59. The clearest single instance of Lévi-Strauss's application of structural analysis probably remains his study of the British Columbian tale of Asdiwal; see "The Story of Asdiwal," in Claude Lévi-Strauss, *Structural Anthropology*, vol. 2 (New York: Basic Books, 1976), pp. 146–97. One might best be advised next to turn to the first of his four volumes analyzing an enormous group of South and North American myths, *The Raw and the Cooked: Introduction to a Science of Mythology* (New York: Harper & Row, 1975). See also *The Savage Mind* (London: Weidenfeld and Nicolson, 1966), *Myth and Meaning* (London: Routledge and Kegan Paul, 1978), and the three volumes that followed upon *The Raw and the Cooked*, all of which are now available in English: *From Honey to Ashes* (New York: Harper & Row, 1973); *The Origins of Table Manners* (London: Jonathan Cape, 1978); and *The Naked Man* (New York: Harper & Row, 1981).

60. Kirk, *Myth*, pp. v–vi.

61. Lévi-Strauss, "Story of Asdiwal," p. 165.

62. Claude Lévi-Strauss, "Structural Study of Myth," in *Structural Anthropology* (New York: Basic, 1963), p. 229. (First published in *JAF* 78 [1955]:428–44.)

63. For example, Roland Barthes et al., *Analyse Structurale et exegese biblique* (Neuchtal: Delachaux et Niestle, 1972); Robert Polzin, *Biblical Structuralism*, Semeia Studies (Missoula, Mont.: Scholars, 1977); Daniel Patte, *Structural Exegesis: From Theory to Practice* (Philadelphia, Pa.: Fortress, 1978). A study that does attempt to interpret an ancient Near Eastern myth in the manner of Lévi-Strauss is my " 'The Contendings of Horus and Seth' (Chester Beatty Papyrus No. 1): A Structural Interpretation," *HR* 18 (1979): 352–69.

64. Lévi-Strauss, *Savage Mind*, p. 117.

65. Note Leach's comments in his review of Lévi-Strauss's *Le Cru et le cuit:* "Anyone who works his way through the astonishing book now before us and still claims that he doesn't believe a word of it has a resolution of disbelief which I must respect, but cannot endorse" (*AA* 67 [1965]:778); and Kirk's summary of the same volume: "When one turns from Lévi-Strauss to any other attempt to analyse these myths, the results look old-fashioned and unconvincing" (*Myth*, p. 63).

66. Lévi-Strauss, *Raw and the Cooked*, p. 341.

67. Burkert, *Structure and History*. Burkert describes his central thesis as the argument that "even structures of the mind are determined by historical evolution in its largest sense, by tradition formed and transforming within the complicated pattern of life"; Burkert thus "does not consider mind as autonomous, creatively organizing itself, but as dependent on the process of cultural transmission" (*Structure and History*, pp. xi–xii). The "basic fact" with which the student of myth deals is for Burkert "not the 'creation,' not the 'origin' of myth," but rather "the transmission and preservation" (p. 2).

CHAPTER 3: GRACE OR STATUS? YAHWEH'S CLOTHING OF THE FIRST HUMANS

1. Gunkel, *The Legends of Genesis,* (New York: Schocken, 1964 [originally published in German in 1901]) pp. 15–16.
2. Edmund Leach, "Genesis as Myth," in *Genesis as Myth and Other Essays* (London: Jonathan Cape, 1969), pp. 7–23. For some of the criticisms that have been leveled against Leach's study, see my "Jacob as Father, Husband, and Nephew: Kinship Studies and the Patriarchal Narratives," *JBL* 102 (1983): 189, n. 2.
3. In both Hebrew and in the versions, Genesis 3:21 is remarkably free of any significant textual variants. About the only dispute on the level of lower criticism is whether to read *lā 'ādām* or *lĕ 'ādām.* See D. O. Procksch, *Die Genesis,* übersetzt and erklärt, 2d–3d ed., KAT (Leipzig and Erlangen: Deichertsche u. Scholl, 1924), p. 30; J. Skinner, *A Critical and Exegetical Commentary on Genesis,* 2d ed., ICC (Edinburgh: T. & T. Clark, 1930), p. 87; C. Westermann, *Genesis,* BKAT 1.4 (Neukirchen-Vluyn: Neukirchener, 1970), p. 254; and R. Davidson, *Genesis 1–11* (Cambridge: Cambridge University, 1973), p. 47.
4. Westermann, *Genesis,* p. 364 *('Strafsprüche').* For a most useful form-critical outline of the entire paradise tale (Gen. 2:4b–3:24), see G. W. Coats, *Genesis: With an Introduction to Narrative Literature,* (ed. R. Knierim and G. Tucker, FOTL 1 (Grand Rapids, Mich.: Eerdmans, 1983), pp. 49–50. Coats labels all of Genesis 3:14–24 simply "Judgment" (p. 50).
5. "J^a" is Procksch's term for this redactor (Procksch, *Die Genesis,* p. 40). B. Jacob, *(Das erste Buch der Tora: Genesis,* übersetzt und erklärt [Berlin: Schocken, 1934], p. 123); Skinner *(Genesis,* p. 87); G. von Rad *(Genesis,* OTL [Philadelphia: Westminster, 1961], p. 93); and many subsequent commentators also find behind Genesis 3:21 a different source from that responsible for the primary narrative here, including the clothing notice earlier in verse 7. Often, both Genesis 3:20 and 3:21 are seen as additions to the central tradition in the paradise tale. See, e.g., J. T. Walsh, "Genesis 2:4b–3:24: A Synchronic Approach," *JBL* 96 (1977):169 (the two verses between the judgment and the expulsion "have no structural connection" with the rest of the scene). Most recently, Coats too lists Genesis 3:21–22 as among "certain secondary elements" that "characterize the latest stage" in the Yahwist's narrative; 3:21 alone is "a delay," one that "appears in every way as literarily secondary" and that "duplicates information already established by the story" (Coats, *Genesis,* pp. 56–57). On the other hand, both Westermann *(Genesis,* p. 364) and N. Wyatt ("Interpreting the Creation and Fall Story in Genesis 2–3," *ZAW* 93 [1981]: 11, n. 5) argue that Genesis 3:21 is a part of the earliest tradition here. The interpretation for the clothing incident offered in this chapter may well imply that Genesis 3:21 is less peripheral than is often suggested.
6. Robertson Smith, *Religion of the Semites,* p. 307.
7. S. R. Driver, *Book of Genesis* (London: Methuen, 1904), p. 50; Skinner, *Genesis,* p. 87 (Genesis 3:21 is a "detached notice describing the origin of clothing").
8. H. W. Attridge and R. A. Oden, Jr., *Philo of Byblos: The Phoenician History,*

CBQMS, 9 (Washington, D.C.: Catholic Biblical Association, 1981), pp. 42–43 (Eusebius, *PE* 1.10.10).

9. Sotah 14a; the translation here is that of *The Babylonian Talmud* (London: Soncino, 1936); cf. M. Jastrow, *A Dictionary of the Targumim* (New York: Judaica, 1971) *sv gĕmîlût.*

10. J. H. Taylor, *St. Augustine: The Literal Meaning of Genesis,* ACW, 42 (New York: Newman, 1982), pp. 165–172; and *Bedae Venerabilis Opera,* ed. C. W. Jones CChr (Turnholti: Brepols, 1967), p. 69.

11. J. Pelikan, ed., *Luther's Works, vol. 1, Lectures on Genesis* (Saint Louis, Mo.: Concordia, 1958), p. 221. Luther's amplification upon this point presages a memorable Puritan theme: So "much effort and expense did men go to in their dress," that "if Adam came back to life now and saw this madness among all classes, I surely believe that he would be petrified with amazement. A pelt was his daily garb as a daily reminder of his lost bliss. But we clothe ourselves flashily and go to extremes in order to prove to everyone that we have forgotten not only the evils out of which we were snatched but also the good things we have received" (p. 222).

12. John Calvin, *Commentaries on the First Book of Moses Called Genesis* (1847; reprint ed., Grand Rapids, Mich.: Baker, 1981), pp. 181–85.

13. John Milton, *Paradise Lost,* ed. S. Elledge (New York/London: Norton, 1975), p. 218 (book 10, verses 211–22).

14. F. J. Delitzsch, *A New Commentary on Genesis* (New York: Scribner, 1889), p. 170 (a translation from the 5th German edition of 1887).

15. Skinner, *Genesis,* pp. 87–97.

16. B. Jacob, *Das erste Buch der Tora,* p. 124 *("ein Nachtrag zur Schöpfung").* Jacob's entire discussion of Genesis 3:21 focuses not on divine grace but rather upon the incident here as an indication of proper, civilized human society, which is thus distinguished from the world of animals. Thus interpreted, the verse becomes "the key to the entire Paradise Story" (p. 124 [*"der Schlüssel zur ganzen Paradiesgeschichte"*]). Jacob's exegesis thus approaches more nearly than does any other analysis of which I am aware the interpretation suggested in part 3 of this chapter. For another study of the paradise tale that emphasizes human clothing as a marker of their distinction from the animal realm, see D. R. G. Beattie, "What's Genesis 2–3 About?," *ExpTim* 92 (1980):8–10.

17. Dietrich Bonhoeffer, *Creation and Fall: A Theological Interpretation of Genesis 1–3* (New York: Macmillan, 1959 [originally published in German in 1937]):-90–91.

18. U. Cassuto, *A Commentary on the Book of Genesis:* part 1, *From Adam to Noah: Genesis I–VI* (Jerusalem: Magnes, 1961), p. 163 (emphasis in original).

19. von Rad, *Genesis,* p. 90.

20. Westermann, *Genesis,* p. 366 *("ein fürsorgendes Handeln . . . der Schöpfer 'beschützt' sein Geschöpf").* As was the case with B. Jacob's comments, Westermann also goes well beyond the conventional view and sees a major theme in Genesis 3 to be that of Yahweh's separating himself from humanity (*Genesis,* p. 364–67). This aspect of Westermann's view, too, is in accord with the position developed in this chapter.

21. C. Westermann, *Creation* (London: S.P.C.K., 1974 [originally published in German in 1971]), p. 104.

22. Davidson, *Genesis 1–11*, p. 47.
23. B. Vawter, *On Genesis: A New Reading* (Garden City, N.Y.: Doubleday, 1977), p. 87.
24. "The Relationship of Genesis 3:20 to the Serpent," *ZAW* 89 (1977):372.
25. "A Man to Work the Soil: A New Interpretation of Genesis 2–3," *JSOT* 5 (1978):10.
26. W. Brueggeman, *Genesis,* Interpretation: A Bible Commentary for Teaching and Preaching (Atlanta: John Knox, 1982), pp. 49–50.
27. *In the Beginning: A New English Rendition of the Book of Genesis* (New York: Schocken, 1983), pp. 17–19.
28. As has been noted in passing earlier, this is not to say that unanimity exists here (or anywhere in biblical exegesis). B. Jacob and Westermann especially move toward the meaning developed later in this chapter, and Coats states explicitly that there is in Genesis 3:21 no "structural or content evidence of interest in labeling this gift a sign of God's grace" (*Genesis,* p. 56).
29. Davidson, *Genesis 1–11*, p. 47.
30. The obvious exception is the use of *'or* in Job 40:31 to refer to the skin of *liwyatan* ("Leviathan") (Job 40:25).
31. The Hague/Paris: Mouton, 1971 (originally published in Russian in 1937). On the work of Bogatyrev, see the introductory essay in this volume by B. L. Ogibenin, pp. 9–32.
32. Bogatyrev, *Functions,* p. 13; see also p. 83.
33. See especially the essays collected in J. M. Cordwell and R. A. Schwarz, eds., *The Fabrics of Culture: The Anthropology of Clothing and Adornment* (The Hague/Paris: Mouton, 1979).
34. M. R. Roach and J. B. Eicher, "The Language of Personal Adornment," in Cordwell and Schwarz, *Fabrics of Culture,* p. 18.
35. The text of Gilgamesh used here is basically that of R. Campbell Thompson, *The Epic of Gilgamesh: Text, Transliteration, and Notes* (Oxford: Clarendon, 1930), with corrections from *CAD* and other sources. For a recent list of Gilgamesh texts, see J. H. Tigay, *The Evolution of the Gilgamesh Epic* (Philadelphia: University of Pennsylvania, 1982), pp. 304–7.
36. Beattie, "What Is Genesis 2–3 About?," pp. 8–10.
37. References to Adapa are to J. A. Knudtzon, *Die El-Amarna-Tafeln* (1915; reprint ed., Aalen: Zeller, 1964), corrected occasionally by *CAD.*
38. On this entire episode, see T. Jacobsen, "The Investiture and Anointing of Adapa in Heaven," in W. L. Moran, ed., *Toward the Image of Tammuz and Other Essays on Mesopotamian History and Culture* (Cambridge, Mass.: Harvard University, 1970), pp. 48–51 (originally published in *AJSL* 46 [1930]:201–203). Jacobsen in fact doubts that Anu's clothing of Adapa is properly an investiture; instead, the clue to understanding this incident (as so often for Jacobsen) is to be found in the mandates of hospitality: "Anu does not know what to do to this new mixture of divine powers and human nature; but at last he decides to treat him as a guest. . . . Accordingly he complies with the laws of hospitality and brings him food, drink, a garment, and oil for anointing" (p. 50). This may well be the immediate motive for Anu's clothing of Adapa, but note that the treatment of Adapa as a *guest* in heaven clearly means that he does not belong and cannot remain in that realm. Given that the garment figures in this marking of Adapa as a guest, and

hence as a mortal, I do not hesitate to label the scene as at least functionally an investiture.

39. J. M. Cordwell, "The Very Human Arts of Transformation," in Cordwell and Schwarz, *Fabrics of Culture*, p. 47.

40. Benno Jacob, who views the clothing incident partly as an indication of human society as distinct from the animal realm, wisely notes that "there are no indications that the temperature beyond the Garden might be anything different" (*"es gibt kein Anzeichen, dass die Temperatur ausserhalb des Gartens eine andere gewesen sei"*) (*Das erst Buch der Tora*, p. 123).

41. Westermann, *Genesis*, p. 377 (*"Das Ziel ist die Vertreibung der Menschen aus dem Garten und damit die Trennung von Gott"*).

42. P. D. Miller, Jr., *Genesis 1–11: Studies in Structure and Theme*, JSOT Supp. Series 8 (Sheffield: *JSOT*, 1978), p. 20 (emphasis added).

43. Thomas Carlyle, *Sartor Resartus: The Life and Times of Herr Teufelsdröckh* (London: Bell, 1900), pp. 89–91.

44. In addition to the observation, documented several times in this chapter, that a number of biblical scholars do approach the particular interpretation offered here, it would be foolhardy to make any claims for complete novelty on behalf of this interpretation. Though I have found none yet, I shall be very surprised if further research does not uncover early statements much in keeping with those made here.

CHAPTER 4: THE PATRIARCHAL NARRATIVES AS MYTH: THE CASE OF JACOB

1. See the discussion in Chapter 2, which treats the issue of definitions of myth at some length. As I note there, though perhaps the majority of biblical scholars will wish to insist upon a major distinction between myth on the one hand and legend or saga on the other hand, this distinction does not appear to be one that can be sustained and is itself a part of the theological tradition discussed throughout the present volume. An earlier version of some of the material in the present chapter appeared in my "Jacob as Father, Husband, and Nephew: Kinship Studies and the Patriarchal Narratives," *JBL* 102 (1983):189–205; I am grateful to the *JBL* editor for permission to utilize that material in the present context.

2. What follows makes no attempt to describe even the most outstanding stages in the development of the historical-critical understanding of Genesis within the theological mainstream. An entry into the richness and sophistication of a century's study of Genesis can be made by looking at three commentaries on this book: Hermann Gunkel, *Genesis*, HKAT 1/1 (Göttingen: Vandenhoeck & Ruprecht, 1901); Gerhard von Rad, *Genesis: A Commentary*, OTL, rev. ed. (Philadelphia: Westminster, 1972); and Claus Westermann, *Genesis*, BKAT 1 (Neukirchen-Vluyn: Neukirchener Verlag, 1966–82). The particular issues of the growth of the various collections of traditions about each patriarch and then of the fusing of these collections are treated comprehensively in Martin Noth, *A History of Pentateuchal Traditions* (Englewood Cliffs, N.J.: Prentice-Hall, 1972 [originally published in

1948]), and, more recently and very suggestively, in John Van Seters, *Abraham in History and Tradition* (New Haven/London: Yale University, 1975).

3. See, for example, his *History of Pentateuchal Traditions* for the material in Genesis, and, for later material, Martin Noth, *The Deuteronomistic History, JSOT,* Supp. 15 (Sheffield: *JSOT,* 1981 [originally published in 1943]).

4. Gerhard von Rad, *The Problem of the Hexateuch and Other Essays* (Edinburgh: Oliver and Boyd, 1966 [originally published in 1958]).

5. For statements of this, see David Daube, *Studies in Biblical Law* (Cambridge: Cambridge University, 1947), pp. 78–79, or E. A. Speiser, *Genesis,* AB 1 (Garden City, N.Y.: Doubleday, 1964), p. 227.

6. Gunkel, "Jacob," in *What Remains of the Old Testament,* pp. 166, 185.

7. Von Rad, *Genesis,* p. 157. See also Speiser, *Genesis,* pp. 211–13. Other examples of the same tendency to answer with reference to the secrets or mystery of Yahweh's free choice could be multiplied easily.

8. Mary Douglas, *Purity and Danger: An Analysis of Concepts of Pollution and Taboo* (New York/Washington: Praeger, 1966), p. 46.

9. Robin Fox, *Kinship and Marriage: An Anthropological Perspective* (Harmondsworth: Penguin, 1967), p. 33.

10. R. M. Keesing, *Kin Groups and Social Structure* (New York: Holt, Rinehart and Winston, 1975), p. 31.

11. See Westermann, *Genesis,* Lieferung 12 (1977):142 for a demonstration of the genealogical "framing" here.

12. A concentration upon the promises to the patriarchs began already with the work of Noth, for whom they comprise one of the five major themes running throughout the entire Pentateuch (Noth, *A History of Pentateuchal Traditions,* pp. 54–58). This issue has then reappeared in the most recent discussions, for example, those of Claus Westermann, "Die Verheissungen an die Väter," in *Die Verheissungen an die Väter,* FRLANT 116 (Göttingen: Vandenhoeck & Ruprecht, 1976) pp. 92–150; of R. Rendtorff, *Das überlieferungsgeschichtliche Problem des Pentateuch,* BZAW 147 (Berlin/New York: Walter de Gruyter, 1977); and of David J. A. Clines, *The Theme of the Pentateuch, JSOT* Supp. 10 (Sheffield: *JSOT,* 1978).

13. Lévi-Strauss, *Structural Anthropology* (New York: Basic Books, 1963), p. 61.

14. Fredrik Barth, "Descent and Marriage Reconsidered," in Jack Goody, ed., *The Character of Kinship* (London: Cambridge University, 1973), p. 6.

15. Fox, *Kinship,* p. 13.

16. In addition to the texts of Fox *(Kinship)* and Keesing *(Kin Groups),* to which reference has been made already, the following can also be consulted for an entry into the tangled issue of kinship: I. R. Buchler and H. A. Selby, *Kinship and Social Organization* (New York: Macmillan, 1968); Paul Bohannan and John Middleton, eds., *Marriage, Family and Residence* (Garden City, N.Y.: Natural History, 1968); Meyer Fortes, *Kinship and the Social Order* (Chicago: Aldine, 1969); and John A. Barnes, *Three Styles in the Study of Kinship* (London: Tavistock, 1971) and "Kinship Studies: Some Impressions of the Current State of Play," *Man,* NS 15 (1980): 293–303. Anyone who proposes to enter into conversation with these scholars would be wise to heed the warning of Barnes that kinship study "has reached a level of sophistication that makes it, more than any other branch of the discipline [of social

anthropology], impenetrable to the specialist in some other branch of social science as much as to the layman" (*Three Styles*, p. xxi). Much of the difficulty lies in the theoretical, even mathematical, nature of recent studies, as is noted briefly in the paragraph that follows.

17. Mara Donaldson, "Kinship Theory in the Patriarchal Narratives: The Case of the Barren Wife," *JAAR* 49 (1981): 77–87. This article, whose conclusions partly coincide with those in the present chapter, is a telling example of the novel but persuasive conclusions to be reached from examining biblical myths outside the confines of theological inquiry.

18. Claude Lévi-Strauss, *The Elementary Structures of Kinship*, rev. ed. (Boston, Mass.: Beacon Press, 1969). This volume first appeared as *Les Structures élémentaires de la parenté* in 1949, the same year, in a striking coincidence, that witnessed the publication of two additional ground-breaking volumes in this same area, George Murdock's *Social Structure* (New York: Free Press, 1949) and Meyer Fortes's *The Web of Kinship Among the Tallensi* (Oxford: Oxford University, 1949).

19. Keesing, *Kin Groups*, p. 79.

20. This definition of endogamy comes from Lévi-Strauss (*Elementary Structures*, p. 45). The opposite of endogamy is exogamy: an alliance rule "which forbids an individual to take a spouse from within the local, kin, or status group to which he himself belongs" (Murdock, *Social Structure*, p. 18, n. 28). All prescriptive marriage rules, of course, are to some extent endogamous and to some extent exogamous. For a clear explanation of these terms, see also Fox, *Kinship*, p. 53.

21. Commentators on Genesis commonly note that the E source alone, and not the Yahwist (J), knows Sarah as Abraham's half sister (Gen. 20:12); see, e.g., von Rad, *Genesis*, pp. 168, 227. Given the present state of uncertainty about the interpretive value (and even the very existence, at least as independent sources running throughout several books of the Bible) of the traditional sources to the Tetrateuch/Pentateuch, the analysis offered here pays greater heed to the frequency with which a given kinship relationship is noted in Genesis than it does to the location of this relationship within any of the traditional sources. It might, however, be of significance that the particular relationship that I accent most, the relationship between Jacob and his mother's brother Laban, is accented both in the P source (Gen. 28:2) and in the J source (Gen. 29:10–13), according to the standard source divisions.

22. Rebekah's father is Bethuel according to Genesis 24:15 and 24:24, but Genesis 24:48 can be read as suggesting rather that her father is Nahor. This issue is discussed by von Rad, *Genesis*, p. 257.

23. For another study that raises in more general terms the same question, see Karin R. Andriolo, "A Structural Analysis of Genealogy and Worldview in the Old Testament," *AA* 75 (1973):1657–69. Andriolo reaches a conclusion about the external versus the internal definition of Israel quite like that reached below ("A Structural Analysis," p. 1663).

24. Leach, *Genesis as Myth*, p. 21.

25. In addition to the literature cited here, see E. R. Leach, "The Structural Implications of Matrilateral Cross-Cousin Marriage," *Man* 81 (1951):23–55; Fox, *Kinship*, pp. 188–207; and Barnes, *Three Styles*, pp. 142–55. Given

the importance of cross-cousin marriage in so many settings, these studies are only a beginning of the material devoted to this issue. Indeed, one might fairly claim that an explanation of the frequency and meanings of cross-cousin marriage is the central issue in Lévi-Strauss's *Elementary Structures of Kinship*. For some comments and criticisms on this volume, see G. C. Homans and D. M. Schneider, *Marriage, Authority, and Final Causes: A Study of Unilateral Cross-Cousin Marriage* (Glencoe, Ill.: Free Press, 1955); Barnes, *Three Styles*, pp. 103–75; and, most critically, F. Korn, *Elementary Structures Reconsidered: Lévi-Strauss on Kinship* (Berkeley/Los Angeles: University of California, 1973).

26. Murdock, *Social Structure*, pp. 260–83; and see Homans and Schneider, *Marriage, Alliance, and Final Causes*, p. 30. Like Lévi-Strauss's *Elementary Structures of Kinship*, which appeared in the same year as Murdock's *Social Structure*, Murdock's statistical approach to kinship studies has provoked much controversy in the past thirty-five years; see Barnes, *Three Styles*, pp. 1–90. Disagreement has also surrounded the issue of the identity of, or difference between, "preferential marriage" and "prescriptive marriage." For example, D. H. P. Maybury-Lewis argues for a sharp distinction between prescriptive and preferential marriage systems ("Prescriptive Marriage Systems," *SJA* 21 [1965]:226), while Buchler and Selby are persuaded rather that any such distinction cannot be maintained, since "it is demographically impossible to have 'true' M[other's] B[rother's] D[aughter] marriage in any society over time. . . . Prescriptive marriage cannot exist empirically" (*Kinship and Social Organization*, p. 126).

27. A. R. Radcliffe-Brown, "On Joking Relationships," in *Structure and Function in Primitive Society* (Glencoe, Ill.: Free Press, 1952), p. 93; see also p. 100 (first published in *Africa* 13 (1940) 195–210).

28. For the former, see Meyer Fortes, *Kinship and the Social Order*, p. 213 (Chicago: Aldine, 1970); and for the latter, B. Farber, *Comparative Kinship Systems* (New York: Wiley, 1968), pp. 104–9.

29. R. F. Murphy and L. Kasdan, "The Structure of Parallel Cousin Marriage," in Bohannan and Middleton, *Marriage, Family and Residence*, p. 185.

30. *Elementary Structures of Kinship*, p. 14.

31. *Elementary Structures of Kinship*, p. 98. Each of the two groups into which tribes are divided for the purpose of exchanging potential spouses is called a moiety (Fox, *Kinship*, p. 182).

32. Fox, *Kinship*, p. 187. By "either unilineal descent system," Fox means just what Lévi-Strauss had meant: under either a patrilineal or a matrilineal system.

33. Donaldson, "Kinship Theory in the Patriarchal Narratives," p. 83.

34. Donaldson, "Kinship Theory in the Patriarchal Narratives," p. 84.

35. Barnes, *Three Styles*, p. 148.

36. Lévi-Strauss, *Structural Anthropology*, p. 39. Lévi-Strauss's focus upon the avunculate in his discussion of the "atom" of kinship is an excellent example of the relatively recent shift to inquiry into systems of alliance. As Barnes observes, "Lévi-Strauss takes this [the bundle of relationships within the avunculate] as his elementary building-block rather than the so-called elementary family favored by all his predecessors in kinship studies, in order to include at this fundamental level the relationship be-

tween brothers-in-law, that is, between the man who gives a sister and the
man who receives her as wife" (*Three Styles*, p. 117).

37. A. R. Radcliffe-Brown, "The Mother's Brother in South Africa," *SAJS* 21 (1924):542–55. This article is reprinted in Radcliffe-Brown's *Structure and Function*, pp. 15–31, from which all subsequent references here are drawn.
38. Radcliffe-Brown, "The Mother's Brother," p. 15.
39. Radcliffe-Brown, "The Mother's Brother," p. 15.
40. Radcliffe-Brown, "The Mother's Brother," p. 16.
41. Radcliffe-Brown, "The Mother's Brother," p. 17.
42. Homans and Schneider, *Marriage, Authority, and Final Causes*, p. 22.
43. M. Fortes, "Descent, Filiation and Affinity," *Man* 89 (1959):208.
44. Keesing, *Kin Groups*, pp. 46, 105. "Close ties," again, should not be taken to imply that a nephew is always fond of his mother's brother, or an uncle fond of his sister's son; these ties refer to a series of conventionalized attitudes in a kinship system and not to what may or may not exist in any empirical instance.
45. On avunculocal residence, see Murdock, *Social Structure*, p. 17, as well as any of the standard texts noted earlier. A residence rule refers to a rule that mandates where a couple is to reside after their marriage; such rules can dictate avunculocal, patrilocal, matrilocal, or neolocal residence, for example. Intriguingly for the Jacob narratives, these residence rules sometimes mandate that residence change only after the birth of a child or after a given period of time has followed the marriage. It is thus quite possible that a key element in the Jacob-Laban dispute is disagreement over a (traditional versus newly instituted?) residence rule.
46. Fox, *Kinship*, pp. 99, 258–60.
47. Lévi-Strauss, *Structural Anthopology*, p. 46; cf. pp. 72–73 and *Structural Anthropology: Volume 2*, pp. 82–112. A further account of the implications of this newly defined "atom" of kinship for the study of myths may be found in my " 'The Contendings of Horus and Seth' (Chester Beatty Papyrus no. 1): A Structural Interpretation," *HR* 18 (1979):352–69.
48. Murdock, *Social Structure*, p. 183; cf. also pp. 201–12.
49. Though such warnings have been voiced by many, the phrase *conjectural history* is that of Radcliffe-Brown, who often spoke of the dangers in leaping from the study of kinship to the reconstruction of history. See on this, Murdock, *Social Structure*, p. 119; and Buchler and Selby, *Kinship and Social Organization*, p. 6.

CHAPTER 5: RELIGIOUS IDENTITY AND THE SACRED PROSTITUTION ACCUSATION

1. Deuteronomy 23:18 in the Hebrew text. The *RSV* (in the edition of *The New Oxford Annotated Bible* [New York: Oxford University, 1977]) is here cited in part to demonstrate the contribution of modern translations in sustaining the charge that several ancient Near Eastern religions involved sexual rites as a part of their cult and that these rites remained a temptation for Israel. The terms translated "cult prostitute" in Deuteronomy 23:17 (Hebrew:

23:18) are *qĕdēšâ* and *qādēš* respectively; this is the standard translation of these terms in most modern lexical works. Some form of this same Hebrew word underlies the standard translations of the verses in Kings, Hosea, and Job cited in this paragraph. In addition, *zōnâ* is sometimes seen as referring to sacral prostitution, as in the story of Hosea's marriage (Hos. 1–3) or of Judah and Tamar (Gen. 38:15).

Earlier versions of the present chapter were delivered on several occasions between 1978 and 1980, and then read as a paper at the national meeting of the Society of Biblical Literature, San Francisco, Calif., December 21, 1981.

2. O. J. Baab, "Prostitution," in *IDB* (New York/Nashville, Tenn.: Abingdon, 1962), 3:933.

3. Georg Fohrer, *History of Israelite Religion* (Nashville, Tenn./New York: Abingdon, 1972 [originally published in 1968]), p. 301.

4. Fredrik Barth, ed., *Ethnic Groups and Boundaries: The Social Organization of Culture Difference* (Boston: Little, Brown, 1969). See especially the "Introduction" to this volume by Barth (pp. 9–38).

5. Barth, "Introduction," in *Ethnic Groups*, pp. 13–14.

6. Barth, "Introduction," in *Ethnic Groups*, p. 14.

7. Rodney Needham, review of W. Arens, *The Man-Eating Myth, TLS* (25 January 1980):75; see the note following for full bibliographical data on Arens's book.

8. W. Arens, *The Man-Eating Myth: Anthropology and Anthropophagy* (New York: Oxford University, 1979). In addition to Needham's review cited in note 7, see those of John W. Burton (*Anthropos* 75 [1980]:644–45) and R. E. Downs (*AE* 7 [1980]:185–86), and, very critically, P. G. Riviere (*Man* NS 15 [1980]:203–5) and James W. Springer (*AQ* 53 [1980]:148–50).

9. Arens, *Man-Eating Myth*, p. 139.

10. Arens, *Man-Eating Myth*, p. 182.

11. Needham, review of Arens, p. 75.

12. Robertson Smith, *Religion of the Semites,* (New York: Schocken, 1972 [originally published in 1889]), p. 455. Note already Robertson Smith's choice of the verb *thronged,* as if exaggerated statement might anticipate any attempts at rebuttal.

13. Karl Budde, *Religion of Israel to the Exile,* American Lectures on the History of Religions, 4 (New York/London: Putnam's, 1899), pp. 70–71.

14. Franz Cumont, *The Oriental Religions in Roman Paganism* (New York: Dover, 1956 [translation of 1911 edition]), pp. 118–20. The practices that Cumont finds so fascinatingly distasteful are established by "irrefutable testimony," e.g., by that of Strabo (n. 41 to p. 118, on pp. 246–48).

15. James George Frazer, *Adonis Attis Osiris: Studies in the History of Oriental Religion* vol. 1, part 4 of the 3d ed. of *The Golden Bough* (London: Macmillan, 1906), pp. 21–24.

16. Frazer, *Adonis Attis Osiris,* pp. 24–25.

17. See, e.g., George A. Barton's article "Hierodouloi," in the widely used *Encyclopaedia of Religion and Ethics,* ed. James Hastings, vol. 6 (New York: Scribner, 1914), pp. 672–76; Barton finds reason to claim the practice of cultic prostitution in Babylon, Syria, Phoenicia and the Punic World, and in Egypt. Max Weber's brilliant portrait of ancient Israelite religion and

society also gives expression to the standard accusations: "Like most ancient agricultural cults, those of Baal were and remained orgiastic, specifically of a sexual and alcoholic character. . . . There were hierodulae *(hekdesh)*
expressly documented in the legal collections, in the legends *(Tamar)* and
by the prophets. . . . From the cults of Baal during his fusion with Yahwe,
sexual orgiasticism invaded the Yahwe cults. The existence of hierodulae
is also ascertained for the Temple of Jerusalem" (Max Weber, *Ancient Judaism*
[New York: Free Press, 1952 (originally published in 1918–1921)], p. 189).

18. William Foxwell Albright, *Archaeology and the Religion of Israel* (Baltimore, Md.:
Johns Hopkins University, 1946), pp. 75–77. The evidence from classical
literature cited by Albright will be surveyed later in this chapter.

19. Albright, *Archaeology and the Religion of Israel*, p. 159.

20. G. R. Driver and John C. Miles, *The Babylonian Laws*, 2 vols. (Oxford: Clarendon, 1952–55), 1:360.

21. Baab, "Prostitution," pp. 932–33. At the outset of the present chapter, we
noted that this article does possess the virtue of noting, though only in
passing, that there is very little data to support the existence of those
institutions so widely denounced in the Bible and elsewhere (p. 933).

22. Gerhard von Rad, *Old Testament Theology*, 2 vols. (New York: Harper & Row,
1962–65 [originally published in 1957–60]), 2: 141–42.

23. James Luther Mays, *Hosea: A Commentary*, OTL (London: SCM, 1969), p. 75.

24. Hans Walter Wolff, *Hosea*, Hermeneia (Philadelphia, Pa.: Fortress, 1974), p.
14. See this same source (p. 14) for an excursus on "The Sex Cult"; Wolff's
chief evidence from antiquity, beyond biblical statements, is drawn from
Herodotus, Lucian, and Augustine. For Wolff's commentary on Hosea 4:14,
see *Hosea*, p. 86.

25. Wilhelm Rudolph, *"Präparierte Jungfrauen" (Zu Hosea 1),"* *ZAW* 75 (1963):
65–73. The research that Wolff cites and to which Rudolph devotes most
of his attention is that summarized in Gustav Boström, *"Die kultische Deutung
von 'iššā zārā,"* pp. 103–55 in his *Proverbiastudien,* Lund Universitets Arsskrift,
NF And. 1, Bd. 30, Nr. 3 (Lund: Gleerup, 1935), and in Leonhard Rost,
"Erwägungen zu Hosea 4, 13f.," pp. 451–60 in Walter Baumgartner et al., eds.,
Festschrift Alfred Bertholet (Tubingen: J. C. B. Mohr, 1950).

26. Helmer Ringgren, *Israelite Religion* (Philadelphia: Fortress, 1966 [originally
published in 1963]), p. 43; note also p. 198, where Ringgren finds the
portrait of "the loose woman" in Proverbs 7 "reminiscent of the cultic
prostitutes of the Canaanite fertility cult."

27. Georg Fohrer, *History of Israelite Religion* (Nashville/New York: Abingdon,
1972 [originally published in 1968]), p. 59; see also p. 106 (the story of
Rahab refers to "sacred prostitution at the local Yahweh sanctuary" in
Jericho) and p. 131.

28. Edwin M. Yamauchi, "Cultic Prostitution: A Case Study in Cultural Diffu-
sion," pp. 213–22 in Harry A. Hoffner, Jr., ed., *Orient and Occident: Essays
Presented to Cyrus H. Gordon on the Occasion of his Sixty-Fifth Birthday*, AOAT 22
(Neukirchen-Vluyn: Neukirchener, 1973), p. 219.

29. E.g., Michael C. Astour, "Tamar the Hierodule: An Essay in the Method
of Vestigial Motifs," *JBL* 85 (1966): 185–96; S. Erlandsson, *"zānāh,"* pp.
99–104 in G. Johannes Botterweck and Helmer Ringgren, *Theological Dictionary of the Old Testament,* vol. 4 (Grand Rapids, Mich.: Eerdmans, 1980); and

Paul E. Dion, "Did Cultic Prostitution Fall into Oblivion During the Post-exilic Era? Some Evidence from Chronicles and the Septuagint," *CBQ* 43 (1981): 41–48.

30. A great deal of this material is collected in Carl Clemen, *"Miszellen zu Lukians Schrift über die syrische Göttin,"* BZAW 33 (1918): 89–91.

31. The text together with a reliable translation of Herodotus's *History* can be conveniently found in the edition of A. D. Godley, LCL (London: Heinemann, 1920); this edition is that cited in the text.

32. Again, for convenience Strabo is here cited from the Loeb edition: H. L. Jones, ed., *The Geography of Strabo,* LCL, vol. vii (London: Heinemann, 1930). Strict chronology might demand our citing the Epistle of Jeremiah between Herodotus and Strabo, but this source has played a much lesser role for ancients and moderns alike. Verse 43 of this fourth-century B.C. satirical letter may make mention of sacred prostitution among the Babylonians. For the Greek text of the Epistle of Jeremiah, see Clemen, *"Miszellen,"* p. 90; a translation can be found in C. J. Ball, "Epistle of Jeremy," pp. 596–611 in *APOT,* vol. 1: Apocrypha (Oxford: Clarendon, 1913). For a recent discussion of the character and date of this letter, see George W. E. Nickelsburg, *Jewish Literature Between the Bible and the Mishnah* (Philadelphia: Fortress, 1981), pp. 35–39.

33. C. Kempf, ed., *Valerii Maximi, Factorum et Dictorum Memorabilium* (Leipzig: Teubner, 1888), II:vi.15.

34. *De Dea Syria,* ed. Harold W. Attridge and Robert A. Oden, Jr., SBLTT, Graeco-Roman Religion Series, 1 (Missoula, Mont.: Scholars, 1976), pp. 13–15, para. 6.

35. For the text and translation, see Claude Mondésert, ed., *Clément D'Alexandrie, Le Protreptique,* SC 2 (Paris: Editions du Cerf, 1949), 2:13.4.

36. Charles B. Gulick, ed., Athenaeus, *The Deipnosophists,* LCL (London: Heinemann, 1933) XII.515d; and Mervin R. Dilts, ed., *Claudii Aeliani, Varia Historia* (Leipzig: Teubner, 1974), 4:1.

37. Otto Seel, ed., *M. Iuniani Iustini, Epitoma Historiarum Philippicarum Pompei Trogi* (Leipzig: Teubner, 1935), XVIII:v.

38. See the translation of Arnobius "Against the Heathen" in the edition of the ANF, vol. 6 (Grand Rapids, Mich.: Eerdmans, 1966), pp. 496–97.

39. Lactantius, *The Divine Institutes,* trans. Mary F. McDonald (Washington, D.C.: Catholic University, 1964), 1:17:10; the Latin text is partly reproduced in Clemen, *"Miszellen,"* p. 90.

40. A portion of the Greek text of the *vita Const.* (III.58) is again to be found in Clemen, *"Miszellen,"* p. 90; the translation cited here is that of the NPNF edition, 2d series, vol. 1 (Grand Rapids, Mich.: Eerdmans, 1952), p. 535.

41. Athanasius, *Contra Gentes,* p. 26; the translation cited here and the Greek text can be found in the edition of Robert W. Thomson (Oxford: Clarendon, 1971).

42. Firmicus Maternus, *The Error of the Pagan Religions,* Clarence A. Forbes, trans., ACW 37 (New York: Newman, 1970), pp. 65–66. Forbes's note to this passage is typical: "Sacred prostitution . . . was certainly a regular feature of the cult of the Cyprian Aphrodite" (p. 174); Forbes's supporting evidence comes from Clement of Alexandria and Arnobius, both of whom we have cited.

43. Augustine, *De Civitate Dei*, ed. J. E. C. Welldon (London: SPCK, 1924), 4:x.
44. Socrates, *Historia Ecclesiastica*, I.xviii. The translation cited here is that in the NPNF edition, 2d series, vol. 2 (Grand Rapids, Mich.: Eerdmans, 1952), p. 22, and a portion of the Greek text is cited by Clemen, *"Miszellen,"* p. 90.
45. Sozomon, *Historia Ecclesiastica*, V.10.7. Again, the translation is that of the NPNF edition, 2d series, vol. 2 (Grand Rapids, Mich.: Eerdmans, 1952), p. 333, for the Greek text of which see Clemen, *"Miszellen,"* p. 90.
46. Walter Baumgartner, *"Herodots babylonische und assyrische Nachrichten,"* pp. 282–331 in Walter Baumgartner, *Zum Alten Testament und seiner Umwelt* (Leiden: Brill, 1959); this article was originally published in *Ar Or* 18 (1950), pp. 69–106.
47. Friedrich Oertel, *Herodots Ägyptischer Logos und die Glaubwürdigkeit Herodots* (Bonn: Habelt, 1970); Detlev Fehling, *Die Quellenangaben bei Herodot* (Berlin: Walter de Gruyter, 1971); and especially O. Kimball Armayor, "Did Herodotus Ever Go to Egypt?," *JARCE* 15 (1978):59–73.
48. Armayor, "Did Herodotus Ever Go to Egypt?," pp. 69–71.
49. A most valuable summary of much of this information can be found in J. Renger, *"Untersuchungen zum Priestertum in der altbabylonischen Zeit,"* *ZA* NF 24 (1967):110–88. See also the article "Inanna/Istar" in the *Reallexikon der Assyriologie* 5.1/2 (Berlin/New York: Walter de Gruyter, 1976), pp. 74–89; and, for the older literature, Bruno Meissner, *Babylonien und Assyrien, II* (Heidelberg: Winters, 1925), ch. 14 ("Die Priester und der Kultus"), pp. 52–101. In this section of the present chapter, I am especially conscious of schematically summarizing some very complex material. This issue, of course, deserves comprehensive treatment from a professional Assyriologist.
50. See Renger, *"Untersuchungen,"* pp. 134–44, and *CAD*, vol. 4 (E), pp. 172–73; and among earlier studies, Driver and Miles, *Babylonian Laws*, pp. 361–64.
51. Brian Lewis, *The Sargon Legend: A Study of the Akkadian Text and the Tale of the Hero Who Was Exposed at Birth*, ASOR Diss. Series 4 (Cambridge, Mass.: ASOR, 1980), pp. 37–38.
52. On the *nadītu*, see Rivkah Harris, "The *NADĪTU* Woman," pp. 106–35 in *Studies Presented to A. Leo Oppenheim* (Chicago: Oriental Institute/University of Chicago, 1964).
53. Driver and Miles, *Babylonian Laws*, p. 366.
54. See Renger, *"Untersuchungen,"* pp. 149–76, and *CAD*, vol. 11, part 1 (N), pp. 63–64.
55. Jacob J. Finkelstein, *Late Old Babylonian Documents and Letters*, YOS, Babylonian Texts 13 (New Haven/London: Yale University, 1972), p. 8; cf. also p. 16.
56. Renger, *"Untersuchungen,"* p. 144–46.
57. Driver and Miles, *Babylonian Laws*, p. 369; see *AHW*, 2:891 for attempts to translate the term.
58. Renger, *"Untersuchungen,"* pp. 181–84.
59. *CAD* 7 (I/J), pp. 270–71. A likely conclusion from a reference in a wisdom text is that the *ištaritu* was dedicated to a temple. The text reads *ištaritu ša ana ili zakrat* = "an i.-woman who has been vowed [?] to a god" (*CAD*, 7 [I/J], p. 271); see W. G. Lambert, *Babylonian Wisdom Literature* (Oxford: Clarendon, 1960), p. 102.
60. *CAD* 8 (K), p. 314.

61. Renger, "Untersuchungen," p. 188 *("Über ihre Functionen wissen wir wenig")*.
62. Maureen L. Gallery, "Service Obligations of the *Kezertu*-Women," *Or* NS 49 (1980): 333–38 (quotation from p. 338).
63. Gallery, "Service Obligations," p. 338.
64. All these texts can be found conveniently in the *CAD*: see, respectively, *CAD* 5 (G), p. 10; 11, part 1 (N), p. 198 (for both the second and third texts cited here); and 4 (E), p. 326.
65. Lewis, *Sargon Legend*, p. 40.
66. J. S. Cooper, *"Heilige Hochzeit B. Archäologisch,"* in *Reallexikon der Assyriologie*, vol. 4 (Berlin/New York: Walter de Gruyter, 1972–75), p. 259.
67. Cooper, *"Heilige Hochzeit,"* p. 266.
68. W. G. Lambert and A. R. Millard, *Atra-hasis: The Babylonian Story of the Flood*, with the Sumerian Flood Story by M. Civil (Oxford: Clarendon, 1969).
69. J. J. Finkelstein, "On Some Recent Studies in Cuneiform Law," *JAOS* 90 (1970): 246 and n. 15.
70. Finkelstein, *Late Old Babylonian Documents*, p. 9.
71. Needham, review of Arens's *The Man-Eating Myth*, p. 76. Needham, of course, is discussing cannibalism and not sacred prostitution, but we have seen in this chapter that these two charges belong together in any culture's battery of accusations used to establish its own identity.

EPILOGUE

1. Walther Eichrodt, *Theology of the Old Testament*, vol. 2 (Philadelphia, Pa.: Westminster, 1967 [1st ed. originally published in German in 1935–39]), pp. 71–74.
2. Gerhard von Rad, *Old Testament Theology*, vol. 1, *The Theology of Israel's Historical Traditions* (New York: Harper & Row, 1962 [1st ed. originally published in German in 1957]), pp. 50–53.
3. Gerhard von Rad, *Old Testament Theology*, vol. 2, *The Theology of Israel's Prophetic Traditions* (New York: Harper & Row, 1965 [originally published in German in 1960]), p. 107.
4. Von Rad, *Old Testament Theology*, vol. 2, p. 110.
5. Von Rad, *Old Testament Theology*, vol. 2, pp. 110–111.
6. Von Rad, *Old Testament Theology*, vol. 2, p. 112.
7. Helmer Ringgren, *Israelite Religion* (Philadelphia, Pa.: Fortress, 1966 [originally published in German in 1963]), p. v.
8. Georg Fohrer, *History of Israelite Religion* (Nashville, Tenn.: Abingdon, 1972 [originally published in German in 1968]), p. 23.
9. Fohrer, *History of Israelite Religion*, p. 25.
10. Fohrer, *History of Israelite Religion*, p. 122. See pp. 121–22 for statements about the "organic development" of such "central ideas" as that of "God's sovereignty and communion with God."
11. Mircea Eliade, "The Prestige of the Cosmogonic Myth," *Diogenes* 23 (1958), p. 11 (emphasis added).
12. Eliade, "Prestige of the Cosmogonic Myth," p. 12 (emphasis added).
13. Mircea Eliade, *Images and Symbols: Studies in Religious Symbolism* (New York:

Sheed & Ward, 1961 [originally published in French in 1952]), p. 169. Lest this appear a momentary slip, it is worth noting that Eliade repeats such assertions in slightly different phrasing elsewhere. For example, in *Rites and Symbols of Initiation* (New York: Harper & Row, 1965 [originally published as *Birth and Rebirth* in 1958]) we read the following: "It is impossible not to realize all that distinguishes Christianity from the Essenes and in general from all other contemporary esoteric cults. . . . The *newness* of Christianity is constituted by the historicity of Jesus. . . . the resurrection of Jesus *could not be* identified with the periodic death and resurrection of the God of the mysteries. Like Christ's life, suffering, and death, his resurrection had occurred in history, 'in the days of Pontius Pilate' " (p. 117, emphasis original). For a bold and penetrating analysis of the theological foundations beneath the works of Eliade, Otto, Van der Leeuw, and others, see now Hans H. Penner, "Structure and Religion," *HR* 25 (1986): 236–54.

14. Claude Lévi-Strauss, *Totemism* (Harmondsworth: Penguin University Books, 1973 [originally published in French in 1962]), p. 177.

15. Jonathan Z. Smith, *Imagining Religion: From Babylon to Jonestown.* (Chicago/London: University of Chicago, 1982), p. 24.

16. Smith, *Imagining Religion*, p. 19.

17. Susan Niditch, "Ezekiel 40–48 in a Visionary Context," *CBQ* 48 (1986): 208–24. Niditch's suggested comparison is equally creative and controlled: The Buddhist mandala's "theoretical framework belongs to its own cultural setting and is, of course, not to be presumed for Ezekiel. Nevertheless, the association of visionary experience with a detailed architectural plan in the Buddhist tradition provides a fascinating analogue helping one to appreciate a similar association in Ezekiel" (p. 213).

Index

Scripture Index